All Y'all

All Y'all

Queering Southernness in US Fiction, 1980–2020

. . . .

HEIDI SIEGRIST

The University of North Carolina Press Chapel Hill

This book was published with the assistance of the Authors Fund of the University of North Carolina Press.

© 2024 Heidi Siegrist
All rights reserved
Set in Charis by Westchester Publishing Services
Manufactured in the United States of America

Library of Congress Cataloging-in-Publication Data
Names: Siegrist, Heidi, author.
Title: All y'all : queering southernness in US fiction, 1980-2020 / Heidi Siegrist.
Description: Chapel Hill : The University of North Carolina Press, 2024. | Includes bibliographical references and index.
Identifiers: LCCN 2024029892 | ISBN 9781469682808 (cloth) | ISBN 9781469682815 (paperback) | ISBN 9781469682822 (epub) | ISBN 9781469682839 (pdf)
Subjects: LCSH: American fiction—Southern States—History and criticism. | Sexual minorities in literature. | Queer theory. | BISAC: LITERARY CRITICISM / LGBTQ+ | SOCIAL SCIENCE / Gender Studies | LCGFT: Literary criticism.
Classification: LCC PS261 .S436 2024 | DDC 810.9975—dc23/eng/20240708
LC record available at https://lccn.loc.gov/2024029892

Contents

Acknowledgments, vii

Introduction, 1
Queering the Queer South

1 Southern-Fried Perversions, 19
   Queer Appetites in the Works of Fannie Flagg and Dorothy Allison

2 Near 'Bout, 54
   Randall Kenan's Swampy Southern Queerness

3 Pornographies of History, 89
   Queer Southern Melancholy in the Works of Monique Truong and George Saunders

4 Southern Gothic Hospitality, 126
   Or, Inviting in the Queer Vampires of Poppy Z. Brite, George R. R. Martin, and Jewelle Gomez

Coda, 159
Dragging Southernness

Notes, 167

Bibliography, 199

Index, 217

Acknowledgments

I can't overstate my gratitude to the many people who made it possible for me to write this book. Beginning as a dissertation at the University of Virginia, this project came to life with the guidance and encouragement of Jennifer Rae Greeson, whose mentorship and advice was invaluable at every stage. I am also indebted to the intellectual generosity and guidance of Mrinalini Chakravorty, Maurice Wallace, Ashon Crawley, Grace Hale, Caroline Rody, Cindy Wall, Rita Felski, Susan Fraiman, and Mary Kuhn. For making the dissertation-to-book process as smooth as I could have hoped, I'm grateful for the editorial support of Lucas Church, as well as everyone on the team at UNC Press. And for their strong support, encouragement, inspiration, and advice during the revision process, I'm indebted to Jaime Harker, Michael Bibler, Jay Watson, and Philip Gordon.

My peers and colleagues in graduate school brought my life joy and inspiration: Bridget Reilly, Jess Swoboda, Jo Adams, Austyn James, Grace Alvino, and Sarah Winstein-Hibbs. And in my time in Charlottesville, my coworkers at the *Virginia Quarterly Review* were invaluable to my growth as a writer and an editor. I'm deeply grateful for the mentorship of Allison Wright and Paul Reyes.

The first seed of this project was planted in the Regenstein Library at the University of Chicago; I'm indebted to the many, many people who gave me an education there. The project would have been unable to grow without the library resources of the University of Virginia and the University of the South (Sewanee). I'm also grateful for the funding that allowed for conference travel; thank you to the Dean's office and to Betsy Sandlin in particular. In the Sewanee English department and in this community more broadly, I've been lucky to have the welcome, the support, and the camaraderie of many friends and colleagues: Matt Irvin, Stephanie Batkie, John and Elizabeth Grammer, Misha Rai, Ross MacDonald, Jennifer Michael, Kelly Malone, Kevin Wilson, and Adam Hawkins.

My students, in all of my semesters teaching, have inspired me with their thoughtful conversation and their openness and generosity with one another. In classes on "The Southern Short Story" (UVA) and "Queer Southern

Lit" (Sewanee) particularly, my students played a crucial role in helping me think from new angles about southernness.

To all the friends and family who have given me laughter, love, joy, inspiration, and encouragement along the way in this process: Katie Fairchild, Ed and Cullen Hicks, Patricia Sammon, Zsofi Valyi-Nagy, Amy Myers, Alan McCormick, Polly Faust, Adam Hannon-Hatfield, Nathan Howell, Urvi Thanki, Caroline Dillon, Elin Crook, Terra White, Millie McKeachie, Sarah Carter, Leigh Anne Couch, Catherine Cavagnaro, Sandy Glacet, Shelley MacLaren, Jim Crawford, and Brooks Egerton. To our dogs, who have blessedly not cared about this book at all: Gilbert, Lucy, Duncan, and Penny.

This book would not exist without my family. Kyle and Delia Siegrist have at every step supported me and loved me for who I am, without judgment; their friendship is a great joy. Ian has brightened hard writing days with his love and laughter, reminding me of the importance of play. Finally, I am unendingly grateful to Lauryl, my partner in all things, my love, my home.

All Y'all

Introduction
Queering the Queer South

・・・

In March of 2020, as we were muddling through the early days of COVID lockdowns in the United States and looking ahead to a deeply contentious election season, the show *Tiger King* premiered on Netflix. I was home in Tennessee with my partner, her child, and her child's father, and we were piecing together haphazard homeschooling schedules and arguing over what should be House Policy when it came to washing our fruits and vegetables. We were fumbling through questions about what our home, and our family, would look like for the next week, the next month, the next year. Along with countless other households in the nation, we watched the first few episodes of *Tiger King* with a sense of schadenfreude, gawking at a world that looked even more confusing and bizarre than ours currently felt.

For the uninitiated, *Tiger King* depicts a kind of Hatfield and McCoy turf war between big cat collectors and conservationists—the former in Oklahoma, and the latter in Florida. Joe Exotic, the eponymous tiger king, is a gay man whose relationships look as exploitative and messy as his business models. In one notable scene, we see him taking part in a polyamorous commitment ceremony involving a straight man whom he has coerced. Everyone involved is wearing a pink suit at some sort of community center.[1] This is decidedly not the cosmopolitan queerness of the ivory tower—it's queerness as spectacle, deviance, predation, tackiness. And although the question of whether Oklahoma and Florida are part of "the South" is a contentious one, it's a phenomenon worth noting that the social media platform formerly known as Twitter had a lot to say, through *Tiger King*, about "the Southern United States[,] . . . the most batshit insane place on Earth" and the pleasure to be taken in the "batshit, chaotic queer content" by "crazy white people" in such batshit insane places.[2] In a moment of deep national insecurity and division, the show exploded into popularity because southernness and queerness, together, served a unifying function, upholding in absentia the dream of "normal" national life in uncertain times.

In the few years since *Tiger King* premiered, LGBTQ rights in the United States have been dangerously curtailed most dramatically and visibly in southern states: Tennessee's attempted drag bans, Florida's "don't say gay" laws, and blocks to gender-affirming care throughout most of the "Bible Belt," to mention a few examples.[3] This trend bolsters the familiar narrative that queer life doesn't belong in the South. But a show like *Tiger King* exploits a contradictory, equally powerful narrative: there is a strange linkage between queerness and southernness in our cultural imagination. This connection is longstanding; "southern" and "queer" are concepts that have attracted and repelled one another in US literature and popular media for more than a century.

These two share associations that, depending on the context, might be embraced or disavowed: otherness, backwardness, perversion. This book explores that fraught and understudied intimacy, and posits that it has important implications for both queer and southern studies. "Southernness," for the purposes of this book, captures any configuration or framing of regional character that cites to a story of the US South as an exceptional space (even in a rapidly changing, globalized world), in some way perverse and, crucially, deviant from national normativity. In US cultural discourse, that exceptionalism is most frequently framed in terms of the legacy of the antebellum plantation and its demise—the endlessly treasured and despised "Old South." It's that legacy that loosely organizes each configuration of southernness I present in this book. By "queerness," I refer to deviance's more stylish cousin, antinormativity, and to a wide range of sexual and gender expressions. Southernness, like queerness, is never a stable quality—it's useful as a term of critical inquiry because it's shaggy, multivalent. "The South" is not a place and "queer" is not an identity—or at least, they're not only that. Queerness and southernness both describe modes of relationality and orientation that are in some way opposed to national, cultural, or social norms. Taking these terms together complicates familiar ways of reading both; southern deviance can be other than culturally familiar and regressive, and queer antinormativity can be other than sleekly urbane and politically powerful.

The "all" in my title refers as much to a multiplicity of narratives and theoretical orientations as it does to a range of gender, sexual, or subregional identities. In the novels and stories I've chosen, the jostling of different stories of queer and southern deviance within the same spaces causes something to spark into being, even if only for a moment—a surprising kinship, a sense of possibility, a shifting balance of power—certainly for characters, and possibly for readers as well. My emphasis on multiplicity refuses readings and arguments that rely on a single definition of "queer" or "southern."

Instead, I insist on the importance of acknowledging competing models side by side: a mode of reading that I hope will add to conversations in both fields of study. The authors whose novels and stories I discuss—from Fannie Flagg to Randall Kenan to Monique Truong to Jewelle Gomez—layer queer and southern deviance as a way of reorienting to the many complicated associations that circulate around both terms, considering the possibilities and limitations of world-building through narrative while grappling with the realities of embodied, racialized identities in those spaces experienced as "the South."

Heading South: Place or Story?

"The South" might refer to a cluster of politically red states; to a region with its own cultural and social histories; to many different homes for many different people. But there is also a great deal of debate over what, if anything, constitutes the "real" South. The question suggests a series of copies, frauds, or fictions that swirl around and obscure some singular, monocultural, uniquely authentic place.[4] Increasingly in the past few years, critics like Jon Smith and Scott Romine have argued that such singular authenticity is, and always has been, a myth.[5] The *truly* southern person, place, or thing is always longed for, and always beyond our grasp.

If the South is a series of places, none any more authentic or "southern" than any other, it is also a series of discursive constructions, a grab-bag of beloved stories and stereotypes spanning back to the nation's founding and even before. The South has always been in some way an imagined place, a region created, fortified, and complicated by representation. Unpacking those representations has been the focus of much of the New Southern Studies (NSS), the endgame of which is sometimes framed as its own demise, its absorption into a wider American studies—as Leigh Anne Duck has put it, a southern studies without the South.[6] But although scholars have done rigorous and important work in unmooring the South from stereotype and making it a more capacious term within academia, southernness is alive and well in the popular imagination. This is, of course, because the idea of the US South as deviant bizarro-land has long done something for those who live, read, and circulate in cultures both within and beyond its imagined borders.

From the eighteenth century onward, the South of our popular understanding has functioned as a region apart. In the nineteenth century, from the lead-up to the Civil War to the devastation that followed, the South occupied two prominent roles in shifting national stories as the United States negotiated its changing relationship to empire: first imperial power, and then disgraced colony.[7] In both these roles, as Jennifer Rae Greeson has argued, the South is positioned as "an internal other" that "lies simultaneously inside and outside the national imaginary constructed in US literature."[8] By the early twentieth century, the South's role in the national imaginary was that of the alienated and backward region, hopelessly separate economically and culturally in the wake of the failures of Reconstruction and the calcifying structures of Jim Crow.[9] As Duck writes, for a nation imagining itself as "an exemplar of civic nationalism," the South constituted a threat that "evoked not only calls for reform and socioeconomic analysis but also a proliferation of Gothic tropes"—tropes with long half-lives, tropes with which writers of southern modernism notoriously grappled.[10]

Throughout the past century, constructions of southernness in the US cultural imagination have provided us with a provincial home, inviting both contempt and nostalgia, for a nation launching itself ever further into "the modern." Because of that affective power, the South is often imagined (and commodified—think banjo soundtracks and Cracker Barrel) as a place where we might find "tradition" and "heritage." Accordingly, the region plays an outsized role in discourses of folkways.[11] The conceptual link between southernness and pastness provides two contradictory ways of understanding the contemporary South relative to a national identity: the region is alternately framed as "moral other, and moral center," as Tara McPherson writes.[12] But even when the South is posited as the heart of the nation, usually in the context of politically conservative discourse, it is framed as exceptional, removed or distinct from "the rest of" the country.[13]

In all of these scholars' formulations, the South is organized discursively, its contours shaped by stories. R. Bruce Brasell puts it well: "no South exists beyond or outside of southern discourse."[14] We might arrive at the South's discursive borders by various paths—through Edward Said's imaginative geography, Benedict Anderson's imagined communities, and Slavoj Žižek's differentiation of narration and historical process.[15] For my part, I echo Greeson's plain statement: "I have no real south to defend."[16] To argue for such a singular entity seems to me at best a lost cause, and at worst a reprehensible allegiance *to* the Lost Cause. But I do aim to demonstrate how popular ideas of southernness—those emerging from a centuries-long story of deviance from national norms—layer onto lived spaces as represented in contemporary fiction. As in fiction, so in life: southernness colors how we understand, discuss, and represent southern communities (which is to say, places in the southeastern United States), as well as people who claim a southern identity or are seen as southern.

A Queer Place

Southernness frequently denotes not only a general deviance, but a uniquely sexual perversion. Consider, for example, the 2003 *Saturday Night Live* skit "Colonel Angus," which opens on a genteel group of men and women waiting on the porch of a plantation house for the return of a beloved comrade. The joke is that, through drawling accents, "Colonel Angus" becomes "cunnilingus." In longing together for this soldier of the Confederacy, this family coheres around the anticipation of oral sex.[17] This is surely one way of distancing the violence of the plantation: it's a space that's always already queer in ways that those within it are laughably oblivious to. Southernness still conjures a very old sense of spectacle: not only general backwardness, lawlessness, and grotesquerie, but a more erotic sensationalism. As Michael Bibler writes, "the South has been portrayed for centuries as a hotbed of sexual obsession and degeneracy: from abolitionists' depictions of rapacious slave owners, to southern whites' mythification of the black rapist during the Jim Crow era, to the darkly comic images of incest and debauchery in the modernist works of William Faulkner and Erskine Caldwell, and the gratuitous sexuality of films like *Mandingo* (1975) and television shows like *True Blood* (2008–14)."[18] The very word "hotbed" suggests simultaneous lascivious growth and decay; this catalogue reveals the persistence of a landscape of southern stories that spawn and gratify perverse desire. What Bibler's list also reveals is that "deranged" southern desire is a story produced and consumed both within and beyond this peculiar region. It's not only Hollywood that constructs the queer South; writers and artists who identify as southern have very often embraced that perception. "Sexual deviance," Jaime Harker argues, "is one of the South's most successful exports."[19]

Queerness flourishes in our imagined South, and yet the region also has a reputation (both from those who do and do not claim the mantle "southern") as the nation's most homophobic region. This reputation has its basis in truth—the conservative politics that consistently turn southeastern states red have historically rejected LGBTQ identities and are doing so now with increasing vehemence—but such trends are hardly exclusive to one area of the nation.[20] To identify homophobia as especially southern can also obscure the queer lives that flourish there. The Southeast is, like any other region of the United States, one where many queer people make their home. This is most obviously true of cities: Atlanta, Asheville, Athens, to begin at the beginning of the alphabet. But it's true outside of these metropolitan areas as well.[21] As Gregory Samantha Rosenthal writes, a rural Appalachian landscape "holds narratives of transness and queerness just as the streets of the Village do."[22] Nevertheless, southernness remains synonymous with both provincialism and conservatism in our cultural vocabulary, despite the wide range of creative, progressive, and complicated southern spaces that scholars and self-proclaimed southerners have come to know.[23] There is still much work to be done in separating queer theory and stories of LGBTQ life from a close association with non-southern urbanity—what Jack Halberstam coined "metronormativity."[24] Queer theory, as academe's hippest child, is all too often conceptualized in terms incompatible with popular understandings of southernness: urbane, cosmopolitan, and elite.

And yet because major threads of queer theory share key connections with ideas of southernness, queer theory offers robust and underused theoretical frameworks through which to understand the South's role in our US cultural epistemology. Queerness takes its power from the critique of naturalized categories of sexuality, sociality, class, race, and nationalism. The forms of queerness used to enact these critiques—Jack Halberstam's theorizations of monstrosity and failure, Heather Love's work on melancholy and the backward glance, and Sara Ahmed's writing on alienation, for instance—are also ideas at work in stories of southernness.[25] Through these concepts, southernness, too, might be in a position to launch a radical critique of normative ideologies—and, by extension, any naturalized idea of "the South." Queer theory, then, helps us place those scare quotes around "the South" as a monolith. It tinkers with the machinery of southernness to bring forth a multiplicity of meanings, many Souths at once— including those with the potential to be more expansive, inclusive, and subversive than we, as readers and cultural consumers, might otherwise be inclined to imagine. This kind of queer framework is useful to the future of the New Southern Studies, which attends to the far-ranging implications of southern exceptionalism and the US South's place in wider discourses of globalization.

Conversely, the relational/anti-relational debate within queer theory stands to benefit from the kind of localized theorizing that southern studies offers. Does the swerve away from the normative build a valuable alternative kinship, or is it solitary, reactionary, destructive? As Tavia Nyong'o writes, the anti-relational strand of queer theory "locates the power of sexuality in its negativity rather than any alternative community it might give rise to."[26] Queerness can be understood as either inherently self-shattering, a challenge to all symbolic order (and therefore incompatible with social organization or world-building), or it can be understood as a tool for imagining utopian worlds and more imaginative forms of community. These two approaches carry dramatically distinct ethical implications, and they demand different ways of envisioning and representing queer life. And yet they merge, as Mari Ruti has pointed out, in the critique and refusal of a wide range of normative paradigms: heterosexual monogamy, capitalism, the idolization of productivity and "success," and dominant humanist ethical frameworks.[27] Moreover, as Tyler Bradway and Elizabeth Freeman have recently argued, both these threads inevitably engage with what they call "kincoherence": the "mutually constituting and complicating forces, desires, practices, relations, and forms that render kinship a horizon of violence and possibility."[28] Southernness—as a constellation of shifting manifestations of antinormativity and kincoherence—offers a way of thinking through how diverse models of queerness might coexist within the same space. Southernness can hold fantasies both annihilating and transformative, kinship as existential threat and refuge, dead ends and paths forward. In other words, we can read some of queer theory's key preoccupations by this strange regional light. If antinormativity risks becoming, as Ruti argues, "a default politico-ethical stance" in queer theory, putting this stance in terms of southernness probes the limits and the context of its stylishness as well as its political force.[29] Narratives of southernness give us case studies of the many ways deviant bodies move through—and create, revise, or reject—deviant spaces. I turn, then, to E. Patrick Johnson's question: "What is the utility of queer theory on the front lines," he asks, anywhere that it fails to acknowledge materiality while the body remains a "site of trauma?"[30]

Racializing Sexuality, Sexualizing Race

Embodiment, here, is key: the joining of queer and southern studies adds complexity to the theorization of race with respect to either term. Queer of color critique, in its work of "highlight[ing] the uneven terrain of bodies and desire," in Martin Manalansan's words, is vital to acknowledging materiality alongside abstraction: to thinking through how stories alter (or don't) lived experiences of otherness in those places experienced as the South.[31] Because "queer" is both theoretical orientation and lived identity, the latter formed by race as well as sexuality, it should be, as Cathy Cohen argues, "a provocation to imagine how we might organize across varied communities defined as 'the other' by the state and/or racial capitalism."[32] Racialization can queer a body seen or experienced as southern, and queers of color must often move differently than their white counterparts through spaces designated as southern.[33] As stories can show us, the ways in which southernness is queered are inextricable from the ways in which southernness is racialized.

Race has always been a key component of the South's perceived deviance. Critics like Siobhan Somerville and Roderick Ferguson have shown how the racial and sexual normativity that came to be naturalized in the twentieth century United States developed in tandem and remain closely entwined. The South, as the "peculiar region" carrying the nation's legacy of slavery and the institution's many physical, psychological, and sexual abuses, provided a useful foil to that developing normativity.[34] As Grace Elizabeth Hale writes, the South has long served as "the darkness that has made the American nation lose its color."[35] This role has cemented contemporary understandings of southern racial identity (in Black and white, but infrequently imagined outside of this color line) as particularly fraught relative to the rest of the nation.[36] The racial deviance of southernness encompasses both white nostalgia and Black trauma—long echoes of the plantation's perversions. And popular representations have long offered scintillating stories of a South that is not only the setting for the production of racial otherness, but is itself the sexualized racial other to a postracial national imaginary. Racial and sexual otherness, as broadly understood categories of difference, constitute the South as deviant. At the same time, specific experiences of sexuality in southern spaces will function very differently for white and Black subjects and those outside this infamous color line.

Thinking queerness and southernness together requires that we resist a single approach that loses sight of either embodied experiences or abstract formulations of race and sexuality. Configurations of deviance can't be siloed at an "atmospheric level" of queer theory, in Sharon Holland's words, that "mires the 'black' in absolute relationship to the 'white' as if their belonging were carved in glacial ice."[37] And yet historical approaches focusing too narrowly on the specificities of any one identity are also limited in that they risk losing the theoretical flexibility and power of making visible the stakes of our attachment to queerness and southernness writ large. My approach seeks to split the difference: the authors I study take the conceptual affinities between southern deviance and queer antinormativity—the perverse, backward, monstrous—as launching points to explore queer embodiment in spaces experienced as southern.[38]

In seeking to join identity-based accounts of southern queerness with more capacious—and thus generative—applications of both terms, I draw on both ethnographical and literary critical works. As E. Patrick Johnson writes, a "reexamination of the queer possibilities of the South" through life chronicles and personal stories "provide[s] not only different perspectives on the relationship between race and region, gender and geography, and sexuality and southernness," but also "serve[s] as an intervention in the prevailing histories of homosexuality in the South and in the nation."[39] Influential ethnographies like Johnson's have explored what it means to live as a southern queer person, interpellated by race and class.[40] The literary monographs exploring these themes, however, have been relatively few. These crucial works have for the most part prioritized "queer" and "southern" first and foremost as identity positions, less so as theoretical orientation or discursive formation.[41] Gary Richards's illuminating *Lovers and Beloveds* argues that the exploration of same-sex desire was a crucial component of Southern Renaissance writing because the South was seen as a permissible fictional setting for sexual deviance. Michael Bibler's *Cotton's Queer Relations*, another essential text in queer southern studies, argues that midcentury southern literary texts "effectively refashion the plantation into an intrinsically queer cultural space"—that is, one in which homosocial intimacies are vital.[42] Despite the latter title, both critics express a wariness of the term "queer"—for Bibler, too expansive in its identification with the antinormative—and prefer an emphasis on same-sex desire at the intersections of race and class. For Richards, "'queer' ironically threatens to reinforce a binarism of normative/queer and thus the notion that there is a stable, finite, knowable normativity."[43] But although this point is well-taken, and although I agree with the value of analyzing same-sex desire across other identity categories, I also hold that the "normative," however illusory, is regularly represented and perceived, and therefore a useful category to engage.

An apparently stable binary of normativity/deviance, after all, is at the root of the conception of "the South" as a region whose exceptionalism can be documented in literature and literary criticism, rather than a region whose exceptionalism emerges through representation. A case in point is the classic southern literary canon itself, the ethos of which might be summed up by Carson McCullers's oft-quoted quip about her position as an artist having left the region: "I must go home periodically to renew my sense of horror."[44] There have been surprisingly few works that answer Brasell's call, in 2002, for "theorists to adopt a queer understanding of the South . . . rather than resist the popular alignment of the South with perversion, [to] embrace it."[45] One important work answering that call is Jaime Harker's *The Lesbian South* (2018), a survey of the 1970s Women in Print movement and its legacy. Harker shines a light on the underestimated importance of radical southern lesbian authors who, she argues, embraced the South's association with sexual deviance. This connection—between a specific sexual identity position and a general sense of regional deviance—is crucial to Harker's project, as to my own.[46] This book is meant to add to that shelf, building out its historical and narrative reach.

Stories on Stories

The 1980s serves as my launching point for a study of queer southernness less for what was happening in the region than for what was happening in the nation. For one, as feminist debates and poststructuralist theories in the academy were laying the groundwork for what would become queer studies, LGBTQ life was entering a new era in American politics. In some ways, the 1979 March on Washington marked the beginning of a shift in gay and lesbian activism, from grassroots to more formalized, professionalized, and high-profile campaigns.[47] Fights for equal rights and more overt representation in the media evoked new questions in public discourse: how do we understand past, present, and future LGBTQ lives in American society? How are those lives experienced and portrayed?

Meanwhile, southernness was becoming increasingly produced and reproducible.[48] In the beginning of the 1980s, pop culture reached unprecedented levels of saturation in American life, through ubiquitous ads and proliferating entertainment options in the forms of television, film, music, and magazines.[49] The visual and print media boom of the 1980s hearkened the growth of syndicated southernness(es) heavy in regional exceptionalism: *Dukes of Hazzard*, *Driving Miss Daisy*, and *Steel Magnolias* on the screen, country music and southern hip hop on the radio, and *Southern Living* annual cookbooks on shelves. The pop culture history that makes a show like *Tiger King* feel already familiar to us has many of its roots in this era.[50] The growth of media channels also delocalized culture, even as media insisted on unique regionalities.[51] As McPherson points out, "the emergence of a new 'Old South'" around this time "coincides both with the political agendas of the Reagan-Bush years and with the economic pressures of late capitalism, reinscribing the region as a site of authenticity and the local at the very moment that globalization blurs the boundaries of the nation."[52] By the 1980s, the modest southern Democratic victories of Carter's term were fading, calcifying our sense of a southernness white, Black, and politically red all over (despite demographic shifts).[53] The stories we tell now about queer and southern deviance did not begin in the 1980s, but they did become more vivid, more available, and more ubiquitous around this time, even as (and perhaps because) the realities became more visibly complicated.

This cultural history provides the backdrop to my study of narrative fiction—accordingly, I make room to explore, in the chapters that follow, how fiction circulates within and at times alludes to a wider media ecosystem. The works I've chosen do not all slot easily into that vague category of "southern literature"; nor do they necessarily belong to the equally vague category of (highbrow) "literary fiction." They are, however, all narratives that reveal and reward an attention *to* narrative. These are works marked by frame tales, labyrinths of intertextuality, formal experimentation that directly engages the reader, and a playfulness about generic convention. These novels and stories anticipate the readership of which Fredric Jameson wrote: "We never confront a text immediately, fresh. . . . We apprehend them through sedimented layers of interpretation."[54] Within the texts I have chosen are characters negotiating old and new stories of southernness, reckoning with the unstable ground that these various layers of stories compose.

In this way, the texts I've chosen are metafictional—by Patricia Waugh's definition, "writing which self-consciously and systematically draws attention to its status as an artifact in order to pose questions about the relationship between fiction and reality."[55] Metafiction can appear in many forms: outright parody, subtler echoes of other forms and conventions, frames, games, and myriad other forms of self-reflexivity in approach to language or structure.[56] In each case, readers play an important role; they become, in Linda Hutcheon's words, "the creative accomplice, the co-producer of the work."[57] The reader is made aware of their role in world-building through narrative—a role that carries a great deal of responsibility.[58]

By invoking metafiction, as well as the constructed or discursive nature of southernness, I come up against two rather fraught terms: the postmodern and (one of its many descendants) the postsouthern. Literary postmodernism has invited, over the years, a wide range of definitions and debates.[59] Those debates are beyond the ken of this book; but it is worth pointing out, as Claire Chadd does in her work on postregionality, that the postmodern and the postsouthern are both often called to answer to the charge that they "lack sufficient focus on the material contexts of history."[60] The postsouthern particularly tends to refer to the sense of being "beyond," in some anxious sense, a literary sense of place rather than any experiential South. Postsouthern writers are, as Michael Kreyling has posited, tasked with the impossible challenge of writing southern literature after the Southern Renaissance, and specifically after Faulkner.[61]

All the texts I offer here are metafictional in some way—but not all of them take a postmodern approach to history, and not all of them grapple primarily or exclusively with a southern modernist literary heritage. As Chadd argues, "we might say that the South has always been 'metafictional'. . . . The issue of defining the real South is not simply a postmodern problem but has preoccupied those writing about the region since at least as early as the 1850s."[62] For these reasons, I have found the postmodern and the postsouthern to be not entirely useful terms for this book. Moreover, my arguments are informed less by postmodern narratology than by directions within queer theory that speak to the paradox that Hutcheon identifies as crucial to metafiction more generally: that "reading and writing belong to the processes of 'life' as much as they do to those of 'art'. . . . On the one hand, [the reader] is forced to acknowledge the artifice, the 'art,' of what he is reading; on the other, explicit demands are made upon him, as a co-creator, for intellectual and affective responses."[63] When life and art are so inextricably tangled, the question of how much power a text's diegetic and extradiegetic readers hold within and beyond the world of a narrative looms large. And this, surely, is an anxious question.

The Politics of Narrative

Metafiction's power to highlight narrativization raises, in neon colors, the question of the political potential and obligations of queer southern stories. In one sense, as I've suggested, queerness can make visible the machinery of the "deviant South," revealing its gears, making them vulnerable to tinkering. This is just what LaMonda Horton-Stallings has in mind in *A Dirty South Manifesto*, which sets forth a "call for a public politics of deviance": by embracing the popular imagining of "the South as a sexual dystopia," we might rewrite the South to become a space of "world-making and cultural creations," a place for "the practice of intersectional politics, critiques of moral authority."[64] And yet to hold aloft a multiplicity of southern and queer narratives and critical orientations, as I do here, does not always accomplish this project—in fact, it often produces more questions than answers. How and under what conditions do metafictional narratives of queer southern deviance challenge or simply reinscribe dominant ideologies? Can the relationships between narrator and reader, teller and listener, create stories dynamic enough to open up more inclusive lived spaces? Should this be what we ask of them? These questions speak to ethical demands upon writers, storytellers, narratees, and readers, and I engage with all of these in this book, although with some ambivalence.[65] It may be, as Wayne Booth wrote, that for both tellers and listeners, writers and readers, "stories are our major moral teachers," but so too are they commodities and sources of entertainment.[66]

It's for this reason that queerness is often framed as conceptually antagonistic to narrative; scholars like Teresa de Lauretis and Leo Bersani argue that the very structure of narrative is inevitably normative, and therefore incompatible with the disruptive power of queerness.[67] If narrative offers a progressive, linear drive, an insistence on order, a consolidation of power, queer anti-narrativity refuses these, urging us instead toward the radical fracturing of ideology and the identities and communities that any ideology organizes. On the other hand, the world-making that Horton-Stallings identifies hinges on queer narrativity of a kind that, as Bradway argues, serves as a mode of connection across time and space: "a form through which queers forge, experience, sustain, renew, and reimagine relationality."[68] As I'll argue in the chapters that follow, narratives of queer southern deviance are not inherently technologies of freedom or generators of community. Rather, it's valuable to both fields of study to consider how these narratives can support a variety (or a combination) of political projects: bolstering the normative, championing the kind of subversive work that queer antinormativity demands, or insisting on the limitations of an idea's influence in the "real world."

My approach does not conform to a single narratological method or ethics, but I do return again and again to the ways that southernness and queerness form and reform one another through narrative, and, in so doing, negotiate structures of power. In that spirit, I have tried to attend here to the ambivalence and the irresolution of many queer southern stories, conversations, and lives taking shape without end or closure. This lack of closure can be discomfiting. But it is precisely what closure precludes that I find most productive: the movement, the contact, and the tensions among shifting formations of queer and southern deviance. For characters, readers, and scholars alike, I believe that there is creative potential in refusing a master narrative that pins down either term; for grappling with the ways abstract figurations and localized experiences spark against one another; for continually reorienting oneself within spaces layered thick with stories.

The habit of theorizing I employ here in insisting on such multiplicity—what I've described as the "all" in "y'all"—is in line with work across queer theory, from, in recent example, Lee Edelman's highly abstracted characterization of queerness as "infinitely mobile as an epithet for strangeness, out-of-jointedness, and nonnormativity," to Ramzi Fawaz's much more relational, identity-based definition of queer forms as "providing opportunities to continually interpret and *re*interpret the meaning of gender and sexuality across countless contexts."[69] This tendency to characterize queerness as a shapeshifter encourages us as critics to refuse the singular reading practice or argument, along with any confidence in the political stability or potency that such singularity would seem to offer. To read queerly is to refuse to limit any idea, including queerness itself, to one pathway, lock it into one box. A body of literature depicting those spaces where contemporary southernness resides—as with other scenes of historicized and localized reading—help us, as critics, to do the kind of reading that queer theory demands, because spatial and temporal limitations (wobbly though they may be) paradoxically allow for queer expansiveness: dissonant definitions and effects can occupy the same space.

In the writing of this book, I have had the experience of throwing myself against the puzzle, the unresolved questions, of my own critical and political impulses. Being queer in Tennessee, I often feel a political urgency: parking my car, with its (commodified, mass-produced) rainbow sticker in the parking lot of the Piggly Wiggly becomes, tediously, not only a milk run but an insistence: *I am, we are.* And yet queer theory feels politically paralyzing: in the simplest and most extreme terms, it demands a choice between walking toward utopia or a gaping void (both, of course, being unreachable destinations, especially compared with the Piggly Wiggly). By emphasizing the way these things feel, rather than what they are or do, I mean to insist on the critical value in uncertainty, contingency, and incompleteness. My readings tend toward a longing for political change: I want those all-too-familiar stories of queer southern deviance to launch us into a space of play that allows for inclusive and surprising ways of thinking, dreaming, and—crucially—living "the South." But I am conscious of Robyn Wiegman's warning of the blind spots that stalk us when, in queer studies, "nothing seems to have escaped suspicion except belief in the political purchase of antinormativity itself."[70] Rather than settling in to either suspicion or belief in the power of deviance, I mean to emphasize the puzzle, the question, of what it might do for us. And (as I realize in my compulsive return to "us" and "we"), I want to work that puzzle, ponder that question, in relation. Looking for that deviant *y'all* is my attempt to do just that. As bell hooks wrote, we seek in the practice of theory "a location for healing" when we are "desperately trying to find [our] way home."[71]

Appetite, Atmosphere, Affect, Abomination

Rather than proceeding chronologically, the chapters in this book are organized as variations on themes at the intersection of queerness and southernness. Each offers a concept where southernness and queerness meet in deviance—that is, where a given configuration of southernness loosely emerging from a story of the "Old South" and its downfall aligns with a theorization of queer antinormativity. These "meeting places" serve as testing grounds for practices of kinship between southernness and queerness, built through narrativity. At these sites, we see a range of possible critical and political effects of this kinship—reminding us that these terms are never singular, and their relationship is never stable, but rather fluid. I begin with the theme of "perverse" queer and southern appetites, in my first chapter, to firmly situate consumption as a throughline. As I argue throughout, we "consume" stories of southernness and queerness in many forms. Those forms include, in Chapter Two, the disordered atmosphere of the swamp; in Chapter Three, melancholy as an affective orientation; and in Chapter Four, aberrant figures of monstrosity—specifically, the vampire. Within each of these forms, I explore how narratives of southernness and queerness are built, unraveled, or reoriented in tandem. And I discuss where these shifting narratives change (or don't) a lived experience of queerness for narrators and characters who—all too aware that they live inside a "South" both conceptual and material—offer and consume stories of deviance.

My first chapter confronts a cultural appetite for queer and southern deviance in literal terms. Southern food has long been a commodified sign of an exceptional region, raising the specter of unhealthy or decadent desires, as well as bringing into view the complicated table at which whiteness and blackness meet. Southernness and queerness, in this chapter, meet in the "perverse" appetite. I begin with three works from the 1980s: the deviant appetites and dangerous tastes of Fannie Flagg's *Fried Green Tomatoes at* the *Whistle Stop Cafe* lead me into Dorothy Allison's stories of southern and lesbian hunger in *Trash*, with a stop along the way at Ernest Matthew Mickler's hit cookbook, *White Trash Cooking*. In Flagg's novel, an older woman and a younger, Ninny and Evelyn, meet over junk food in the antiseptic whiteness of a 1980s nursing home to share stories of Whistle Stop, Alabama, where during the Depression two women, Idgie and Ruth, built a life together as well as a restaurant business. In Ninny's telling, white female queerness is conflated with a queer and abject blackness. The novel's narrative frame encourages readers to work up an appetite for this conflation, as much as for the decadent biscuits and fried green tomatoes of the novel's title, from a safe distance. A "perverse" southern appetite for racial and sexual otherness is paradoxically crucial to the novel's production of nostalgia for what is, finally, a fantasy of "traditional" (white, heteronormative) small-town southern life. But there remains a spectral blackness and queerness that the novel doesn't resolve—leftovers that unsettle an otherwise consumable story. These irresolvable appetites for sexual and racial otherness, and the always-unsatisfied hunger for just the right story of "southernness," echo across Dorothy Allison's work. In *Trash*, Allison's narrator grapples with her own deviant appetites—for adventurous queer sex and for unhealthy, "trashy" southern food. Allison's narrator, as a white, poor lesbian from North Carolina, is all too aware of how these appetites make her into the "wrong" kind of feminist and shape her capacity as a storyteller of "southernness" for hungry audiences. Ultimately, her longing for a table where southern heritage and queer identity meet in inclusive harmony through deviant desires never becomes a reality, but it remains a cherished dream and vital political project.

The table of shared hungers is an apt way of envisioning the fiction of Randall Kenan, but in my second chapter, southernness and queerness are joined by atmosphere rather than appetite. Specifically, these concepts meet in the swamp: a place of wildness, tangled roots, and endless capacity for disorientation. In Kenan's work, published across the past thirty years, it's in the swamp and the town it becomes, Tims Creek, that the possibilities of rural Black queer southern life are alternately hidden and revealed, refused and celebrated. I posit the southern "swamp" as material geography, metaphor, and queer mode of reading in Kenan's novel, *A Visitation of Spirits*, and his story collections *Let the Dead Bury Their Dead* and *If I Had Two Wings*. The atmosphere of the swamp suggests a general southern deviance (the South is often framed as "the middle of nowhere," wild and fecund, half-uncivilized) as well as the historical fugitivity of communities of bondspeople who escaped the reaches of the antebellum plantation. Similarly, the historical and associative meanings of "swampiness" are particularly generative for queer theory: disorientation, rhizomatic connections, sedimented archives, radical anti-capitalism, strange temporalities. I argue that Kenan's work embraces the swamp in order to offer his readers a South that is not only home to the ghosts of Dixie, but also a territory to be claimed for queer Black life. Kenan's work is intertextual, filled with past stories and storytellers; taken together, his works weave together many imaginings of southern space, asking the reader to engage in a constant reorientation. Accordingly, I offer the swamp not only as a geography but as a queer framework for thinking across Kenan's works: layering texts, temporalities, and interpretations.

As Kenan's swamp shows us, stories can build a refuge, but that refuge is never complete; accordingly, my third chapter explores the possibilities and limitations of narratives in which queerness and southernness are joined by melancholy. A deviant affective orientation relative to the optimism that characterizes national progress narratives, melancholy's backward glance is not only attuned to the past. Whether the melancholic gaze is on the Lost Cause or lost queer histories, it also demands alternative ways of orienting to the future and to the political present. I take melancholy as an affective hinge for constructions of queer subjectivity as well as southernness in two recent novels: Monique Truong's *Bitter in the Mouth* and George Saunders's *Lincoln in the Bardo*. I argue that Saunders's novel, although not in any concrete way about the South, structures the "bardo" as an implicitly southern and queer space, one affectively organized by melancholy and the backward glance, ultimately impotent and necessary to relinquish for national cohesion. The novel's unusual form suggests a melancholic orientation toward history as well—that a "true" history is something that we could narrativize, use, and learn from, if we could ever grasp it. The "lost cause" of historical narrativization leads me to Monique Truong's *Bitter in the Mouth*, in which melancholy becomes, for a Vietnamese adoptee growing up in North Carolina during the Vietnam War, a way to construct her own historical archives, navigate her experiences as a racialized southerner, claim a queer community, and reinvent her own story, past and present. In Truong's novel, the queer uses of melancholy make visible the possibility of more inclusive "southern" stories, but the power of this affect to effect material change is limited. I end with a brief analysis of Saunders's story *CivilWarLand in Bad Decline*, in which the political weakness of melancholy of any stripe—and the inefficacy of narrative as a way of altering the track of history—appear especially stark.

I end my third chapter with a ghost, and I begin my fourth with a vampire. These are not unexpected guests; the most infamous form of southern deviance, the Gothic, has long been a productive site of queer study. In this last chapter, I explore the centrality of monstrosity to imaginings of southernness as well as queerness. Specifically, the narrative I explore here is that of the southern vampire, who has shown up quite frequently in novels (and other popular media) of the past four decades. The vampire figures the queer possibilities of border crossing, and the southern vampire specifically alternately functions as an object of intrusive horror (queer predation encroaching on the isolated region) and alarming contagion (southern perversions extending outward, replicating outside the peculiar region). Moreover, s/he calls humanism into question in her refusal of the dichotomies that borders enact, invoking the monster's potential to spur radical epistemological change. In a survey of post-Anne-Rice "southern vampire" texts, most notably George R. R. Martin's *Fevre Dream*, Poppy Z. Brite's *Lost Souls*, Jewelle Gomez's *The Gilda Stories*, and Grady Hendrix's *The Southern Book Club's Guide to Slaying Vampires*, I argue that the vampire and the South are both cluttered with convention, metaphorically over-available, and monstrously queer. In my readings of these texts, I identify a self-consciousness to the way that southernness spills out over generic and national borders. In this spillage, these narratives are at times hospitable—if tenuously so—to queerer, more expansive formations of family. Queerness adds layers of political and critical complexity to what are often overly familiar conceptions of southern monstrosity, just as southernness provides a space from which to hold aloft conflicting formulations of queer monstrosity.

I end with a return to our contemporary political scene, discussing Tennessee's recent "drag bans" and concluding with a brief meditation on Lizzo's 2023 performance in Knoxville, Tennessee. In our current political climate, as LGBTQ rights become increasingly precarious, "southern" and "queer" appear ever more in tension, and yet more linked in deviance as well. As I see it, that makes the need to dig into a queer, southern kinship—and the stories it can tell, the worlds it might imagine, the lives it might affirm—all the more crucial.

1 Southern-Fried Perversions

Queer Appetites in the Works of Fannie Flagg and Dorothy Allison

....

In October of 2016, my partner and I were driving through Florida to Tennessee, taking a series of back roads prescribed by Google Maps, and hungry. We hadn't seen anything but Trump signs for miles when we came across It Don't Matter Family Restaurant. Among other white families, plus the Halloween skeleton in the corner, we had a classic southern lunch of sweet tea, turnip greens, and chicken and dumplings from the buffet. I think about that restaurant a lot. We went in unafraid because of some serious privilege: we are white women, and we can, when we feel vulnerable, pass for friends or sisters. And yet the restaurant's name suggests a kind of existential shrug that claims any guardedness is without reason. We wondered what the name meant. What doesn't matter? The food you eat? The family you choose? *Anything*? It was a bizarre denial of what I've felt to be true of the marketing of southern food I've encountered within and outside these states, and which only seems to have become truer in the years since: southern food *matters* to people. Matters because it suggests history and politics and culture, because it raises the question of what counts as the "authentic" South, because we love to believe that we are what we eat.

In this chapter, I explore two texts that situate southernness and queerness in terms of deviant appetites: Fannie Flagg's novel *Fried Green Tomatoes at the Whistle Stop Cafe* and Dorothy Allison's story collection *Trash*. In these texts, different kinds of appetites shift and overlap: for decadent food, for queer intimacies, and for narratives that cater to problematic white fantasies. Eating so-called southern food not only connects characters to the nation's peculiar region, but represents an active embrace of peculiarity or perversion. In both Flagg's and Allison's work, the appetite for "bad" or unhealthy southern food becomes aligned with queerness—an expression of the "wrong" kind of desires. In Flagg's food-centric novel, white queer appetites are routed into blackness, which must finally be cannibalized by the narrative to provide a palatable pose of racial innocence that nonetheless remains attached to a nostalgic white ideal of small-town southern life. But an abject remainder endures, interrupting narrative coherence. Flagg's novel—with a somewhat changed plotline—became a hit film, one whose logical gaps viewers were, for the most part, willing to swallow. In both novel and film form, *Fried Green Tomatoes* is politically complicated: a narrative that places queerness in the South through the framework of deviant desires, but troubling in its use of that framework to imagine past and present southern racial dynamics.

The dynamic of who and what is eating and eaten speaks to the larger political stakes of demand and consumption in publishing. Accordingly, I offer a brief discussion of Ernest Matthew Mickler's runaway 1980s hit cookbook, *White Trash Cooking* (contemporaneous with *Fried Green Tomatoes*), and the fraught history of "white trash" as a notorious version of southernness before transitioning into Dorothy Allison's story collection *Trash*. For Allison's narrator, the experience of being perceived as "trash" is inextricable from her exploration of the politically radical possibilities of "perverse" sexual appetites, which she also associates with cravings for "bad" southern food. Across the collection, Allison's narrator spins stories of familiar versions of "trashy" southernness even as she longs for more inclusive configurations of feminist and regional identity—configurations that would embrace "perverse" appetites and recognize them as potentially loving and inclusive. But finally, hunger for a harmonious southern queer identity—unconstrained by the expectations set upon it by either constricting feminist politics or damaging stereotypes of southernness—remains, by and large, an unfulfilled craving. Although Allison's collection longs toward the possibility of reimagining "trash" as a widely inclusive identity that embraces queerly antinormative appetites, it also highlights how rigid regional and sexual identity positions can be in practice. For both Flagg and Allison, queerness—as abstraction and embodied experience—begets a more nuanced view of southernness and vice versa. And although the "deviant appetite" isn't always politically progressive, these works do ask us to consider how our appetites for certain stories take shape.

Eating Identity

Food is never politically neutral—and "southern" food in particular taps into a host of associations, emotions, memories, and even value judgments. The food we eat, crave, and write about speaks to both local and global networks as well as subtle gradients of identity and history. As Scott Romine puts it, "the *discourse* of the foodway makes it possible to eat the South"; it offers a "*perform[ance]* of a kind of Southernness" (emphasis original).[1] Two recent works on southern foodways, for example, assert that "food is a text upon which the history and values of the southern people are written" and that "by sharing and celebrating the stories of Southern Foodways, but more importantly sharing the actual food, Southerners are able to focus on similar histories and traditions, despite the division that has plagued and continues to plague the region."[2] The word "southern" gets a workout here—southern is what these people are already, an identity reinforced by enjoying southern food, somehow swallowing the pleasant taste of tradition *and* digesting the difficult complexities of history.

What, exactly, is southern food? Increasingly, scholars and chefs dedicated to southern foodways have expanded the menu, acknowledging that what constitutes the fare of the region might range from tamales to crawfish étouffée and far beyond, acknowledging the global influences of African, European, and Indigenous roots.[3] But suffice it to say that when it comes to popular cultural understanding, southern food is like porn—we know it when we see it. Food and drink like sweet tea, pecan pie, buttered cornbread, and barbecue still click strongly into myriad hazy cultural networks populating the table of southernness.

That table, despite holding many dishes historically rooted in Black culture,[4] satisfies otherwise-disallowed appetites in the sense that "southern" food has often been marketed as a means of indulging nostalgia for a "simpler time"—hear, here, the racist dog whistle. Fantasies of white southernness, especially nostalgia for a lost Old South, have very much been shaped by a discourse around food. As Marcie Cohen Ferris writes, from the end of the nineteenth century through the first half of the twentieth, "white southerners struggled to retain the racial constructs of the Old South" through "an invented tradition of Southern food . . . sweeter, richer, 'mysterious.'"[5] Advertising icons like Aunt Jemima and Uncle Ben construct palatable fictions of Black labor in the southern kitchen and make the fruits of that labor a hyper-accessible commodity nationwide.[6] Cookbooks featuring smiling white faces and humid-looking verandas have done the work of forging a narrative about what people and foods belong at the southern table, and various national restaurants have for decades catered to a revisionist southern history. Cracker Barrel was decorated with Confederate paraphernalia until the 1980s—an association that still echoes in the ham and biscuits on the billboards along the interstate.[7]

The kind of beloved southern food I've been describing has a reputation as both delicious and dangerous, something you might crave but avoid eating often. It won't appear in any health food aisle, loaded as it is with salt, fat, and sugar. Although Ferris identifies the 1970s and 80s as decades of a "national resurgence in regional cuisine" that eschewed rich "Dixie" cooking in favor of fresh local ingredients, a trend that has only grown in the decades since, the popular narrative of southern food as artery-clogging holds strong.[8] Consider this 2004 Simon & Schuster release, *Suddenly Southern: A Yankee's Guide to Living in Dixie*: "The four basic food groups in the South are beans, bacon, whiskey, and lard. Yes, the salads are more grease than green."[9] Despite a longstanding natural foods movement in southern states, the stereotypical plate of "southernness" endures, denoting both comforting nostalgia and ambivalent anachronism, delicious indulgence and toxic craving.[10]

Queering the Southern Plate

The terms we apply to physical appetite, especially for food that's "bad" for us—indulgence, craving, comfort—are also ones we frequently apply to sexual appetite. Although Sigmund Freud's theories of the role of the mouth in sexual development didn't come until the end of the nineteenth century, the antebellum period was marked by a flurry of both dietary and sexual reform movements—in Kyla Wazana Tompkins's words, a coextensive "mapping of erotic and alimentary pleasure."[11] The moral body was a body with the "right" appetites. In Tompkins's theorization, *queer alimentarity* describes how "eating functions as a metalanguage for genital pleasure and sexual desire[,] . . . [aligning] between oral pleasure and other forms of nonnormative desire."[12] This linkage extends far beyond the antebellum period. Food is, as Lauren Berlant has argued, one of our few controllable pleasures (along with sex) in late capitalist American life.[13] And socially, there are rules around both food and sex that dictate what is proper and improper.[14] It's best to be careful, then, about one's appetite: to hunger for the wrong thing is to live queerly, perhaps dangerously, to have wants spill out over the boundary that divides body from soul, self from other. This kind of spillage suggests Darieck Scott's definition of the abject: the "inescapable slippage across necessarily porous but desperately defended boundaries: the boundary between the ego and what it excludes in order to constitute itself."[15]

Through appetite, Tompkins writes, "we . . . recognize our bodies as vulnerable to each other in ways that are terrible—that is, full of terror."[16] While the AIDS epidemic was ravaging queer communities against the backdrop of hostile conservatism in the 1980s, the public was also becoming increasingly aware, for the first time, of a different "epidemic": America's obesity epidemic, caused by just the sort of foods we call southern, and its counterpart, a spate of eating disorders that emerged acutely in the public imagination partly due to the death of Karen Carpenter from anorexia in 1983.[17] In other words, queer appetites, poorly controlled appetites, and pathological appetites were seen to have potentially deadly consequences.

To eat into southern culture, then, can be seen, perhaps especially during this period, as in some sense to eat into queerness: eating as a turn away from the normative "laws of health" that make people "strong . . . morally";[18] eating associated with the state of fatness, a body of "overabundance[,] . . . bad taste[,] . . . out of bounds";[19] eating our anxieties about authenticity, realness, *naturalness*; and eating as a way of flirting with disavowed "Old South" nostalgia and fantasy. Flagg's *Fried Green Tomatoes* and Allison's *Trash* are filled with descriptions of southern food as it is prepared, served, eaten. These are works about queer appetites: in terms of extreme or inappropriate pleasures in food, sexual desires between women, and longings for impossible pasts and distant futures. And crucially, these are works obsessed with how readers or listeners "consume" stories of southernness—and why it matters.

Hunger for stories of white southernness was strong in the 1980s. As McPherson writes, "the 1980s and 1990s saw countless television reruns of *Gone with the Wind.*"[20] During this period, the belle, that icon of white southern femininity, proliferated in magazines, books, and movies—expressing a nostalgia for the Old South's bygone "charm" and domesticating the racial violence that constructs and sustains her. If nostalgia is one key affective register of southern feeling, the flip side, of course, is guilt. One response to white guilt, as I will discuss in further detail, was the fetishistic celebration of "white trash" as a site to contain southern racism. In focalizing around white southern women and all that they hunger for, consume, and serve up—and in raising the question of who does the cooking—Flagg and Allison circulate self-consciously amid popular narratives of southern femininity.

Fried Green Tomatoes and *Trash* are concerned with appetite in every sense of the word: as sexual desire, alimentary craving, and market demand. As different as these two texts are, they both layer and slide among these different "appetites." Moreover, there is a nesting doll quality to eater and eaten in these texts. The character who harbors a "queer" appetite (for the wrong kind of food or sex) looks like a tempting meal to characters interested in a juicy story from a self-righteous distance.[21] The reader, accordingly, finds herself indicted by this storytelling dynamic, making visible the way our reading practices are shaped by market demand. When we read, we participate in larger cultural appetites—perhaps for the belle serving up a simpler, moonlit world on a silver platter, masking the Black labor behind the tasty morsel, and perhaps for the "white trash" that buoys middle-class moralism. These texts lead us into such familiar fantasies of white southernness by way of our stomachs: Ruth and Idgie, in *Fried Green Tomatoes*, begin their romance over biscuits, fried chicken, and honey, and Allison's unnamed protagonist first seduces women over red velvet cake. These texts solicit the reader's interest in queer hungers to invoke (and to either critique or linger within, as we'll see) culturally disavowed forms of white southernness. Where we think we are reading about characters' deviant desires, we find, ultimately, that we are reading about our own appetites for stories of "the South."

Fried Green Tomatoes (and Other Southern Flavors)

Fannie Flagg's 1986 novel *Fried Green Tomatoes at the Whistle Stop Cafe* is beloved as a classic of contemporary southern popular literature—equally so is the film version from 1991. While I'll return to the film, it's worth lingering a moment on the reviews of the novel, to give a sense of the kind of reception it received: "a real novel" (the *New York Times*), a "literary enterprise shin[ing] with honesty, gallantry" (the *LA Times*), and "first-class" (Erma Bombeck).[22]

If the glowing reviews of *Fried Green Tomatoes* (novel and film) tell us anything, it's that there is very much an appetite for this kind of fare. As Roger Ebert put it, "You have been to Whistle Stop before, in a dozen other books and movies."[23] Predictably, many critics described the film in flavorful terms: The movie is "sweet" if not "downright sugary" (*Tulsa World*); something you "could get a craving for" (*Washington Post*); at its worst, "ham handed" (*Variety*). The novel, too, is deeply food-centered, opening with an ad for the cafe in a character's newsletter and ending with a list of recipes—for fried green tomatoes, biscuits with butter and honey, pecan pie, lemon icebox cake—but not, importantly, barbecue. A quick and dirty summary explains why: Idgie and Ruth, the novel's two protagonists and "close friends" (a special emphasis on those scare quotes), run the Whistle Stop Cafe beginning in the 1920s. When Ruth's cruel estranged husband and KKK leader Frank Bennett comes over from Georgia to try to steal Ruth's baby, Whistle Stop's best cook, Sipsey (who is Black), protects the baby and kills Frank by whacking him over the head with a cast-iron skillet—and Sipsey's son, Big George, cooks him into barbecue to hide the evidence. Surely, there is not much "sugary" about this, but it is familiar. Flagg is not the first to link southern food with violence—after all, in *To Kill a Mockingbird*, Scout Finch's confrontation with Bob Ewell occurs while she's dressed as a ham. In fact, Harper Lee's review of *Fried Green Tomatoes* (included in the edition of the novel I cite here) is worth quoting: "Airplanes and television have removed the Threadgoodes from the Southern scene. Happily for us, Fannie Flagg has preserved a whole community of them in a richly comic, poignant narrative that records the exuberance of their lives, the sadness of their departure. Idgie Threadgoode is a true original: Huckleberry Finn would have tried to marry her!" In three sentences, Lee accomplishes quite a lot. She establishes the incompatibility of "the Southern scene" with modern life; she frames, with words like "preserves" and "records," the Threadgoodes as extinct anthropological subjects rather than fictional characters; and she makes two unsupportable claims. For one, Idgie Threadgoode is not a true original. She is, if anything, a descendent of Lee's own Scout Finch. Like Lee's protagonist, Idgie is a "tomboy" with an interest in racial justice. Both characters even share an affinity for sticking a hand into a hole in a tree and pulling out treasure. If that sounds suggestive, it should—more on that later. For now, I want to move on to Lee's second claim, which is that Huck Finn would have tried to marry Idgie. To project romantic intentions onto a fictional child is rather strange, and more so the impulse to describe Idgie, a character more plainly queer than Lee's Scout, as *marriageable* to that child rather than simply similar to him. Lee's comments try to mitigate a discomfort with the novel even as they identify it as belonging to "the Southern scene."

Her review points to an important problem: although this bizarre novel makes a theme of southern fare, something about its very desire to be consumable sticks in the craw. Structurally, the various narrative levels function at first to offer the reader the prospect of consuming white southernness guilt-free: reveling in the imagined taste of biscuits and the nostalgic backward gaze into "simpler times" without having to confront any ideological problem with such an impulse—but this structure finally collapses. As I'll argue, the project of "consuming" the southern story in just the right way is an impossible one for the novel's principal characters and its implied reader, who gaze back in time from the vantage point of the flavorless, antiseptic space of a Birmingham nursing home. Although perverse appetites (for indulgent food and for stories trafficking in racial and sexual otherness) are crucial to building a distinctive southernness in the novel, the deviant morsels on offer (violent blackness, white queerness) must finally be disavowed in the project of making southernness appear palatable—that is to say, heteronormative, racially innocent, and even calorie-free. Narrative coherence falls apart somewhat under the strain of this project, ultimately lending the novel a fractured temporality and a hasty, ill-fitting resolution that reveals something indigestible and artificial in the meal on offer. *Fried Green Tomatoes* can't, ultimately, serve up a South that is both sensationally deviant and innocently wholesome; and it's the text's capacity to give some indigestion on this account that is critically valuable. To either celebrate *Fried Green Tomatoes* as a subversive queer novel or dismiss it as a problematic piece of southern fluff is to miss a crucial piece of the story. The text's formulations of queerness and southernness are inextricable, connected by way of starkly racialized deviant appetites.

(De)constructing Whistle Stop

Structurally, the novel depends on distancing its reader from the problems with white southern nostalgia—while still providing the "taste" of it. It must only tease the satisfaction of this deviant craving. The novel's plot emerges through three components: a storyteller, a (fictional) historical archive, and an omniscient narrator. The storyteller, Ninny Threadgoode, is a woman in a Birmingham nursing home slowly losing her memory. Over the course of several months in 1986, she tells the story of the quaint small town of Whistle Stop, Alabama, to Evelyn, a discontented housewife in her forties who feels somehow out of step with the modern world: "things had changed so fast[,] . . . she had gotten lost somewhere along the way."[24] At first, Ninny seems to begin speaking to her apropos of nothing, a miraculous fount of story whose driving force is a strange murder that happened in the small town in the 1920s—but over time, as her bond with Evelyn deepens and her memory fades, it is Evelyn, as active listener, who keeps the story going, returning to visit Ninny and coax her into storytelling with offers of food.

The town of Whistle Stop captures in its name the space of an idealized southern past of which Ninny is delegate. As a term for a small town, "whistle stop" came into popularity in the 1950s, but it dates from the 1920s, describing a station small enough that a train would stop only on signal.[25] The town of Whistle Stop, then, is unique and yet already a shorthand for the quintessential American small town. More specifically, this is the fantasy of a specifically southern culture—where life is slower, more "traditional"—a romance that arises out of the more complicated history of the region's lagging economy after the Civil War.[26] The train, as the motor of industrial capitalism and therefore modernity, gives Whistle Stop its name, its cafe, and its story, but it also sets in motion the end of that story.

Ninny's home in Whistle Stop is with the Threadgoodes, a large family who lived in a "great big two-story white-frame house with a big front porch that wrapped all the way around to the side," once framed by wisteria and sweetheart roses but now fallen into disrepair.[27] This description taps into the potent fantasy of the plantation house, Tara in decline. It's not only the war that diminishes this grand Old South, but industrialization. Twice, the train cuts off southern virility at the roots, killing Buddy, beloved eldest of the Threadgoode family, and taking the arm of Buddy Jr., thereafter christened "Stump."[28] Although Ninny professes her love for "watching the trains go by," it's their relentless forward motion that finally produces the blandness of Rose Terrace nursing home.[29] As a true southern town, the charm of Whistle Stop is that it is always already dying, always threatened by the sterility of late capitalism.[30] Rose Terrace, by its very name, is an imitation of the "real" terrace that once housed the southern lady and the Old South— and Ninny, "a rather sweet-looking old lady in the faded blue flower-print dress," a woman "living on . . . dreams," is a pale imitation of the "real" southern lady.[31]

With her stories, Ninny invites Evelyn into a negotiation of what white southern womanhood in the modern world might mean. Ninny's diction and dialect is old fashioned, with an Alabama twang ("You cain't smell anything they've got cooking out here. . . . I wouldn't give you a plugged nickel for anything boiled, would you?"[32]). And her homesickness for the "little town . . . out by the railroad yards" prompts in her initial stories a backward gaze into a time and place full of what she understands as community and ease: a big, happy family, a town where Black people happily take care of white, and simple pleasures.[33] Yet the storytelling mode here is not only a backward gaze, but, as Sarah Gilbreath Ford puts it, "a way of performing regional identity, that changes it in the process."[34] Evelyn, through questioning Ninny, supplying her with snacks, and prodding her when she begins to go off on tangents, becomes a co-creator of her story, which ultimately revolves around the protection of Ruth. In Ninny's description, Ruth fits perfectly into the Old-South haze of the Threadgoode house as its adopted belle, adored by the Threadgoodes' devoted servant, Sipsey, and embodying the belle's beauty and manners. Ruth "had light auburn hair and brown eyes with long lashes, and was so sweet and soft-spoken that people just fell in love with her on first sight. . . . She was just one of those sweet-to-the-bone girls. . . . She was raised real strict-like."[35] While Ninny might be "sweet-looking," she isn't the *real* belle, but rather a substitute, a wallflower moved by necessity to center stage.

Ninny ventriloquizes the story of Ruth's arrival, her romance with Idgie, and the progress of their lives because, having "nothing better to do," she has served largely as a conduit for whatever "juicy" stories arrive in the small town; she has had the leisure to sit and listen to other stories at the cafe. All the Whistle Stop storytellers are the ones who have, quite literally, a seat at the table—the white members of the community. This dynamic briefly flares into visibility: On a day when Evelyn is absent, Ninny begins telling her story to Geneene, her Black nurse, who, taking a moment to rest her feet and apparently taken aback by this barrage, can only respond with "What?" and "Who?"[36] Ninny proceeds to tell a rambling story, with only these two questions from her otherwise silent interlocutor. It's clear that Geneene is not a co-constructor of the nostalgic story of the bygone southern world. Rather, she performs the invisible labor that provides the space and leisure for Ninny and Evelyn to negotiate white femininity past and present. Geneene is "tired[,] . . . working a double shift" while Ninny expresses to her a concern for the happiness of Evelyn, a bored housewife.[37] This dynamic further evokes the belle through her counterpart, the "mammy" figure; as Kimberly Wallace-Sanders writes, "When we reimagine the antebellum plantation as the body politic, we see how the mammy's body serves as a tendon between the races, connecting the muscle of African American slave labor with the skeletal power structure of white southern aristocracy."[38]

Just as the co-construction of Whistle Stop is a white endeavor between Ninny and her listener, so does the novel enlist a white reader with an appetite for nostalgic—and flavorful—white southernness. Ninny's paternalistic racism is abundantly clear, but like everything else that comes out of her mouth, it's figured as adorable or at least excusable because it is quaint, belonging squarely in the past—as though her horror at a Black boy at the supermarket "cutting his eyes" when asked to carry a white woman's groceries, or her amusement with Geneene's "talk[ing] as big as you please" is no different from and no more consequential than her outdated belief that a Coke only costs a nickel.[39] Evelyn never engages with these comments, and so the novel invites a reader who might feel similarly excused from having to confront Ninny's racism—rather than offended or excluded on the basis of it. Ninny is every white southerner's racist grandmother, the embodiment of the "belonging to a different time" argument, and her often-referenced childlike innocence and her sepia-toned stories of Whistle Stop suggest that this "different time" was harmless, and that it is simply dying out rather than changing shape or growing stronger. Even her name asks the reader to concede that Ninny—along with the southern belle she constructs through story—is an innocuous figure.

The novel seeks to place its reader at an appealing middle-distance from Ninny's nostalgia by employing a series of archival documents. Relative to Evelyn, the reader approaches Ninny at a remove; nothing communicates this better than the gustatory pleasure that accompanies narrative pleasure in Ninny's storytelling. Whether lemon icebox pie, Cracker Jacks, or Taco Bell—Ninny's first foray into "foreign food"—alimentary pleasure is capable both of sparking memory and speech, or of interrupting it, as when Evelyn has to prod Ninny several times to tell her the story of what happened with Ruth and Idgie because Ninny is distracted (ahem) by the size of her taco.[40] Evelyn has something the reader obviously lacks—the experience, the literal *taste* of the story at its source. But the reader has something that Evelyn lacks—access to the story beyond Ninny's diminishing capacity to tell it. As Ninny increasingly loses her memory (and, to use the novel's own pun, the "thread" of her story), the reader gains "objective" knowledge. Interspersed with Ninny's tales at Rose Terrace Nursing Home are chapters dated and headed as news items: from the *Weems Weekly*, Whistle Stop's main newsletter; *The Birmingham News*; *Slagtown News Flotsam & Jetsam*; and *The Valdosta Courier*. This kind of archival simulacra produces what we might call, in reference to Lee's review, a preservation effect.

If the reader is able to consume the *feeling* of southern nostalgia at a remove through Ninny and Evelyn, she is also able to play the part of historian, unearthing artifacts of southern life, through these publications. As a historian, she reads asynchronously, at a far temporal distance from those who are supposedly reading the paper on its date of publication. Presented as its own chapter rather than clearly embedded within the narrative, the newspaper article asks the reader, and the reader only, to bear witness to what is "preserved," an entire community that would otherwise be lost to time. However fictional, this archive places the novel in historical terms, invoking real communities of lost whistle stop towns. And the single news strip, rather than a full layout, suggests a story and a region alone and unto itself, captured at a moment, unsullied by a wider network of geopolitical relations.[41] The full story the article gestures toward is visible only to the reader, who renders this "document" part of a narrative whole. Unlike Ninny, a newspaper is, presumably, not subject to slips of memory, to bias, to nostalgia. Framed in this way, these chapters ask the reader to participate in historical scrutiny, to see what things were *really* like back then, rather than descend fully into Ninny's reminiscence. By positioning the reader as historian, the novel suggests that the reader, unlike Ninny and Evelyn, occupies a "modern" temporality: a space of objective knowledge, of unsullied appreciation of the clearly glimpsed past. Of course, this very conception of history is another fantasy offered to the reader, another way to claim distance from the Jim Crow South.

Finally, it is the outermost narrative layer—the omniscient narrator—who provides complete access to scenes beyond Ninny's awareness *and* the historical record, positioning the reader as a detective uncovering the "real" (in the sense of that which is hidden or secret and also the most authentic) story of Whistle Stop.[42] In connecting Ninny's stories to the archival artifacts, this voice lends the novel its dramatic appeal. Stories of a sleepy old southern town and yellowing newspaper articles are not, of course, innately interesting; it is the murder mystery that drives the narrative. Who killed Frank Bennett, and where did he disappear to? Did those intimate women friends have anything to do with it? Ninny, in her innocence, knows very little of the answer. And just as Evelyn approaches Ninny with an affectionate awareness of her limitations, holding her tongue when Ninny wears her dress inside out, the omniscient narrative voice positions the reader to regard Evelyn in much the same way. Evelyn's biggest fear is of not knowing things that others do know (for instance, the cause of death when it goes unlisted in obituaries—newspapers do not reveal narrative to Evelyn in the same way that they do for the reader). Knowledge, made scarce, is power. In this way, Whistle Stop becomes the reader's, apparently wholly available for our consumption alone—but it won't go down smoothly. The story of the murder in Whistle Stop is organized around a titillating story of white queerness, routed into a frightening blackness; this, finally, becomes the abject remainder alongside the novel's guilt-free "taste" of nostalgic white southernness. With this lingering otherness, the southern fantasy the novel offers is, on close inspection, not wholly palatable.

Sinful Stories

Through Ninny's stories, Whistle Stop becomes markedly queer. Ninny has an appetite for disturbing stories; her innocence as a white southern woman feeds on a fevered racial imaginary and anarchic gender trouble. In the simplest terms, oral pleasure and illicit hunger are crucial to the storytelling dynamic between Ninny and Evelyn. From the first story Ninny tells, food is figured as deeply personal, even intimate: "I used to love my buttermilk and cornbread, in the afternoon. I like to mash it all up in my glass and eat it with a spoon, but you cain't eat in public like you can at home[,] . . . can you?"[43] Evelyn, who has hidden in the nursing home visiting room to furtively enjoy a candy bar, must understand the feeling. As Ninny and Evelyn tell stories and eat together, that intimacy becomes something shared. The nature of this secret pleasure is perhaps most visible on Easter, when Evelyn brings Ninny a chocolate rabbit. The story Ninny elects to tell that day is that of Mr. Pinto, the famous murderer whose corpse traveled through Whistle Stop on the train. As the omniscient narrator affirms, Mr. Pinto is hardly good conversation for a religious holiday; when a mischievous boy tries to photograph Mr. Pinto, he is so shaken upon glimpsing the murderer's electrocuted stare that he manages only a blurred photograph. Here, as in the larger murder mystery of Whistle Stop, the thrill in discussing Mr. Pinto ("like the bean") is in gobbling sordid or violent stories and then pushing them away. As she bites off the head of her chocolate rabbit, Ninny reflects that "I guess I'm the only one out here that's having myself two Easters. It may be a sin, but I won't tell anyone if you won't."[44] The "sin" to which she refers, and the shared secret of that sin, seems to have to do less with Easter than with her rapacious and clandestine appetite for both chocolate and violence.

In biting the head off her rabbit, Ninny reenacts two stories of decapitation she has previously told to Evelyn. The first beheading is a lively anecdote of what happens when a woman's hormones are left to run wild: a young woman in Georgia, finding herself in an early menopause, cuts off her mother's head and throws it atop the courthouse steps, shouting, "Here, this is what you wanted."[45] The other scene of decapitation is less murderous, but certainly not less significant. In her introduction to Sipsey, the caretaker for the Threadgoode children and the source of the cafe's recipes, Ninny explains that "the thing she was the most deathly afraid of in the world was the heads of animals," burying hundreds in the garden to ward off their spirits, which might otherwise possess their human killers.[46] When Ninny bites into her Easter candy, she joins and enjoys two moments of queer and Black otherness.

The tale of the woman who decapitates her mother is in the first place a "queer" story in the old sense of being strange, but it is also a story of the female body made sexually queer by lack of proper balance. Like a dream, it feels overdetermined in its signs, designed for psychoanalysis. The mother, as the figure of heteronormative futurity, buoys the state. The woman in early menopause, only thirty-six, is at the right time in her life to step "naturally" into that role of motherhood; and yet she is so hormonally off-beat, out of step, so to speak, that she grotesquely parodies this role, chopping off the head in the kitchen in order to provide the courthouse with what it "wants" quite literally. She "prepares" femininity as a meal to give to the state, a kind of drag by which she repeats the domestic performances of her mother with a violent difference—perhaps an extreme example of Butlerian gender trouble.[47] One way to read this is that in castrating the mother figure, the woman frees herself to occupy a different role; another way to read this is that menopause will make you a murderer if you're not careful.

In telling the story, Ninny solicits both these readings; she savors the anarchic possibilities of female sexuality as excessive, radical, and destabilizing of social norms even as she disavows these possibilities. She presents the story as a cautionary tale for Evelyn, whose depression and overeating Ninny attributes to menopause. Exacerbated by the early death of her own mother, Evelyn's excess of emotion and appetite occasions the courthouse story when Ninny finds her "eating a Baby Ruth candy bar, with big tears streaming down her face."[48] Ninny recommends "Stresstabs Number 10" to get Evelyn's hormones back in order, but she hardly reinstates the role of the lost mother, paragon of appropriate female moderation.[49] On the contrary, she reinscribes female excess—and her interlocutor's appetite for it—through queer story, most remarkably that of Ruth and Idgie. It seems no coincidence that Evelyn is devouring a Baby Ruth bar when Ninny tells her about the woman at the courthouse, nor is this the first time that sweetness links associatively to queerness. At Ninny and Evelyn's first meeting, Evelyn is eating a Butterfinger when Ninny first introduces the murder: "[Idgie] was a character all right, but how anybody ever could have thought that she killed that man is beyond me."[50] Inexplicably, Ninny believes that "it all started" on April Fool's Day of 1919, which Idgie, at this point a child, celebrates by coming to Sunday dinner with a rather phallic prank: her finger presented in a box with a hole in it. As everyone is eating cobbler, she announces "out of a clear blue sky" that she will never wear a dress again—and goes and puts on her brother's clothes.[51] Ninny's vague linkage of Frank Bennett's murder, Idgie's gender expression, and April Fool's Day dinner connects sweetness and hunger, queerness and violence, sexuality and play—connections that overflow from the diegetic world on the current of the near rhyme of cut-off finger / Butterfinger.

Queer sexuality, though, is never explicitly named in Ninny's storytelling. The closest she comes is her account of Idgie's declaration at dinner ("I'm never gonna wear another dress as long as I live!"), like the inverse of a marriage promise, when she suddenly refuses her white dress.[52] Like Idgie's frequently retold story of a lake that freezes over and is carried away by the ducks who were floating there (resulting from a radical temperature drop that likewise purportedly happens "out of a clear blue sky"), her queerness is both of the world of Ninny's story and impossible in it.[53] What Ninny most emphasizes in Idgie is her playfulness, a quality adjacent to Ninny's own often-mentioned childlike innocence and therefore desexualized. Idgie is, to Ninny, "a character," someone who performs a role for laughs.[54] Although Ninny narrates Idgie's and Ruth's relationship openly, remembering Sipsey's proclamation that "that ol' love bug done bit Idgie," neither woman's sexuality ever becomes an explicit topic of conversation.[55] To acknowledge sexual queerness, as opposed to desexualizing and domesticating "the love bug," is to venture too close to endorsing deviant hungers—appetites that risk unsettling heteronormative structures.

Similarly, rather than speak explicitly about the racial dynamics of Whistle Stop, Ninny gestures to an unknowable and essentializing blackness in her stories—of Sipsey in particular. Sipsey's practice of burying heads in the garden is a "spooky" ritual, born out of a fear that the spirit of the animal will otherwise come to possess her.[56] Although Ninny doesn't pause to speculate about this practice, the "spookiness" lingers in Ninny's inability to firmly place Sipsey in space and time. She states that "you never know where colored people come from," suggesting her anxiety about Sipsey's connections to a deep and dark history.[57] Ninny does, in fact, know—and says— that Sipsey's mother was enslaved, but this fact seems too uncomfortable to sit with. Instead, she constructs blackness as a black box, inscrutable and therefore potentially dangerous.

In eating the head of the chocolate rabbit, Ninny performs what she effectively enacts in every session of storytelling: the consumption of the Black body, its internalization into her white subjectivity and history of Whistle Stop, to make it less of a threat.[58] Ninny's description of Sipsey follows a familiar cultural script: her pride in her son, George Pullman Peavey, after Poppa has "taught him how to be a butcher[,] . . . slaughtering hogs when he was only ten"; her playfulness; her wonderful cooking at the cafe.[59] Her garden produces "the biggest tomatoes and okra and squash in town," and her culinary skills are literally magic: "Even at eleven, they say she could make the most delicious biscuits and gravy. . . . Her dumplings were so light they would float in the air and you'd have to catch 'em to eat 'em."[60] Sipsey's cooking brings white customers through the front door and Black to the back, inciting Idgie's bravery in standing up to the KKK.[61] It's not difficult to see how in Ninny's account of Sipsey, blackness becomes a "natural" resource for labor and a vehicle for white goodness and bravery.

The reader's apparently superior position to Ninny allows her to see how Ninny's "innocence" is produced through the simultaneous consumption and disavowal of white queerness and abject blackness.[62] Although the reader is given endless accounts of the tastes that Ninny and Evelyn share—in food and stories—the reader is excused from taking on the accompanying ideological and literal weight of this kind of white southern nostalgia and pointed, instead, to Ninny's blind spots. In their first conversation, Ninny explains to Evelyn that "I brought a picture with me that I had at home, of a girl in a swing with a castle and pretty blue bubbles in that background . . . but that nurse here said the girl was naked from the waist up and not appropriate. . . . I never knew she was naked."[63] This odd disclosure suggests an overdetermined whimsy in Ninny's preferences, and the kind of disavowals of knowledge that her stories will repeat. Meanwhile, Evelyn's visits to Ninny, as well as the snacks she eats in the visitors' lounge, remain a secret from her husband Ed. As this covertness suggests to the reader, fully sinking into the southern comfort of indulgent white nostalgia and food is hardly healthy. And yet it is not just Ninny but the omniscient narrator who savors and disavows the abject other, enlisting the reader, like Evelyn, in a clandestine queer alimentarity.

The omniscient narrator eats her words most obviously in the construction and erasure of a frightening blackness in the figure of Sipsey's grandson Artis Peavey. Born "so black he had blue gums," Artis's blackness is figured as vicious, lascivious, exotic, and, ultimately, threateningly unknowable.[64] He is inclined to violence (in childhood, he stabs his light-skinned twin brother, Jasper, simply because it "felt so good I just couldn't stop"), as well as extreme sexual appetite; as an adult, he satisfies these desires in the Black Birmingham neighborhood of Slagtown, which, as Michael Dunne points out, houses many of the novel's "unresolved racial attitudes."[65] For the most part, that "exotic sepia spot," full of the debauched appeals of the city, is set in contrast to Whistle Stop.[66] But if Whistle Stop's purity is constructed by its border with Slagtown, Artis is a border-crosser. He is the one to eat the barbecue that Big George makes out of Frank Bennett.[67] He enjoys Frank, along with a Grapico, alone in the woods, far from the cafe and its friendly back-door service.[68] Cannibalism has long signaled a Western fantasy of the Black primitive savage, but the trope of cannibalism is also built into our discourse around democracy and race: the ideal of whiteness and fully realized Western modernity, ever a specter of the future, requires the continual incorporation of the raced Other.[69]

Understood this way, the text cannibalizes blackness. The omniscient narrator, either in exploring Whistle Stop or roaming through the contemporary world of the 1980s, is after a kind of bland multiculturalism that would dilute histories of racial oppression without destabilizing white supremacy. The narrator's stories of interracial affection and friendship across generations in Whistle Stop—Big George carrying Stump all the way to the hospital after his accident and Idgie helping bring an elephant to Big George's daughter Naughty Bird, to take two examples—*could* be Ninny's stories. They are accounts of "friendship" between Black and white that promise warm feelings while avoiding more complex histories and affects. It's a model of "friendly" non-engagement epitomized by Idgie's celebrated willingness to serve the Black community barbecue out the back door of the cafe.

Blackness in Evelyn's world, the contemporary world of the 1980s, is most clearly cannibalized by whiteness during Evelyn's adventure into a Black Birmingham church. This experience is presented as a kind of de-racist cleansing for Evelyn, providing her with the revelation that Black is beautiful and that she "could never know" what it's like to be Black.[70] And yet the peace and understanding that the joyful service brings her is revealingly one-sided; when the woman next to her greets her with "God bless you," Evelyn replies, "Thank you."[71] Although she perceives herself as "the Pillsbury doughboy in the belly of the snake," it's really the Black church that is being consumed by the white narrative.[72] The church becomes a platform for Evelyn's self-knowledge and although her knowledge of the woman whose hand she shakes is denied, the same is not true for the reader, who is given access to the woman's full lineage: she is the daughter of Jasper Peavey, son of George Pullman, son of Sipsey. The novel's multi-generational account of its Black characters (not its white ones) feels proprietary.

And yet blackness can't be fully consumed—it remains to an extent foreign, abject. As Zita Nunes argues, because the meaning and power of whiteness depends upon blackness, some aspect of blackness must remain always outside the body politic: a remainder.[73] If the woman whose hand Evelyn shakes in church is connected by blood to Jasper, she is also connected to Jasper's dark twin, Artis. The suggestion of blackness-as-primitivism is visible in the description of the church's energy, which spreads physically through the room as the preacher "dances and struts" and the room "throbs" with enthusiasm under Evelyn's astonished gaze.[74] The novel's fervent endorsement of "friendship" is incompatible with the fever dream of blackness that Artis represents.[75] The words lifted up to God at the church—"There is no resurrection for bodies gnawed by the maggots of sin"—captures the pleasure the narrative offers in the queer specter of bodies chewed, blackness internalized by a thousand white bites.[76] But Artis remains outside the church, out of reach.

Black/Queer

Like Ninny biting the head of the Easter rabbit, the broader narrative links blackness to queerness through a process of consumption. Narrative hunger for and disavowal of white queerness (as violent unbalance) and blackness (as violent unknowability)—is made visible through the strange and repeated elision between the two. In a pivotal romantic scene, Idgie leads Ruth on a picnic, inducting her into "secret" knowledge by sticking her hand into a hole in a tree and coming away "covered from head to foot with thousands of bees. . . . By the time she had gotten back [to Ruth], almost all the bees had flown away and what had been a completely black figure was now Idgie . . . with a jar of wild honey."[77] Ruth, who has "slid down the tree onto the ground and burst into tears" watching this spectacle, is "still shaky" when Idgie tells her, "I just wanted for us to have a secret together, that's all."[78] After they've eaten the fried chicken, potato salad, and biscuits, along with the honey, Idgie is, with the "clear blue sky" reflected in her eyes, "as happy as anybody who is in love in the summertime can be."[79] Ruth is so overcome by Idgie's secret as to appear physically spent, and the suggestive honey pulled from the tree coats their decadent meal. It is difficult *not* to read this as an erotic queer moment. It is also one in which Idgie, in pursuing queer pleasure, becomes covered in blackness—a blackness that, while not covering the more passive, feminine Ruth, certainly touches her as she shares with Idgie the food Sipsey has packed.[80]

Idgie's secret identity as Railroad Bill reinforces the linkage of queerness and blackness; as a vigilante hero, she takes on radical hungers in blackface. Railroad Bill is Whistle Stop's Robin Hood, throwing food from passing trains to the needy. His blackness is dramatically emphasized in a conversation at the cafe in which the men of the town speculate about how to catch "that black son of a bitch."[81] In the next chapter, Stump, as a grown man, recounts the day he learned of Idgie's secret identity: "Aunt Idgie was still drying her hands and face. . . . The sink was still full of coal dust."[82] Stump has until this point believed that Artis is the culprit, based on his being "about the right size"—and, of course, Black. Here, the quiet queer-coding of the word "aunt" slides into the historical use of the word to refer to Black women.[83] The rationale for Idgie's choice is unclear. What use for her, or anyone else, is there in playing the vigilante Black? The answer is that the novel's displacement of her queerness into blackness renders Idgie herself harmless. She takes on radical socialism and perverse desire only when she puts on blackface, and although she tells Ruth she would "kill" for her love of her, this violent appetite is ultimately transferred into the Black body, leaving Idgie herself innocent. It is Sipsey who kills Frank (protecting Ruth and her infant son), and Big George who cooks him (again, out of protection); in their naturalized labor, they clean up, so to speak, Idgie's queer intentions. But the dirt must go somewhere, and finally it is concentrated in the body of Artis.

Artis, in devouring human barbecue, also devours—absorbs—queer perversity. After the meat is gone, all that is left of Frank are his bones and glass eye. That cold, hard blue eye, those stripped and cleaned bones, evoke powerfully Frank's whiteness. If cannibalism is the incorporation of the "loved or desired and feared object," what Artis desires and consumes is not only Frank's whiteness, but something else: his "perverse" sexuality.[84] While alive, Frank is described as going to great lengths in the styling of his hair and clothes, and although he makes many sexual conquests, these are an expression more of violence than desire. The origin of his violence is a scene in childhood when he catches his father having sex with his mother (to whom Frank, as a child, is extremely bonded). The inability to properly "stomach" heterosexual sex, identification with the mother, dandyism—these all code Frank as queer. When the Valdosta police come to Whistle Stop looking for the missing man, Grady, the sheriff, calls them "sissified," a description that the narrator appears to endorse by describing the sheriff as speaking in a "high, tight little voice."[85] In denigrating homosexuality, Grady names it, locates it as intruding from outside Whistle Stop, and demands its elimination. Artis's consumption of Frank, then, is a simultaneous incorporation and destruction of a foreign and potentially violent male queerness.

What is left in the resolution of this story, finally, is that which is feminine, passive, and white. Although Idgie seems to replace Frank in the role of husband and father (disciplining Stump, she firmly admonishes him that "your mother and I didn't raise you to be an ignorant, knothead redneck"), the novel also displaces her from that role, refusing to make her relationship with Ruth overtly queer.[86] When Ruth dies of cancer, the role of besotted mourner is given not to Idgie but to Smokey, the local itinerant: "He had never touched her[,] . . . had never kissed her."[87] He and Idgie are set in parallel. They mourn Ruth together, silently. If Ruth "never knew" how Smokey loved her (romantically and sexually, that is), the suggestion is that Ruth "never knew" how Idgie loved her either. The final word about Ruth's death, and about the love in her life, is told through Smokey's perspective, denying Idgie a voice in mourning. Smokey functions, in essence, as a smokescreen for the queer relationship that can never be named.[88] But for all Idgie's antics as a "character" next to Ruth's conventional femininity, it is Ruth who threatens to "out" the quite-visible relationship. In committing herself to Frank and then Idgie, Ruth is the object—and the subject, although less overtly—of queer desire twice over, threatening its proliferation, and suggesting, like Artis, the porousness of Whistle Stop's borders. Because of Ruth, queerness must be figured as timeless (endemic to certain "sissified" Valdosta men) even as the novel demands that we think of it as historically located (post-Whistle Stop).

Finally, the novel's temporality comes to a stutter around Artis and Ruth: together, they represent blackness and queerness as abject otherness, the excluded and haunting remainder of a narrative seeking to uphold Whistle Stop as the repository of what is finally a white, heteronormative—and yet innocent, healthy even—southern nostalgia. Accordingly, the narrative seems to choke up around these two. Ruth dies a painful death while still young, wasting away slowly from cancer, and Artis dies an undignified one as an old man in a Birmingham hotel. But in a text peppered with dates, only two apparent errors in the timeline appear—in the 1940s, concentrated around Artis and Ruth. In such a date-focused, chronologically oriented novel, these singular mistakes around these characters appear more as significant puzzles, an unwitting unraveling of narrative cohesion, than simple misprints. The effect of these two temporal slipups is disorienting: they suggest that the "omniscient" panorama and the historical "archive" of southern story are just as fallible or fictive as Ninny's fading memory, upsetting the reader's apparently stable position.

In 1949, Artis is arrested for helping a dog escape from a pair of dogcatchers in Slagtown. And yet in 1948, Idgie helps get Artis out of Kilbey Prison, where he has been incarcerated for said dogcatcher episode. This second anecdote appears just a few pages after the first, both related by the omniscient narrator. A similar issue occurs in Ruth's narrative: the omniscient narrator first relates that she dies of her long illness in 1947, with help from a well-timed morphine dose from Sipsey, but a few chapters later, in the discussion of Smokey's and Idgie's mutual love for Ruth, her death date is given as 1946. Both episodes are organized around imprisonment. Artis's desire to preserve a dog's freedom leads to his own capture; and when Ruth, increasingly imprisoned within her own body, finally passes away, she is locked away, made inaccessible, in another sense.

These date slippages, although perhaps unintentional, nevertheless speak to the ways in which Artis and Ruth escape imprisonment from a straightforward temporality, pointing to a larger threat: the "simple time" of the bygone South that Ninny and Evelyn (and the reader, from a safe distance) long for is not simply remembered, but rather created by the lights of the present. The dream of Whistle Stop's pre-lesbian intimacy and interracial friendship in the isolated small town (a time in which a woman could dress like a man, proclaim her love for another woman, and raise a child with that woman without anyone thinking anything *modern* of her) is simultaneously the nightmare of an already-present future in which "sissy" men sully the purity of that innocence, and ravenous Black men, dissolving the proper boundaries between bodies, carry that stain into the depths of the growing city. The town newsletter, the *Weems Weekly*, ends with a lamentation of the town's descent into Birmingham suburbia in 1969 and a vague gesture toward the political and cultural importance of that momentous decade. The civil rights movement and second-wave feminism loom large, although the newsletter doesn't mention these changes. Nor does Evelyn refer to the larger national events of her time—but it's difficult not to see the craving for a "simpler time," from her world of the 1980s, as a reaction against the dramatic political and social changes of the intervening years. Rather than showing the gradual fading of an innocent world, the stutters of the novel's progression through time has the effect of creating an overlap between past and present.[89] Like Mr. Pinto passing through from Mobile, the horrors approaching from "modernity" are unnameable, uncapturable, and nevertheless already present, a blurry trace, as though future creates past rather than the other way around.

Southern-Fried Perversions 39

Decadent Recipes

The novel's conclusion presents an additional problem: to situate the legacy of the southern belle firmly and harmlessly in the past, Ninny must eventually fade away completely, but in death, she upsets the narrative structure. As Evelyn attempts to retreat with Ninny back into the past, into stories, Ninny is coaxing Evelyn into the present—encouraging her to go on hormonal medication, suggesting she begin a career, and assuring her that life has not "passed her by"—aligning her with the modern world. In this way, the source of their intimacy is also its unraveling, and it is no surprise that Ninny dies while Evelyn is away at a weight loss program in California. Her trip has taken her away from the South temporally as much as geographically. Her changing relationship to food at the program is indicative of her changing relationship to the past: it no longer provides her with a comforting nostalgia, but it also doesn't laden her with weight literal or metaphorical. At the "fat farm," Whistle Stop recedes from view: "The most important thing on their minds was what exciting low-cal dessert would the cooks come up with tonight?"[90] The paucity of the present is stark; in contrast to the rich narrative texture of Ninny's stories, we are given a brochure for a life filled with preprogrammed days that start at 8:30 with "Wake-up exercises, done to the recording of 'I'm So Excited,' by the Pointer Sisters" and end at 7:30 with "arts and crafts . . . [and] still life (using artificial fruit only)."[91]

For all the derision such details invite (Evelyn's favorite lo-cal dessert is Fitness Flan), Evelyn is also *happy*, filled with a sense of community and agency, not to mention losing weight. She's newly "healthy," free of her appetite for fattening (southern) foods and perverse (southern) stories. Her new happiness, along with Ninny's exit from the frame, unsettles the reader's superior position, which has depended upon Evelyn's ill-fit with modern life and Ninny's limited understanding of the contemporary world. Upon venturing to Whistle Stop to retrieve what Ninny has left her, Evelyn finds a ghost town and a note: "I love you, dear little Evelyn. Be happy. I am happy."[92] The "preservation effect" that the novel has built up exclusively for the reader is rather suddenly replaced by what Evelyn inherits from Ninny: the picture of the naked girl, the Mason jar of Ninny's gallstones, and a shoebox filled with various forms of documentation (funeral programs, birth certificates, and photographs). Evelyn's visit to Whistle Stop collapses the three diegetic levels—the omniscient narrator recounts the storyteller's listener digging into the historical archive. What the reader is left with, in the place of Whistle Stop's story, is the physically real town. But it is quite literally hollow: the abandoned Threadgoode house, its trellis "entirely covered with thousands of little pink sweetheart roses, blooming like they had no idea that the people inside had left long ago," is an Old South fantasy, colorful but empty in the middle of contemporary Birmingham suburbs.[93]

What the novel's conclusion serves up—anticipating the hungers of the market, certainly—is white southernness as depoliticized commodity. If Evelyn arrives on the "modern" plane with the reader, it is worth noting that she *also* reinvests in the emptiest version of Ninny's nostalgia. Ninny has, in essence, shown her how to live in the world of the 1980s while clinging to an imagined innocence of the early century. Gone are Evelyn's most interesting qualities: her fleeting interest in feminism, her wild and freeing anger, her hunger. In its place is a contented and demure femininity that brings her success in the "modern" world and yet aligns her with the past; she works for Mary Kay, a Houston-rooted company notoriously invested in "traditional" femininity and its accompanying values.[94] Evelyn puts on Ninny like she would put on a costume, and takes her off just as easily: at the spa, finding that her Alabama accent is unexpectedly "adorable," Evelyn "play[s] it for all it [is] worth, holding court at night by the fireplace."[95] In "playing at" Ninny, she sells a taste of southernness in exchange for intimacy with her new friends. Her weight loss quite literally transforms her: at Ninny's grave, she remarks that a friend, upon seeing a photo of Ninny, exclaimed over how much Evelyn looked like her mother. Finally, white southern femininity, accompanied by its nostalgia for an "innocent" past, is reduced to an obviously artificial scene of repetition. Wherever you are, southernness is a commodity that can be engineered and endlessly reproduced for entertainment and profit.[96]

With Ninny gone, Whistle Stop is vacated of perverse appetites and titillating stories—but in the novel's overdetermined insistence on palatability, the resolution on offer looks more like a still life of artificial fruit than a plate of fried green tomatoes. In Evelyn's visit to the cemetery where Ninny is buried, the novel offers us a final reassurance of Whistle Stop's bygone innocence. Evelyn makes the trip out on Easter, a day of "spectacular [floral] arrangements of every color" rather than sinfully bitten chocolate rabbits.[97] And she notices, by Ruth's grave, an Easter card that is signed, "Your friend, The Bee Charmer."[98] Nothing here, in this peaceful place, but simple friendship. Evelyn assures Ninny that Geneene at Rose Terrace (who always reminded Ninny of Sipsey) misses her. And, having inherited from Ninny all Sipsey's recipes from the cafe—except for Big George's "secret sauce," presumably—she tells Ninny, "I use those recipes all the time. Oh, by the way, I've lost forty-three pounds since the last time you saw me. I still have five more to go."[99] The order of these disclosures begs the question: How does one lose weight and yet regularly return to recipes for pecan pie, fried ham with red-eye gravy, and skillet cornbread? Although Evelyn now seems to be able to take in southernness without the calories—the novel's promise to its reader—this appears, finally, as an impossible feat, an insincere and empty resolution. But in closing with a series of recipes (labeled as Sipsey's recipes, but "courtesy of"—that is to say, owned by—Evelyn Couch), the novel once again insists upon its offer of an appetizingly innocent southernness for the white reader: yours to consume—cleansed of the queerness, the blackness, and the human barbecue. The reader might well close the book suspicious of such an offer.

Nevertheless, the popularity of *Fried Green Tomatoes* has tended to mask the strangeness of its mix of cannibalism, lesbianism, and Old South nostalgia. It spent thirty-six weeks on the bestseller list and was quickly transformed into a beloved "feel good" movie, suggesting a market all too hungry for queer southern deviance that might slide, somehow, into a normative nostalgia for the "innocent" small town.[100] The fraught construction of a palatable white southernness is at the heart of the 1991 film, which accomplishes its project simply by erasing much of the blackness and queerness so crucial to the novel. The film's structure is, as Roger Ebert writes, that "a couple of people sit around in the present, discussing a story that took place in the past, and then we get flashbacks showing the earlier story." His "built-in resistance" to this structure is that he "can't see what the point is: Why not just tell that story from the past and be done with it?"[101]

The point is that, much like in the novel, we *can* reinhabit the past, can, as viewers, jump seamlessly between two separate temporalities—whereas only a glimpse of this is available to Evelyn, in a scene where she discovers Mrs. Threadgoode's bedroom, outfitted with paper roses and old photos of Ruth and Idgie. The film's approach to these characters is to finally reveal that Ninny was really Idgie all along. This resolution domesticates Idgie's queerness with a marriage and child after Ruth's death, at which point she apparently traded in her bowler hats for floral dresses, but it is deeply sloppy: why would Ninny/Idgie speak about herself in the third person and adopt a new name? A great deal of the conversation about the movie centers around the question of Ruth and Idgie's ambiguity throughout the film (Ebert, for example, bizarrely speculated that although Idgie and Ruth are almost certainly a lesbian couple, it's anybody's guess "how clear that is to Ruth").[102] The inability to believe that *Ruth* could harbor queer desires aligns with her belle-like performance; Mary Louis Parker plays her role with such a slow drawl that she seems truly trapped in her own distinct temporality. The film tiptoes up to romance between Ruth and Idgie, but never crosses that line: Chris Holmlund points out the "murmured fear of lesbianism" in the film's handling of the women's "relatively blissful if asexual life of longing looks together."[103]

This "murmured fear" is also the film's attitude when it comes to race, presenting the Black citizens of Whistle Stop as perfectly happy to live in friendly service to the whites—except for those pesky KKK visits. For Jeff Berglund, the "uncanniness" of the "secret cannibal cover-up" stands in for the broader circulation of secrets about race and gender; the film erases Artis entirely, as well as any comments about the "sissified" men of Georgia.[104] Another movie critic, in analyzing the "comfort zone" that the movie tries to produce, shrewdly points out that "rather than dealing with race and relationships honestly, the film attempts to appeal to whites' attitudes about blacks and to straight peoples' attitudes about same sex partnerships."[105] But despite the fact that the movie successfully caters to an appetite for a heteronormative white southern nostalgia, it's also linked to progressive politics. John Egerton, as recently as 2006, aptly categorized *Fried Green Tomatoes* as one of many "food Southerns"—a genre "deal[ing] with food in the South"—that "turns on matters of race, class, gender, and sexuality."[106] He suggests that such a movie can "make us laugh, cry, rage out of the theater ready to right the wrongs."[107] Egerton's review points to the appeal of a text like *Fried Green Tomatoes*: its racial and sexual politics relegate those "wrongs" to the past, already righted. A southernness queered by deviant sexual and racial appetites—and then apparently vacated of those appetites—might be sufficient to satisfy consumer cravings.

Ernest Matthew Mickler's "Trash" Food

Fannie Flagg's *Fried Green Tomatoes* coincides with the publication of Ernest Matthew Mickler's wildly—and unexpectedly—successful *White Trash Cooking*, a glossy, spiral-bound cookbook that features everything from oven-baked possum to drunk man's pudding, accompanied by pictures of the rural southern poor and their homes. As different as they are, both these works testify to an appetite for a particularly aestheticized white southernness of one brand or another—"white trash" just as appealing as the not-so-innocent small town. Although John T. Edge's introduction to the cookbook's twentieth anniversary edition praises the work as "a marker of movement beyond the constraints of stereotype," I tend to agree with critics who argue that it risks reinscribing the stereotypes of "white trash," a figure that has only grown more interesting to us over the past few years. Nancy Isenberg's 2016 history, *White Trash: The 400-Year Untold History of Race in America*, for instance, was a bestseller, arriving in an election year that saw much discussion of low-income white voters—especially rural and southern ones.

As Dina Smith writes, although it may be argued that white trash identity is destabilized through its commodification, "we may well remember that aestheticization is not always subversive. . . . White trash . . . is presently-produced poverty turned into a cultural commodity."[108] Mickler's work, particularly in its reception, is not so different from Flagg's in that it seems to attract a readership eager to gawk at a particularly "queer" kind of southernness from a safe distance.

Harper Lee, who was certainly busy on the review circuit in the mid-eighties, called the book "a sociological document of such beauty," a compliment suggesting its link to James Agee's and Walker Evans's 1941 work *Let Us Now Praise Famous Men*, which documented, through photographs and experimental prose, the lives of poor southern sharecroppers. These works fulfill a similar demand: the distant poor provide delicately arranged food for thought for the middle class. This is, after all, the gist of the cookbook's reviews.[109] Writers from NPR, the *New York Times Book Review*, and *Vogue* sang its praises in elevated vocabulary, keen to identify the book's white trash recipes as "authentic" from a well-classed distance: "I read cookbooks like some people read music scores and I can hear the recipes sing!"; "Intriguing . . . a delight to peruse . . . one of the few unvarnished cookbooks around"; "a marvelous and genuine book—not camp."[110] Others found the book "funny," albeit disturbing: "really amusing . . . but, surely, people don't eat that stuff?" The reviews authenticating the recipes are from *former* white trash who have risen to seats of power: a governor from North Carolina and a senator of Arkansas, who found the book to represent "what I am" and "my favorite of all cuisines," respectively. Although Mickler's work is refreshing in its turn away from the many health-conscious cooking tomes of the eighties, the photos he chooses—notoriously, the woman on his book's cover sued over the use of her image—might capture Mickler's own heritage, but they also cater to an impulse to gawk at the way some strange people live *now*.[111]

I'm less interested in the impossible question of whether the book's representation of white trash cuisine is "authentic" than in what this demand for authenticity suggests—a market for touring "white trash" life. The cookbook presents its recipes (from "Indian succotash" to "tar babies" to "potato chip sandwich") with folksy directions in prose, alongside photographs of "trash" in their natural habitat.[112] In his introduction, Mickler differentiates soul food from white trash cuisine (the latter has fewer spices but more variety) and "common" white trash from White Trash, before claiming a few favorite white southern heroes—Faulkner, O'Connor, Hank Williams, and Maybelle Carter among them—for the latter clan (distinguished by its manners and pride).[113] But this is an unstable distinction—manners and pride are not particularly emphasized in the book's glossy performance of "white trash" as a novelty and something of a joke. And certainly, the murkiness around Mickler's definition of the term and the cuisine it claims points to the concept's fraught relationship to race and class.

The naming of "authentic" white trash performs a function: it can locate white victimhood and contain racism within a single demographic. At the turn of the century, poor southern whites were, as Smith puts it, seen as a "a buffer labor zone, an inanimate virgule, between black/white and feminine/masculine culture."[114] Increasingly after the progressive era, as the South came to be defined by Jim Crow, "white trash" became an image that could be supplied to abdicate responsibility for racism: W. J. Cash's *The Mind of the South* (1941), for instance, offers "an apology for white southern privilege that inevitably still privileges whiteness through the location of white victimhood."[115] "White trash" has served as a convenient place to attribute white mob violence, differentiating the civilized southern gentry—as well as a rational-minded, progressive nation—from the illiterate, angry racist hordes.[116] Violence inheres in the very term. The word "white" layers, rather than shifts, the terms of an already racialized trash. As William David Hart argues, "blackness is what whiteness throws out[,] . . . the normative trashiness against which that abnormality called white trash is imagined."[117] Human "trash" raises the specter of eugenics—what to do with trash (abject, contaminated and contaminating) but dispose of it? By the early twentieth century, the term *poor white trash* had not only come to symbolize degeneracy, but to normalize it as part of the natural order of things—particularly in the South.[118]

White Trash Cooking offers a taste of "trash" from a well-glossed distance. As Cami Sublette and Jennifer Martin argue, the appetite for "white trash" and its food in American popular culture (including "white trash dinner parties") endures precisely because it provides the middle-class with a reassuring foil to its usual healthy-eating (and living) practices.[119] The popular idea of the white trash diet attends less to poverty than to moral condemnation: "whatever is worst for bodies and health," eaten by those who have no regard for their bodies.[120] We tend to hop from cheap whiskey and fried squirrel to racism and illiteracy quicker than a duck on a June bug. *White Trash Cooking* is slippery in this way: it can be seen as a politically suspect celebration of southern culture, a subversive rejection of snobbish 80s diet tomes, a highly commodified novelty cookbook playing at authenticity, or some combination of these. If its reception is any indication, it satisfies appetites for southern deviance from a safe distance without provoking much critical engagement with those appetites. But to have a *real* appetite for the foods in *White Trash Cooking*, rather than merely an interest in culinary slumming, is to be *really* white trash: backward, disposable, perverse. Tying value to eating practices is a way of determining which bodies matter, and which are disposable—an urgent question also in considering queer histories. Mickler was openly gay; he died of complications of AIDS in 1988, the same year his second book, *Sinkin Spells, Hot Flashes, Fits and Cravins* was published. Within its title lurks an unsettling suggestion of queer precarity in the midst of the parodic celebration of "trashy" southern eating. This link—between deviant queer and southern appetites—is precisely what Allison tackles in her collection *Trash*.

Lesbian/Trash Appetites

When the term "trash" enters into the literary market, it takes on another valence: "trashy" literature is not only insubstantial, but lurid, catering less to the mind than to the appetites of the body. Trashy *southern* literature, certainly, points to perversion. Dorothy Allison openly embraces these associations in *Trash*, published two years after Mickler's first cookbook. As Harker writes of Allison and her circulation within feminist presses, "the line between literary and trash was permeable."[121] Such lines of division appear frequently in Allison's work, only to be troubled. The semiautobiographical collection draws heavily from her experiences as a self-described "southern writer" and a notorious participant in the "Sex Wars" of the late 1970s—in her words, a battle over "who, in fact, defines feminism and what, in fact, is feminism[,] . . . trying to figure out what kind of pervert I really was. . . . It is a feminist issue."[122] These anxious questions of how we assert the rules and boundaries of personal identities and political orientations swirl through Allison's stories in the overlap of expressions of southern and queer deviance.

In the collection's repeated return to scenes of performance and storytelling, reception and readership, Allison critiques the desire for an exoticized, sensationalized white trash southernness—and celebrates "perverse" queer and southern appetites. Her stories call into question the logic by which some desires are deemed worthy of validation (certain normative forms of lesbianism) as a means of living a feminist life, while others are condemned (kinky sexuality, hunger for southern food) as a way of disavowing racism, poverty, and political backwardness.[123] Her project is an expansive one, but in these stories, there is also a recurrent sense of frustration. No matter how rich the overlapping ground between her visions of queerness and southernness, Allison's narrator can't resolve her disparate identities and communities into a longed-for harmony. "Trash" holds, for her, the subversive potential of a radical feminist *and* a woman deeply influenced by her southern upbringing, but her communities are too culturally separate for the narrator to bring these two identities together in an inclusive political project.

Across Allison's short stories, "trash" cites to both a cultural joke or fantasy about ignorant white southernness, and to the harsh realities of a traumatic childhood. The first story in the collection, "River of Names," sets the terms of the narrator's upbringing in North Carolina, marked by poverty and abuse. The narrator hears stories from her girlfriend, Jesse, that encapsulate health and white privilege in tasty terms: "her grandmother who always smelled of dill bread and vanilla . . . fairy tale[s]."[124] In exchange, the narrator tells "terrible stories" of her own past. As children, "we were so many we were without number and, like tadpoles, if there was one less from time to time, who counted?"[125] Metaphors for her childhood sense of her family's disposability swing between abject blackness—a cousin who hung himself, "his face as black as his shoes," and cheap whiteness—"pale carbons of each other in shades of blond."[126] Sexual violence becomes a cliché and a joke: "What's a South Carolina virgin? 'At's a ten-year-old can run fast."[127] Telling stories in bed—what might be a scene of intimacy between the narrator and her girlfriend—is instead a performance. When she tells the stories, "it comes out funny. I drink bourbon and make myself drawl, tell all those old funny stories."[128] But these tales that her girlfriend experiences as "funny" fill the narrator with secret rage.

The narrator continually steps into and rebels against performances of this kind of southernness: she sees a market for stories of this identity that others both pity and fantasize about. But as storyteller, she becomes both victim and villain for a white middle-class audience who can see themselves, through the narrator's "trashiness," as more cosmopolitan and sophisticated. In "Monkeybites," the narrator's new experience as a college student with a cool "bar dyke" girlfriend returns her to her past through her girlfriend's English class. Toni, an English major, teases her about the "drawling lies" she tells for laughs: "You think about what a queer sort you are, girl. . . . You southern dirt-country types are all alike. Faulkner would have put that stuff to use."[129] Although Toni is also from a working-class background, "another scholarship student," she identifies and distances herself from the narrator's class "type," specifically her poor *southern* background. As in "River of Names," the narrator's performance of "drawling" stories, which Toni calls "just too much Southern Gothic," is a way of flattening the deep pain of her experiences—in performing southernness for her girlfriend, she avoids making herself vulnerable.[130]

The story that Toni latches onto most is the narrator's tale of being bitten by a monkey: a "dirty-furred, gray-faced creature kept caged by the lake where my stepfather would go on Sunday to try for a catfish dinner. . . . She had an old red collar with a bell on it."[131] Given that Toni gives the narrator a copy of Flannery O'Connor's short stories, the link to O'Connor's "A Good Man Is Hard to Find" is resonant: in the classic story, a family stops at Red Sammy's for a barbecue lunch before continuing their ill-fated vacation. At Red Sammy's, the children are captivated by a "gray monkey . . . chained to a small chinaberry tree."[132] It is Red Sammy who gives the story its title, in a conversation with the grandmother about the way the world is changing—they agree that one can't "know who to trust," a sentiment that Red Sammy's wife doubles down on, with a suspicious gaze at her husband.[133] The humor in O'Connor's depiction of Red Sammy hinges on recognizable "funny" markers of "white trash": the whiff of a public display of matrimonial discord; Sammy's laziness as he "lies on the bare ground . . . with his head under a truck"; his and his wife's adjacency to racial otherness, red and brown from working in the sun; their pathetic debasement in the service economy (RED SAMMY'S FAMOUS BARBECUE. NONE LIKE FAMOUS RED SAMMY'S! RED SAM! THE FAT BOY WITH THE HAPPY LAUGH! A VETERAN!).[134] Although white trash functions to provide levity for the reader of O'Connor's story—and for Toni, as the removed listener to the narrator's tales—to be read as a "southern country dirt type" is a source of deep pain for the narrator, whose real-world dealings with monkeys leave a physical scar and expand the metaphor lurking in O'Connor's story. The monkey on a chain, made to be a source of entertainment, is deeply sad.

The space of the university demands this kind of southernness not only as literary trope, but as exoticized poverty that buoys white middle-class righteousness. In "Steal Away," the narrator, at college on a scholarship, is fawned over by the president's wife with her "pink flesh hand" and the sociology professor who "demonstrated for civil rights" but who gazes onto less fortunate groups (or perhaps less "civilized" groups) from afar, reading Malinowski's *The Sexual Life of Savages* in a comfortable office—a professor who "did not want to hear about my summers working for the mop factory, but . . . loved my lies about hitchhiking cross-country."[135] These details situate the "right" kind of poor white student as a coveted token in the university space, perhaps a safe stand-in, in the eyes of these academic do-gooders, for the "exotic" Black student. Although the narrator knows exactly how to play to the university community's demand for her as intriguing foreign object, she is enraged by it, and takes to stealing. Although she has lunch with the sociology professor, and sees her gazing hungrily at her, "biting her lips," she lets the professor's appetite go unabated, involving herself with the sociologist just enough to steal and mark in her books—to mar her privileged stories even as she appears to cater to them.[136]

Sexuality, in Allison's stories, is often framed through the lens of food and hunger. The women who surround the narrator have an appetite for a fantasy of southernness, but only—as in Flagg's novel—from the safe distance that storytelling provides. Sexual desire, however, demands a closer intimacy. And queer appetites, through the metaphor of food, call into question arbitrary lines dividing proper and improper, healthy and perverse. In her sexual exploration, Allison's narrator embraces the deviant appetites through which she can claim her own southern, queer identity, but she finds that her desires are regarded with contempt and fear. In "Muscles of the Mind," the narrator, renting an apartment in Tallahassee after college, is hyper-aware of her "trash" background and her sexual preferences for "bar dykes" in the environment of the "Women's Center," where the working class is purely a theoretical abstraction, no one is supposed to fantasize about sex, and everyone dresses "like they belonged to the same gypsy troupe" and eats sunflower seeds—a naive, health-conscious, and presumably very white group.[137] The narrator, on the other hand, goes out with butch women; they drink Jack Daniels and enjoy stock car races, "eating boiled peanuts and pissing into an open trough behind the bleachers."[138]

She bristles at the judgment that her appetites receive from the members of the Women's Center; queerness is not an escape from normativity in this space, but rather constrictive, linked to a mode of feminism that requires conforming to a reductive set of rules.[139] The feminist collective, as Allison represents it, designates which appetites are healthy or normative in order to establish superiority to a "perverse" set of appetites. Out on a date with her girlfriend, the narrator runs into a group from the Women's Center and feels both anger and shame after feeling the women's eyes on her and her butch girlfriend. It's as if they are—as in "Monkeybites"—trash, "animals in a cage."[140]

The relationship between queer sexuality and the wider southern community in this story is defined by opposing but parallel conceptions of inappropriate desires. "I could tell you," the narrator's "dyke hippy" landlord Anna tells her, "the name of the boy who firebombed the last two gay bars, and exactly what year his daddy was appointed sheriff."[141] The prejudice of a conservative southern community against so-called perversion—people who love, act, and dress the wrong way—finds a surprising (although less violent) echo in the Women's Center community's vehement judgment of the wrong kind of lesbian (butch women, women who have casual sex, southern working-class women) and schemes to shut down the pool bars that they frequent. The narrator experiences both her southern and her queer identities as wrong in some way—but in her practice of karate, she "frees" herself by disciplining her ability to access these many facets of herself, rather than disciplining her desires in order to conform to one community: "What did I imagine was wrong with me anyway?"[142]

Likely the most remarked-upon story in the collection is "A Lesbian Appetite," which depicts the narrator's many cravings, for both sex and food, and invokes the possibility of the radical, loving, inclusive southern queer identity glimpsed in her karate practice in "Muscles of the Mind." In this story, the narrator recounts various sexual experiences, especially those whose appeal lies in power play and sadomasochism—the "wrong" kinds of lesbian sex, according to the likes of the Women's Center—through metaphors of rich food: bodily fluids are "thick cream[,] . . . musky gravy."[143] As Antje Lindenmeyer has written of the story, "Allison sees the discourse of 'bad food' as closely connected to a discourse of 'bad [perverse] sex'."[144] The bulk of the narrative depicts preparation for the Southeastern Feminist Conference, which is all about "good" food and "good" lesbians. The narrator is helping her wholesome femme girlfriend Lee, who "look[s] like the mother in a Mary Cassatt painting," host the conference.[145] After spending an agonizing day chopping mountains of vegetables into "bite-sized" pieces for hungry vegetarian feminists, the narrator ends up sharing a YooHoo and the dream of barbecue with a butch woman after Lee disappears to flirt with another woman over the benefits of macrobiotic cooking.[146] The implications are clear: the divisions over what lesbians are allowed to eat, look like, and want are laughable.

For the narrator, however, these rules are deeply ingrained; she feels that her desires are bound up with a "white trash" identity that signifies unworthiness. When the narrator gets tired of Lee's health food regime, she secrets herself away to read Carson McCullers and eat a Snickers bar (a poor substitute for a Moon Pie[147]) in shame and homesickness. In this scene of reading, she is also anticipating and rehearsing how her appetites will be read: "Poor white trash I am for sure. I eat shit food and am not worthy."[148] These two sentences are remarkable: stylistically unique, almost incantatory, they reverse the correct order of operations (eat food, shit) and suggest white trash as abject. The clichés of white trash—racist, stupid, criminal, incapable of self-control—haunt the term. Ironically, the narrator has developed an ulcer from an overabundance of Vitamin D in childhood, which she consumed to develop her brain so that she might escape her imagined white trash fate. But in adulthood, her ulcer turns her stomach against the more "virtuous" foods that supposedly signify her ability to rise above trashiness and access her progressive queer future. It's the belief in a fated identity that causes the narrator's ulcer, and the easement of restrictions on identity that will cure that gnawing, angry hunger—not a forced change of appetite.

Real health, Allison suggests, is not about diet plans and doctrines, but an ethical relationality that comes from loosening the link between appetite and identity. As Christina Jarvis points out, through the "repeated conflation of hunger/appetite with sexual desire . . . the story explores a variety of lesbian relationships, opening up experimental space for the narrator to perform several lesbian subject positions."[149] In celebrating a range of sexual desires and alimentary appetites, the story identifies and pushes against the way the "body becomes socially interpolated in terms of class, race, sexual preference, etc."[150] Health-consciousness can function as a form of class oppression, just as feminist ideals of sexual expression can function as a form of censorship. The narrator's depictions of finding joy in different kinds of sex and foods—what "sweetens [one's] mouth and feeds [one's] soul"—begin to take on a listing quality; together, these experiences suggest a freedom to be found in the absence of interpretability, the refusal to read for a singular identity, the embrace of a multiplicity of hungers.[151]

"A Lesbian Appetite" is a deeply intimate story, offering explicit accounts of sex and food of all types—a smorgasbord of the narrator's *own* appetites, rather than a carefully curated dish for someone else's appetite, whether a fellow lesbian activist or the reader expecting southern fantasy. As critics have pointed out, Allison refuses in "A Lesbian Appetite" to align herself with one queer identity—this story describes *a* lesbian appetite, *many* lesbian appetites, even, but not *the* lesbian appetite; the same could be true of the story's depiction of southern appetites. As Jaime Cantrell writes, the story is expansive in the possibilities it suggests, "illustrating how lesbian hypervisibility" might ideally "accommodate other forms of sexuality and enable new conceptions of national subjects through the regional."[152] Finally, there is no "authentic" lesbian identity determined by adherence to a set of arbitrary rules, and the narrator's performance of southernness as deviant white trash is just that—a performance, ultimately meant to destabilize smug notions of the normative.

The story ends on the narrator's dream of a potluck that, as Lindenmeyer puts it, emphasizes the story's "utopian possibilities": a big and heterogeneous group comprising both the narrator's feminist community and her big North Carolina family, where "everybody is feeding each other."[153] Although the racial politics of this dream are unclear, presumably "everybody" might gesture toward a more welcoming and equitable future for feminist southern life. Rather than being the object of a hunger for "trashy" southernness, and certainly rather than understanding herself (or anyone else) as "trash," the narrator is free to follow the bliss of her many appetites and "have a little taste" of everything.

But the narrator's utopian dream of the crowded table is just that—a dream. Her experiences of being southern "white trash" and a radical feminist and lesbian are also experiences of trauma, failures of communication, the struggle to make ends meet. The vision of a more expansive, communal, and politically progressive queer southern deviance is glimpsed only distantly, through the harsh realities of the present. And it is, importantly, a private dream, a vulnerable, intimate one that seems to lack the market appeal of all those "funny" stories of southernness told in a bourbon-facilitated drawl. How can a different kind of southernness match that appeal? As Allison wrote in a 1988 letter, "most 'lesbian' fiction . . . sits on the shelf like stale white bread."[154] Allison's fiction—often boldly sexual, never stale, instrumental in the growth of queer fiction in the South[155]—stirs up hunger for a better vision of queer, southern life. But crucially, it also acknowledges the ways that such a hunger often goes unsatisfied.

Michael Twitty, a culinary historian who writes about his experience as a queer, Black, Jewish southerner, is particularly attuned to the market appeal of stories of southernness that intersect in complicated ways with lived experience. In his culinary memoir *The Cooking Gene*, Twitty writes that "the Old South is a place where people use food to tell themselves who they are, to tell others who they are, and to tell stories about where they've been. The Old South is a place of groaning tables across the tracks from want[,] . . . a place in the mind where we dare not talk about which came first, the African cook or the European mistress, the Native American woman or the white woodsman."[156] Twitty recognizes many ways of defining "southern" in relation to Old South fantasy—some of which he reiterates on the Netflix series *High on the Hog*. This popular documentary series explores the history of southern food, tracing the roots of many dishes to Africa and to the legacy of slavery. Even so, all too often in the popular imagination, as in the works I've explored here, southern food—and the desire for it, and stories about it—are more attached to whiteness, either in the form of Old South fantasy or an easily denigrated "trash." It's not only that food tells stories, but that stories about food negotiate what comes of a "deviant" appetite: more expansive imaginings of what "southern" might mean, or the reinstantiation of white heteronormativity? We need the discourse of queerness to fully see the ways the answer can be both, and thus to critically engage with both possibilities. Queerness takes us beyond what are at this point overly familiar narratives about southern foodways, just as southernness lends historical and ideological complexity to the reflexive celebration of deviant desires. Reckoning with our appetites as readers for queer southernness—to put it in the terms of that restaurant in Florida—matters.

2 Near 'Bout
Randall Kenan's Swampy Southern Queerness

Boggy Readings

In an interview, Randall Kenan contemplated that the writers he most admired had constructed their own geographies: "It just made a lot of sense to have your own little postage stamp that you could reinvent whenever you wanted to, manipulate any way you wanted to. It appealed to me."[1] Faulkner's "postage stamp of native soil," that phrase beloved in discussions of southern literature, denotes the hyper-regional but also suggests the metropolitan and the cosmopolitan. It evokes an image of pure nature—soil—as well as something as constructed, modern, and abstractly meaningful as the postage stamp. With that stamp, Faulkner erects borders to fence in the "native" soil, and he also extends himself across borders, sending out this "soil" to mean, to communicate—even to function as a kind of currency for—an elusive elsewhere. Randall Kenan spoke of his work as a continuation of Faulkner's. And Kenan's fictional Tims Creek is kin to Faulkner's Yoknapatawpha in that it constructs, across texts, a South both real and imagined, hyper-local and expansive across time and space. Tim's Creek is a town that grew out of a maroon colony: men and women who escaped enslavement by building a home in the swampy wilderness adjacent to the plantation. I'm interested in the way the swamp, as a space of deviant southernness with rich potential for Black queer life, expands across Kenan's two short story collections, *Let the Dead Bury Their Dead* (1992) and *If I Had Two Wings* (2020), and his novel *A Visitation of Spirits* (1989). In this chapter, I argue that Kenan returns again and again to the swamp as a space of escape from the legacies of the plantation; this is a space that holds dangers as well as possibilities for queer forms of Black southern community. "Swampiness" can also be understood as a mode of reading and storytelling that embraces intertextuality and eschews linearity and hierarchy. In "swampy readings," we find many ways of thinking through southernness and queerness. Tims Creek, then, is not a singular place, nor is it a utopian one—but it's through engaging with the many stories that organize a "postage stamp of native soil," Kenan's work suggests, that tellers and listeners, writers and readers, might collect the materials to dream a more livable world for queer, Black southern life.

In his geography of Tims Creek, Kenan enters into a complex constellation of associations and understandings of "the swamp" both as physical space and symbol of deviance. The swamp is home to a southernness entirely wild, untamed, unlawful, fecund, even maddening. If the American project is to tame and conquer the wilderness in the name of man's progress, the great swaths of southern swampland refuse that civilizing project.[2] The Southeast has long held the honor of being the swampiest region in the US. In Monique Allewaert's history of the swamp ecology in American plantation zones, she writes that in the nineteenth century, swamps were "often described as unnavigable territories"—hence unmappable—which "compromised the order and productivity of imperial ventures" with the sheer impenetrability of their dense, overwhelming, and threatening abundance of plant and animal life.[3] The swamp's perverse insistence on untameability is perhaps best encapsulated, in our contemporary discourse, by any number of memes about Florida and its unlawful, snake-loving residents. But it's not, of course, just Florida—as Anthony Wilson argues, swamps have long been, and are still, associatively linked to the South, an association that appears regularly in popular culture. Watching an episode of the popular cartoon *Avatar: The Last Airbender* with my family, for example—a show situated in a future far beyond our current geopolitical formations—I was interested to see the protagonists find themselves in a spooky swamp populated by "swamp benders" with distinctly southern accents, their boisterous movements accompanied by a cacophonous, twangy soundtrack.[4] The southernness of the swamp readily connotes disorder, wildness, a perverse fecundity.

The terms of the swamp are also frequently the terms of queer theory. Queerness, like the swamp, is productively disorienting: in Sara Ahmed's words, if the normative body "appears 'in line,'" correctly oriented, the queer one is spatially errant in some way.[5] As Ahmed points out, the word "queer" derives from a word for "twist": to twist is to turn in a way that allows one to "inhabit different worlds"—possibly more expansive ones.[6] This has rich implications for queer of color critique; Kara Keeling, building on Eve Sedgwick's oft-cited formulation of queerness as an "open mesh of possibilities," offers a theory of queerness as a "structuring antagonism" of normative institutions and practices.[7] For Keeling, given that "the quotidian violence that holds existing reality in place does so in part by making the concepts 'queer' and 'Black' appear as aberrations," Black queerness holds a kind of radical creative agency in opening up visions of life beyond the exclusionary normative regimes of white supremacy.[8] Queerness is that which is "eccentric and errant[,] . . . proliferat[ing] connections . . . unaccountable[,] . . . ungovernable."[9] Certainly, these descriptions of queerness align with the imagery and ethos of the swamp.[10]

Not only does the swamp encapsulate an atmospheric queer and southern deviance, it is—as a physical space—important to the history of Black southern resistance. The swamp exists figuratively and historically alongside the plantation, as a space of otherness threatening the plantation's hegemony as site of the romanticized white family structure and locus of control over Black labor and the environment. Swamps were often on or adjacent to plantation grounds, and yet starkly opposed to the plantation's structures of control.[11] So close by, and yet such a radically separate space, the swamp held some power to defy the plantation's naturalized racial order. We can think of the swamp not only in terms of Keeling's theorization of queerness, but Katherine McKittrick's formulation of a Black geography: a "*terrain* of political struggle itself[,] . . . location of black history, selfhood, imagination, and resistance" that offers "real and possible geographical alternatives" to spaces of white supremacy—that is, the antebellum plantation and its legacies.[12]

In many cases, the swamp was a very real refuge for enslaved people. Stephanie Camp, for example, counts the swamp as one "rival geography" by which bondspeople established "alternative ways of knowing and using plantation and southern space."[13] These "maroons" were cast by imperial regimes (first European explorers and, later, white Americans) as militants, potential agents of dangerous revolution.[14] Between the seventeenth and the nineteenth centuries, dozens of southeastern swamps were home to generations of maroon communities. Although we know this much due to the work of archaeologists and anthropologists over the last century, these communities are largely absent from the historical record.[15] They remained, and remain still, outside of the surveilling, instrumentalizing gaze of the "plantation space whose commodity production fueled the Enlightenment's quantifying projects," as Allewaert puts it.[16]

What we do know about the structure of life in these spaces helps us think about the swamp's function as a territory of resistance. In a history of the Great Dismal Swamp of eastern North Carolina, Daniel Sayers describes the swamp as a site in which "thoughtful and influential transformational social resistance [was] possible and actionable" through modes of relation and labor that "critiqued the racialized capitalistic world" of the plantation.[17]

These maroon communities sustained themselves both as hunter-gatherers and through raids on nearby plantations; they relied on both natural resources and the plantation's stolen wealth. Such histories raise the question of how maroon communities may have conceptualized time and space through noncapitalistic frameworks—and lived by epistemologies other than those dictated by the plantation.

Even so, I am wary of speculating overmuch about the revolutionary function of swamps as historical sites. Although they offered an escape, these were spaces to which people of color were driven by terror and torture, and which provided in turn their own terrors: countless dangerous forms of animal and insect life, extreme heat, the constant threat of hunger, and fear of capture. But I take from this scholarship the usefulness of swamp-as-metaphor: a queer southernness to counter the geography of the plantation. The swamp provides a way of imagining the subversion of oppressive normative configurations of white supremacy and capitalism, offering alternative kinship structures and distinct ways of conceptualizing time and space.

In writing his own geography in the form of Tims Creek, Kenan locates a swampy southernness: a complicated terrain, to be sure, but one that might be claimed and embraced for blackness and queerness. As Susan Thananopavarn argues, "Kenan's work uses the swamp in an overall trope of inversion, both in the sense of emphasizing black histories . . . and in the sense of inversion as queerness. As a site of 'otherness,' the swamp binds together African American and queer histories and insists that they are integral parts of the past."[18] So, too, are they integral parts of the present. In Kenan's work, the swamp becomes a space of shifting and accreting stories of all that is "other" to the adjacent plantation. These stories often come into conflict and tension; not all are salves to those who tell them or hear them. But it's through the swamp's many stories, its multivocality, that there emerges a resonating insistence on forms of intimacy—between Black men and interracially—that make possible more loving, more joyful, gentler, and more powerful systems of relation more broadly.

In embracing the swamp in this way, Kenan revises narratives of the South as a place from which escape is the only reasonable option. In the twentieth century especially, the South operates as a starting point for a familiar narrative shared by blackness and queerness: migration to the metropolitan North. This narrative relies on the idea that within the South's amorphous but powerful borders resides "the past"—the South is provincial and atavistic, always a place to be escaped for a more modern future.

As Colin Johnson argues, "because metropolitan space has proven to be so obviously and overwhelmingly significant to the story of modern lesbian and gay identity formation, there continues to be an assumption among many that nonmetropolitan space"—the South and the rural Midwest, in Johnson's formulation—"can and should be treated as anterior to that story in a temporal, geographical, and conceptual sense."[19] This multifaceted understanding of the South's anteriority is also at work in narratives of American blackness; Farah Jasmine Griffin points out that the "dominant form of African-American cultural production" arises from the slave narrative's "notions of ascent from the South into a 'freer' North" and portrays the South as "an immediate, identifiable, and oppressive power . . . unsophisticated in nature" even as it remains the site of the ancestor, who provides a "black birthright to the land, a locus of history."[20]

If US histories of queerness and blackness share a familiar narrative of geographical momentum, it's because southern states have long been inhospitable to people of color and non-normative sexualities. The political entity that is the "New South," in Horton-Stallings's words, "continues to depend upon anti-Blackness, sexual morality, and dehumanization of the poor for its growth and support."[21] But the South also continues to function as a powerful set piece citing much further back: the mythologies that swirl around the plantation, "the South's most iconic institution," in Michael Bibler's words, "operate as a powerful and elaborate discourse about race, sex, and sexuality in American culture" more broadly.[22] The plantation South denotes a system of violent surveillance. The home it makes for whiteness is structured by strict gender roles and sexual norms that displace all deviance onto the Black body.[23] Even the nature that surrounds this "home" is drenched in ideology: lynching trees, magnolias, and beasts occupy the southern pastoral. It's this mythology, in all its contemporary power, that Kenan's work cites to and revises.

As Kenan's essays suggest and his fiction bears out, he understands the South both as physical space and as abstraction, one that can be shaped and changed through intellectual work. As he writes in a letter to himself in his posthumously published essay collection: "Black, Southern, Queer[,] . . . the sooner you start seeing your background, your reality, as a diamond mine, the sooner you will see yourself as a force to be reckoned with."[24] The swamp, like that mine, is a natural space that yields its treasure only to those who know how to work within it. Tims Creek, after all, is loosely based on Kenan's own upbringing in Chinquapin, North Carolina, by his description on "the northernmost edge of the Angola Swamp."[25] But although

Tims Creek remains a stable locale across his fiction, it is composed of complicated webs of temporalities and choruses of voices and epistemologies. It is a place where borders become shadowscapes, and landscapes shift under the spell of magic that wavers somewhere between metaphor and material reality.[26]

In my readings I mean to acknowledge, and in fact embrace, the organizational difficulties that a territorial survey of Kenan's work presents. Kenan's work plays with genre and engages the reader in many different ways. It invokes textual predecessors from several styles and traditions, but is completely its own. Kenan inherits North Carolina, as Trudier Harris writes, as "a land saturated with tales of revenants and conjurers, and overrun with legends and myths" in its "very soil."[27] He also inherits the tradition of the speakerly text, and (like Henry Louis Gates Jr. argues of Hurston before him) celebrates "the sheer play of black language" for its power to signify on sedimented ideas of Blackness.[28] Kenan plays on story-saturated soil, in the swamp and the town it becomes, to claim that land for Black southern queerness.[29]

In what follows, I first track how Kenan dramatizes the ramifications of toxic "Old South" mythologies for contemporary Black southern life in *A Visitation of Spirits*. In his two subsequent story collections, *Let the Dead Bury Their Dead* and *If I Had Two Wings*, he revises the story that the South is a place that must be escaped. Instead, in his representation of the town of Tims Creek and its history, Kenan embraces the legacy of the swamp to imagine a sustainable Black, queer southernness that exists alongside and destabilizes the oppressive spatial configurations of the plantation and its afterlives. Kenan's deviant swampy geography revises the dominant narratives of home, nature, and surveillance that emanate from the plantation South. The counternarratives that emerge in the swamp are not necessarily utopian, but in their proliferation and their entanglement, they do create space for hope. As I trace these revisions, I do so by the light of the methodology that the swamp suggests: thinking through several stories, as well as the novel, from multiple angles and with attention to different kinds of details—constellations of small and interconnected analyses rather than the more heuristically driven focus of an argument with a singular thread.

Rewriting Souths

In Kenan's 1989 novel *A Visitation of Spirits*, specters of the Old South prove overwhelming to a Black, queer boy in rural North Carolina, obscuring any vision of a South that could be a real, sustainable home to him. This critically lauded novel gives us the story of the community of Tims Creek, but more specifically, it is the story of Horace Cross, a Black boy who, upon entering adolescence, can't reconcile his queer sexuality and his family's dreams for him as the "Great Black Hope" of their future.[30] After attempting to escape this unsolvable problem by conducting sorcery to transform himself into a hawk, Horace experiences a kind of break from his everyday reality—he wanders through the town and through his own memories, visited by spirits and demons, before finally taking his own life.

One of the memories Horace revisits is of his time spent working on the set of a play being staged in Crosstown (the white town neighboring Tims Creek). In his work, he spends time around a group of mostly queer traveling actors from New York. These urbanites, frustrated and "isolat[ed] from city lights," look "askance and aloof at sleepy, backward Crosstown."[31] Their initial conception of Crosstown as "backward" is enforced by the play in which they are acting—the "cliche-ridden drivel, the doggerel verses and the melodramatic romanticizing of southern American history" in a play called *Ride the Freedom Star*.[32] The poster describes the musical as "the saga of an American Family. Their trial through the Revolution, through the Civil War[,] . . . the American Story."[33] Of course, this story is represented as a white one, nearly parodic in its romanticized history, its sloppy cliché. The poster, relying heavily on idealized gender roles and Othered blackness, depicts "men . . . hearty and robust like comic book characters[,] . . . the women . . . either voluptuous or petite[,] . . . frail and feminine. . . . Off to the right of the group stood three black people, . . . horse-muscled" and bearing "out of place" grins.[34] The effect is grotesquely performative, sexualizing racial difference. The actors step into more than costumes to play these roles—the lodgings provided for them are in an old school renovated to be modeled after a southern plantation home.[35]

The New York actors live as well as work on a set piece, so it's no wonder they can't (or don't attempt to) distinguish Crosstown—and its inhabitants—from the South of layers of cliched revisionist history. Horace begins sleeping with one of the actors, a New Yorker named Antonio, who eventually suggests they sneak into an old, abandoned house that evokes yet another plantation space: "a large house . . . reminding Horace of the haunted houses of his childhood fears," with an "overpowering smell of dust, decay, rotting wood."[36] Antonio is sure its design "dated back to antebellum craftsmen," a comment that leads to discussion of Horace's own family's history in slavery.[37] Antonio begins calling Horace "boy"—a development that Horace first allows, "unsuccessfully suppressing a smile" as he refuses the term, but then protests in earnest ("Stop! Damn it!") as Antonio pins him in a wrestling hold and announces his plans to "rope [him] up."[38] Performance veers into threat; despite his disdain for the play, Antonio is taken in by its story as he attempts to force Horace into the role of slave. The appeal of "sleepy" Crosstown, for him, is the thrill of dabbling in "backward" histories that he can just as quickly leave behind.

But for Horace, the set feels as confining as Antonio's hold. His experiences of the play are reminiscences narrated in fragments, culminating with the memory of the actors' postproduction orgy, which takes place in the old town cemetery. Walking like a ghost through his memory of that night, Horace looks beyond the graves of Crosstown's early Scots-Irish settlers and the bacchanalia of queer sex for his own grave. He finds "what he had led himself to see[,] . . . hard and soft, black and white, cold and hot, smooth and dull, took light and gave light. . . .": a series of impossible binaries that suggest his own alienation as a queer Black teenager in a southernness composed of either violently sexualized queer plantation fantasy or deeply heteronormative family allegiance.[39] Queerness, in this space, is aligned only with death. Contemplating this riddle, he turns around to see—and shoot—his double, who appears in harlequin makeup. Antiwan Walker argues that this moment suggests to Horace his own "white face minstrelsy"—an alienating racial performance that would allow him a way of embracing his sexuality, but would also take him out of his home in rural North Carolina along with the actors.[40] But the life that Horace craves is not that of migration to the big city.[41] Instead, his dream is to live stageless and unmasked in his own home: "he had to stay here."[42]

Horace's dream—for the southern home that should be his already—is deeply poignant, resonating across the novel. When Horace commits suicide, his memories, rather than fading, repeat themselves insistently on the page, building a southern geography infinitely more complex than the temporarily amusing set that appears in the eyes of the actors or the family land that would exclude him: "I remember the first time I saw Granddaddy kill a chicken. . . . I remember watching men, even as a little boy. . . . I remember dark nights at home. . . . I remember studying Einstein's theory of relativity. . . . I remember me."[43] After Horace's death, these memories—the insistent repetition of "I remember" on the page—accrue the solidity of a memorial, insisting on a queer, southern presence even after his body is gone.

The possibility of Black queer life in rural southern space, rather than an imperative of escape to the metropolitan North, returns in Kenan's subsequent story collections, *Let the Dead Bury Their Dead* and *If I Had Two Wings*. In both, Kenan challenges anti-Black and anti-queer geographical and conceptual binaries. "Foundations of the Earth," for example, focalizes around an elderly Black woman, Maggie, whose grandson Edward has died in a car crash "up North" in Boston, where he moved to live authentically as a gay man. He returns to Tims Creek in a coffin, accompanied by his boyfriend, Gabriel, "like an interpreter for the dead."[44] But although North and South are formulated as opposite poles, and Edward only returns to North Carolina in death, Maggie's pain in the experience of their lost relationship, and the depth of her love for her grandson, knocks loose the binary. In the same way that she visualizes the Earth as "a monstrous globe floating in cold nothingness," she reflects on Edward's move up to Boston as his being "gone" to "the cold North," as if the coldness of beyond-the-South, away-from-home, is as vast and as densely negative a space as the nothingness beyond the Earth.[45]

This galactic vision of the North unmoors the South, too, displacing Maggie from her experience of home. When she mourns that "Edward had been gone away from home so long without seeing her," it is the absence of *his* solidifying sight of *her* that provokes anxiety.[46] She has always felt that he "moor[ed] her to the Earth," and without him she feels herself to be floating.[47] It's this unmooring that allows Maggie to reconsider her understandings of sexuality. Although her beliefs are informed by the church in her deeply religious community, it's a more destabilizing experience with the divine, a dream of a God speaking in terms of wild and natural love, that finally holds sway: "A voice, gentle and sweet[,] . . . spoke to her from the whirlwind . . . of the myriad creations of the universe, the stupendous glory of the Earth and its inhabitants."[48] A fish asks her, "Who asked you to love? Who asked you to hate?" and the dream ends when "Maggie . . . slip[s] down into the water, down, down, down, sinking . . . into the dark unknown of her own mind."[49] A reckoning with Edward's queerness disorients her from the formerly familiar Tims Creek, transforming it into unknown territory and attuning her to new voices there.

After this dream, Maggie's South becomes, rather than the oppressive end of a binary, a set of rituals, practices, and directions that can support ever-greater depths of exploration. Instead of staying at the level of "shallow and pleasant talk" with other churchgoers that begins the story, she moves along a trajectory of depth, "watch[ing] the sun begin its slow downward arc" and "feeling the baked ham and the candied sweet potatoes and the fried chicken with the collard greens and green beans and beets settle in their bellies" as she ventures below the surface of hospitality to welcome and try to understand Edward's boyfriend Gabriel.[50] Southern comfort food becomes a surprising fuel for a cold voyage into the depths of a foreign land where she "would have to begin again, to learn . . . all the laws and rules" of her world, as well as to negotiate a relationship with the white man who loved her grandson.[51]

Kenan's story "Resurrection Hardware," from *If I Had Two Wings*, is self-conscious about the literary circulation of southern food as comforting, catering to a fantasy of or nostalgia for home. Kenan employs that self-consciousness in service of the building of a new kind of Black, southern, queer home. The story's protagonist, an academic named Randall, returns home to North Carolina to work on an edited collection on southern food called *Lard & Promises*, a colorful (and, one imagines, marketable) title with an inescapable connection to *The Carolina Table*, the real, more buttoned-up collection of which Kenan was editor.[52] Randall's past (he grew up poor in North Carolina, "well loved[,] . . . never ever hungry") takes the reader beyond the food tourism of *Lard & Promises* and into more complicated, and more private, negotiations of region, cuisine, and family.[53] The story's teasing proximity to autobiography, of course, is immediately clear. Although not set in Tims Creek, the house Randall chooses in "Resurrection" is just outside Durham, but so out of the way that Randall warns his friends that their GPS might fail to direct them. The effect of this autofiction is that the unmappable outskirts of Durham appear fictional—no more or less real than Tims Creek. In this way, the story cues us to geographies that slide between fiction and truth, holding as-of-yet untold stories and more livable homes just out of sight.

When Randall first visits the antebellum country home that will eventually become his own, it's at night, for a conference on southern food, when he is still a New Yorker planning on spending the rest of his life in what he will later think of as "the 21st floor of some urban engine."[54] By a darkness literal and figurative, the house appears to his New Yorker's sight "in the middle of nowhere"—rural life occupying the very center of a sphere of overwhelming nothingness, as unknown as the depths in which Maggie finds herself.[55] But by that same non-determinacy, the "nowhere" of rural southern life seems to open out into space and possibility, geographies and scripts yet to be formed. The house transforms along with Randall's changing perspective on what he might find in this place down South.

Just as "nowhere" becomes "somewhere"—Randall's home—the ghosts of the house's centuries-old past emerge from nothingness into visibility quite literally. He begins seeing and hearing enslaved people roaming the grounds and offers them food and drink. His means of showing love to his contemporary visitors, a group of queer friends from New York, is much the same: he hosts Thanksgiving dinner. At the story's end, Randall is alone; his friends have left, and the first ghost who appeared has been rowed away to freedom by a spectral Quaker boatman after offering Randall "one of the most free-hearted and brotherly waves" he has ever seen.[56] Randall's solitary enjoyment of southern food after all these guests have left (eggs, grits, and red-eye gravy) is a complicated recipe of love, gratitude, community, grief, and loneliness that nonetheless asserts his belonging: "I think of my mother, I think of my lover, I think of home."[57] *Southernness* here is not a culinary diversion, a cleverly packaged fantasy to be distributed and enjoyed by the New York publishing scene, but a swampy space of possibility for a home off familiar maps. His house, at first "too *Town & Country* for my tastes[,] . . . preordained back when John Adams or Thomas Jefferson was president," changes shape quite literally as Randall begins to see the ghostly geography he inhabits.[58] His home becomes, rather than commodified white antebellum aesthetic, a private and healing refuge for queer Black life.

We could read both these stories as representations of southern homes haunted by queer and Black deaths; but they are also stories that reorient their readers spatially and temporally in order to insist upon, and to celebrate, the possibility and reality of past and present Black queer southern life as real and thriving—or at least capable of being in some way "resurrected." From Crosstown to Tims Creek to the suburbs of Durham, Kenan invokes conceptions of the South as the domain of white plantation romance and a narrow Black home life, haunted by historical trauma and overwhelmed by contemporary social stagnancy. But just as surely does he offer alternatives to those conceptions. There are many possible ways of seeing southernness together with queer kinship here; these stories refuse to stabilize their readers within any singular vision that would relegate Randall's ghosts or Maggie's fish to a negligible flash in our periphery.

Swampy Spaces

Across Kenan's novel and story collections, the metaphorical swamp is a space where southernness, Blackness, and queerness join, building and rebuilding homes through stories. More than this, the swamp offers a fruitful mode of queer reading and analysis. To access the swamp, we have to abandon a reliance on limited modes of knowing and rigid adherence to linear temporalities. The roads into Tims Creek are roads into the swamp: they insist that getting turned around is the only way to begin, as Saidiya Hartman puts it, to "imagineer a free territory, a new commons."[59] As I expand on this "swampy" reading practice, the best place to get turned around is surely the titular story of Kenan's 1992 collection, *Let the Dead Bury Their Dead*. Not only does this story tell the tale of Tims Creek's history as a maroon community, but it is formally swamplike in its complex ecosystem of voices distinct in tone, intent, context, and temporality. In working through the story and various readings of it, I'm interested in how "Let the Dead Bury Their Dead" can serve as a guiding text for the queer practice of reading in/through the swamp.

The story opens with a preface by the academic "RK"—Reginald Kain[60]—who introduces the Reverend James Malachi Greene, ethnographer and historian (and a character who travels across Kenan's oeuvre). Greene, Kain tells us, has patched together the history of Tims Creek from a hodgepodge of sources.[61] These include the transcribed storytelling of his uncle Zeke and Zeke's sister-in-law Ruth; academic footnotes from deep research into secondary sources; Greene's own lyrical reflections on Zeke and Ruth; excerpts from the antebellum journals of Rebecca Cross, wife to the slaveholder Owen Cross; and the letters of the Crosses' youngest son and famed gay botanist, Phineas. Together, these interlocutors piece together a story that includes descriptions of the present-day community of Tims Creek, rumors and theories about the town's history as a maroon community, and a wild tale of an apocalyptic night of demonic possession and neighbors raised from the dead. This accretion of stories and voices, all vying for narrative authority, suggests an almost overwhelming number of interpretive possibilities.[62]

"Let the Dead Bury Their Dead" sustains all these possibilities by insisting on multiplicity when it comes to the "real" story of Tims Creek. The Reverend Greene's goal is to separate the "mythic" from the "real" maroon community at the center of Zeke's wild tales, but his death (a car accident just after crossing the boundary into Tims Creek, after returning from a conference in Atlanta) suggests a powerful, almost occult force at work in refusing the separation of these two forms of knowledge. In his investigation into Tims Creek's history, the Reverend Greene references several historical monographs (all by white men) on maroon communities and concludes that "these communities were never able to sustain high populations and were often found out and eradicated."[63] Greene's knowledge here is contested by Zeke's testimony that a large community *was* in fact developed; a man named Pharaoh led a slave revolt and an escape to the swamp, organizing a community there and "learning em to love themselves and the world round em."[64] The reader is left to consider that the swamp is a site that escapes the official archive, just as the people making up its community escaped plantation surveillance. Then again, the accuracy of Zeke's folk archive is also suspect. He tells Greene that he's related the tale of the maroon community "word for word," but he shifts from this exactitude, in the story's last words, with a repeated addendum: "near 'bout."[65] Near 'bout is proximity to proximity—it's an ever-receding destination, a suggestion that getting to the most accurate history wasn't ever the point.

To find one's footing as a reader in this story of stories is surely to simplify in some way, to trust a single voice or to puzzle out a secret truth, a definitive "point," from all this archival material. To put it in spatial terms, our impulse is to orient ourselves. It's a tempting challenge: the story of the origins of Tims Creek, as Doris Betts put it, is also a "game" for the critical reader.[66] The word suggests rules, strategy, and hierarchy—that in mapping a path through the text, we might "win" it, succeed where Greene failed at resolving myth and history. And yet the text's authorial recursivity chastens the impulse to simplify, keeping us always within the game, never above it. When we interpret a text, we prioritize one reading among many, and therefore do hierarchical, even authorial work. But to act as a critical/authorial reader is to see ourselves mirrored by fallible readers within the text. We are reading the work of Reginald Kain, who is reading and curating the Reverend Greene, who is reading and curating his family stories. Of course, "Reginald Kain" not only shares his initials with Randall Kenan, but scans and nearly rhymes with "Reverend Greene." And Reginald Kain's efficient analysis of Greene's "major preoccupations" in his work on his hometown's history anticipates and parodies the critical emphasis on Randall Kenan's own work: "his family's slave past; the intermingling of the two Cross families, black and white; folklore and the supernatural[;] . . . community leadership and decay."[67]

Through the prefatory frame of Reginald Kain, academic, Kenan demands a critical reading even as he parodies it; Kain announces that Greene, as a historian of Tims Creek, has "taken great liberties with the established patterns of oral history," but Kain has allowed his "oddly positioned" textual excerpts and his liberty-taking oral history to remain in the text, "with the exception of three minor passages."[68] Of course, the minor instantly becomes the major to the academic reader, trained to attend to the negative spaces that draw attention to the politics of curation.[69] In this way, the introduction begs the question of who gets to shape a text, and to what end. In attempting to ground ourselves through critical reading, we're implicated by the text. Like an Escher print, the writer sketches the story of his own writing, at once establishing his authority and calling attention to the fictionality of that authority.

If the text is a "game," satisfaction—and critical reward—is not to be found in mastery, but in the destabilizing play that sucks us in. The story's narrative layers invite readers to think about the authority of institutional knowledge and methodologies, as well as the limitations of reading solely through this framework. Several critics have identified the kind of work that Kenan does in this wild mix of archive and methodology. As Uzzie Cannon puts it, there is no "master reality" to be found; a hierarchy of authoritative knowledge crumbles.[70] Lindsey Tucker also discusses how Kenan "destabilize[s] the concepts of field, ethnographer, and informant[,] . . . bring[ing] into writing a strongly contested site marked by long-standing political, racial, and religious struggle and . . . assert[ing] that the documentation of the origins of any village—of whatever name—will remain irrevocable."[71] As Thananopavarn points out, destabilization "works both ways": we can't trust Zeke's tale (he is constantly interrupted by Ruth, who declares him to be lying), but we also can't trust the written historical sources.[72] And through the very act of engaging with Kenan's text, the literary critic (including myself here) participates in or at the very least aligns herself with just the kind of institutional archive that she praises Kenan for destabilizing. The work of the swamp is that it gives the critical reader no solid ground on which to stand.

To curate the story's archive too neatly by attempting an interpretation along a straight line is to risk losing a disorienting but generative swampy ecosystem. It's for this reason that I believe Ruth, for example, gets short shrift in readings of this story. Although Ruth is, as the story quietly establishes, Zeke's sister-in-law, at least two critics have identified her as his wife, a misreading that eschews wider and more complicated ties of kinship. Zeke's and Ruth's disagreement on the history of Tims Creek, when framed as "the husband and the wife's differing accounts," translates well to an argument about the split in the perception of community along gendered and domestic lines. Alternately, when the argument is that the story radically and productively *reimagines* community, the "interruptive spats with the narrator's wife" suggest that the reimagining is principally a univocal male one.[73] The substitution of sister-in-law for wife is a small misreading, but it matters. The urgency of interpretation, which demands that we select our details, risks organizing those details into too-familiar heuristics. As Kain notes in his introduction, the conversation between Zeke and Ruth "took place . . . at the home of Mrs. Cross."[74] Ruth alone provides the porch—the page upon which this story is written—and yet she is also, as these critics note, a resistant listener. This isn't because she is bound by holy matrimony to listen to her husband holding forth on *their* porch. These two defy our expectation that family storytelling takes place within the context of marriage. And yet they are both kin and antagonists, and Ruth's interjections ("Horror, my left tit," she says, when Zeke gets to the fiery, apocalyptic chapter of his story) in one sense protect the story by debunking both Zeke's claims and Greene's academic supplements.[75] "Now you are going to hear," quotes the story's epigraph from Hurston, "lies above suspicion."[76]

If lies rise above suspicion, footnotes burrow (quite literally on the page) below it. For instance, when Zeke introduces the character of Pharaoh, who led a slave rebellion at the Cross plantation, directing his community into the safety of the swamp, Ruth interjects that "No such man ever existed," and Greene footnotes the moment, informing us of "some accounts" by which this slave might be named Menes, Sultan, or Prince, and directing us, for further reading, to "see Reginald G. Kain's monograph *Tims Creek Chronicles* (Oxford, 1999)."[77] Of course, to borrow Ruth's words, no such monograph ever existed—not least because its publication date is set in the future. The effect is that the site/sight/cite of the truth—what we can possibly know about this swamp community that became the community of Tims Creek—moves up and down this vertical axis, in and out of reach.

Because a "clean" interpretive reading becomes suspect in the swamp, I'm also wary of readings that align this space too easily with all queer sexuality. As much as the swamp functions as a space of inversion, it also remains a material landscape of Black struggle—a fact that gets lost in readings that claim belonging for Phineas there simply by merit of his sexuality. A botanist who uses his share of the family wealth to study in London, Phineas Cross comes back to North Carolina to explore the swamp, looking for the exotic Venus fly trap, and finds the area "a paradisio."[78] For Thananopavarn, Phineas's response suggests his "real respect for the indigenous species and land," his sexuality and general eccentricity in the story marking his belonging in the swamp's subversion of plantation order.[79] It is, she argues, an "Eden" both for Phineas and the maroon community.[80] But although Phineas is gay, earnestly loves the swamp's flora and fauna, and disapproves of the institution of slavery, he nevertheless sets out into the swamp looking very much like the imperialist explorer. He searches for and names plants as he goes, and regards the Black girl with whom he comes into contact with a similar approach: "She looked at me with indescribable fright, just as the deer and heron had, and fled. . . . If Providence had not placed an above-ground stolon at her feet I might never have made my discovery, for she tripped."[81] Overtaking her, he disregards her fear to ask questions, christening his new territory after the Thames and likening himself to Adam. Despite his essentializing impulse upon coming into contact with Pharaoh, that "mysterious" African, Phineas shows far more respect than the rest of his family, and is given mercy, allowed to live as long as he never speaks a word of his experience in the swamp.[82] Instead, he writes about it, and his experience of the swamp forms a single layer of our understanding as readers. Phineas suggests the importance of understanding queerness in the swamp as multivalent, composed of more than sexuality alone. Phineas's "deviance" as a gay man may lead him into the swamp, but this hardly reads as a "natural" fit; after all, this space of anticapitalistic disorientation defiantly refuses his presumptive taxonomizing.

"Let the Dead," with its many competing stories that accrete on the single swampy landscape of Tims Creek, captures in miniature the experience of reading Kenan's story collections and novel. The swamp resists any dominant narrative, ideological hegemony, or single conceptual orientation because the space insists on getting lost—we sink into these swirling stories, "get into the weeds," as with Kain's and Jimmy's labyrinthine footnotes. The result is an expansiveness of interpretive possibility that refuses simplification. To read Kenan's works together, to take them as rhizomatically connected, is to read according to the rich, accumulative landscape of the swamp. This kind of "swampy reading" insists on many formulations of queer southernness—and the generative critical implications of that multiplicity.

In an attempt to read in a way suited to a swamp archive, I've chosen, rather than bordering off separate texts, to explore ideas connected across texts, hoping to build out a geography that I believe a focus on a single text might miss—attuning always to the possibilities for play between story and reader. A swampy queer southernness is a space of creation and resistance, insisting on many stories. I've chosen to focus on three themes—home, nature, and surveillance—that are, as I have identified, key to a potent "Old South" mythology that writes itself onto southern landscapes like Tims Creek. In the sections that follow, I attempt to show how Kenan does the swampy work of dismantling and revising narratives along these themes, building other forms of southernness in which Black queer joy and intimacy are possible. To bear witness to Kenan's narrative transformations is, I hope, to take part in his creation of swampy spaces in Tims Creek and beyond.

Reorienting Nature

Across his work, Kenan taps into the many roles of "nature" in discourses of the South—roles that extend far beyond the physical landscape. The South is frequently aligned with nature, and, even now, with the agrarian vision of *I'll Take My Stand*. As Christopher Rieger argues, the pastoral mode has been used to construct, both within and outside the region, "nostalgic versions of the Old South that offer the plantation regime . . . and its pleasant rural peace . . . as an alternative to the confusion of the materialistic New South. The antebellum plantation is portrayed in these works as a refuge of order and stability, a harmonious blend of city and country."[83] The southern pastoral, surely, has proven to be an enduring set piece.

Such a view of the natural world shapes which social systems are deemed "natural"—it's not only the magnolia under the moonlight that falls within the "natural" landscape, but the white family tree and the lynching tree. The rise of evolutionary thought and scientific racism in the nineteenth century increasingly linked blackness and queerness with "natural" inferiority and "unnatural" degeneracy, respectively.[84] Nature is hardly a neutral term—all the more so because, as Catriona Mortimer-Sandilands points out, "landscapes have been organized to produce and promote (and prohibit) particular kinds of sexual identity and practice," as well as racial identity and practice.[85] Kenan, in his engagements with this ideologically crowded territory, cultivates what Mortimer-Sandilands calls a queer ecology, using the modern rural landscape of Tims Creek to rewrite familiar narratives of a "natural" southern domain.[86]

In "I Thought I Heard the Shuffle of Angels' Feet" (2020), Dax Cross's land in Tims Creek is under threat from Percy Terrell and the Terrell Corporation—a white company eating up Black land for luxury condos. Dax has had to move to an assisted living home after having his foot amputated due to diabetes, and Dax's gay nephew Cicero, a kind of prodigal son, is coming home from the city to help organize the move and sell the land. Dax's desire to hold onto his home is about more than property; it's about refusing a long history of exploitation and white encroachment onto Black land. Accordingly, the problem appears in epic terms: Dax is "rolled out of the only home he'd ever known, ancestral, fruit tree-surrounded, lushly carried-for and tended and mended over the years; now ushered into the anteroom of the great undiscovered country. Not so great."[87] The ancestral, fruit-tree laden home is a kind of Edenic image, resonant of a family line, but what is it to be "carried-for"? "Cared" would seem to fit better there, but to "carry" for something, lushly or otherwise, has different implications. You might carry a child for the ancestral home, carry responsibility, carry a legacy. The word emphasizes the weight of the Cross bloodline as well as Cicero's deviance from its demands. In DC, Cicero has built a house with his partner Jacson (both are architects) that epitomizes the cosmopolitan: large, expensive, and eclectic, a fusion of global styles. He has effectively traded his family kingdom for a "queerdom"—a neologism that Cicero uses to indicate not just identity but its corresponding designated dominion outside of the rural South.[88] Instead of evoking futurity in the form of the child, Cicero's and Jacson's domesticity is a state that Jacson, from the time of the house's construction, associates with his own death—he "carries" HIV. If Dax's "ancestral, fruit-laden" land is the generationally (heteronormatively) dependent homeplace, its endangerment is linked to queerness. Dax's missing limb becomes Cicero, the hacked-off limb of the family tree, hobbling not only himself, but the continued survival of the family and their land.

As for the "great undiscovered country," in linking the afterlife with pristine nature, even the wilderness is given structuring ideologies. The anteroom of the "great undiscovered country," the assisted living home, has no windows to the awe-inspiring landscape the phrase suggests.[89] In fact, it is the antithesis to nature, with its "dull industrial carpet," "framed posters of kittens and puppy dogs and baby pigs" (along with Bible quotes), and "stain-resistant upholstery."[90] These images evoke meager modern comforts, reifying the sentimental reverence of youth in the holding cell for death. Occupying these chambers and obsessed by a metaphor that substitutes the real fruit tree for a family tree, Dax is far removed from nature, and yet sure of his religiously informed ideas of "the natural," telling Cicero, even after he decides to keep the family land, "'I'm done with your black faggoty ass.'"[91] The anteroom might not have a window to the undiscovered country, but if the framed Bible verses on the walls are an indication, we like to think of the afterlife as not-so-undiscovered—or at least reserved for the right kind of people. The heteronormative narrative upon which Dax insists is connected to confining religious moral geographies, but when Cicero makes the decision to stay in Tims Creek, these are not the geographies that he claims.

Cicero's choice to keep the family home is rooted in a different kind of belonging: a surprising, tender reunion with his high school friend, Tony, kissing in his kitchen "in the April-bright North Carolina light that streamed through the lemon curtains."[92] This natural light, shining upon queerness, seems to bring Cicero a similarly "natural" insight. His moment of decision, to keep the family land and come back to cultivate a relationship with Tony, is a moment in which he aligns himself with the natural world beyond the fraught metaphor of the family tree, in a kind of kinship with the young cornstalks on the side of the road. Symbol of rural life, they strive, like Cicero, both for attachment and utopian flight: "the green so young, so struggling to take to the sky. Immature things but too big for crows to pluck."[93] In a revision of Billie Holiday's haunting lyrics from "Strange Fruit," nature becomes the scene of queer Black strength rather than pain and violence.

The ghost of the lynching tree lingers in "Run, Mourner, Run" (1992). As Suzanne Jones has pointed out, the opening and closing images of Dean, the poor, queer white boy at the center of the story, swinging from a tire swing on a sycamore, rhyme strangely with that too-familiar violence.[94] *Rhyme* is a key word here; Dean thinks in terms of folktales and nursery rhymes, and the landscape around him acquires a magical agency, threatening in its silence.[95] The "burnt and brittle-colored maples" are highlighted against a red sky that does not, as the old adage promises, presage either delight or warning.[96] He wonders if he could have been saved from Percy Terrell's plot—to seduce Ray Brown, a rich Black man, so that Percy might have blackmail material with which to coerce Ray into giving up his land— "if he'd had some warning from a crow or woodchuck."[97] But the natural world refuses to intervene in Dean's human affairs. What he remembers, from his days with Ray, is a different stance: Ray confidently recruiting nature for his seductions and mumbling to Dean that "all flesh is grass, my love."[98] This line, Biblical and Whitmanesque, gestures to life as both transitory and ubiquitous—it claims the natural world for queer intimacy and places queer intimacy in the natural world.

Ray and Dean both straddle two distinct ecosystems: a kind of utopian ecological collective and a capitalist system with its roots in slavery. Percy promises Dean that, should he "do [his] bidding," he'll get a promotion.[99] Dean's attachment to Ray is made of both genuine affection and desire for wealth: he imagines damask sheets on a big, beautiful bed they share. And Ray, invested in his booming business and his appearance as a family man, can only ever use his family homeplace as a clandestine meetup spot, vulnerable to Percy's blackmail. Dean's and Ray's relationship is one of a power differential, on the one hand, and a secret exploitation, on the other: "Is this where you take your boys?" Dean asks, to Ray's affirmation, and on entering, hears "the voices of old black men and old black women screaming for his death" as Ray pulls him into bed.[100] But Dean's and Ray's time in the homeplace seems to shift (however briefly) the frameworks of race and class, offering an alternative to the capitalist world in which they reside. They see "the daffodils and the crocuses and the blessed jonquils," a "mist about the meadow and the pond" while they lie "intertwined in dreams and limbs."[101]

These brief moments offer the glimpse of an environment unstructured by racial and economic hierarchy, holding the potential to reconceive the heteronormative family tree—not with a limb cut off, but with limbs grafted, protected, and growing in many directions: an image of queer kinship. The ethereal morning mist, and the idyllic and mysterious route to the homeplace, suggest the swamp that Tims Creek once was, the natural refuge against slavecatchers, resistant to maps and conquest: "down narrow back roads, through winding paths, alongside fields, into woods, into a meadow Dean had never seen before, near Chitaqua Pond."[102] It's a fleeting but significant glimpse of peace before Percy Terrell catches them in bed together and blackmails Ray into giving up his homestead. Although an alternative ecosystem might still be visible at dawn, by the time the sun comes up, heteronormative capitalist geographies reassert themselves, and Ray and Dean find themselves vulnerable to Percy's approach. Through the fog, the looming voices and dogs are reminiscent of slavecatchers.

Dean's vision of the cold and silent woods at the story's opening evokes two different gazes onto the woods in *A Visitation of Spirits*—two different ways of understanding the wilderness in relation to queerness. Shame and fear can imbue the natural landscape with a moral darkness: demonic, chaotic, deathly. These are the woods as Reverend "Jimmy" Greene sees them, beyond the football field, after Horace shoots himself. Jimmy spends the novel, and apparently his life, in the role of the good son, suppressing his queer impulses, becoming a preacher to make his family and community proud, and, it seems, convincing himself of the rightness of the role he steps into. To play the part of "the Great Black Hope" is to be to some extent unhappy and unrecognized, and yet both men understand it to be the only possible option. Their experience of community, as structured by their church, aligns with Ashon Crawley's theorization of the queer Black body as occupying a peripheral space: "constantly in danger of slipping away, of being erased from memory and knowledge."[103] Jimmy's gaze into the woods—"cold and incomprehensible," the space of "wild things," "futility

Near 'Bout 73

and waste"—suggests everything about Jimmy's fear of being "out of place," peripheral, beyond the geographical borders of God and into the damnable (queer) wilderness.[104]

This alignment of a God-forsaken wilderness with a doomed queerness reflects a naturalized narrative of queer tragedy. Like Cicero, both Horace and Jimmy have been conditioned to believe that the only way to live authentically is to trade their kingdom—in this case, the kingdom of God, as well as their earthly Black community—for a (sinful) and white queerdom, unimaginably distant. Between these two constricting options, only death presents an alternative. But there is no "great undiscovered country" in Horace's death, no liberated afterlife, only the horror of a body destroyed by gunshot.[105] Kenan's visceral descriptions of the organic processes of death mock the idea that Horace's suicide could be understood as a "natural" event—the religious demarcations and divisions of borders and identities is, on the contrary, deeply unnatural. As Lucy Littler points out, Kenan's representation of Horace's death discourages "readings that focus on the transformative power of Horace's suicide," which "risk reifying the dominant narrative that employs Exodus rhetoric to limn a model of progress through sacrifice"; it's potentially damaging to read Horace's death as "naturalized, a necessary part of community's transformation."[106]

Horace never thinks of transforming his community, but rather of transforming himself, hoping that he can banish what he believes is unnatural in him (his sexuality) by banishing his humanity and becoming what he imagines to be an agent of pure nature (a hawk). As Sharon Holland argues, "in a racist society," only "the ultimate erasing of black subjectivity" can "actualize a queer project."[107] Unlike Jimmy's gaze onto the woods, Horace's imagined hawk-eye gaze is one of inhuman and therefore unraced power. The hawk's "murderous" eyes narrow in on its helpless prey, and he flies unharmed through "a storm sky, black and mean, full of wind and hate, God's wrath."[108] But although Horace fails to transform into a hawk, just before this experiment he is able to adopt a different kind of understanding, one that also takes refuge in the natural world but allows him to keep "his humanity, his flesh, his blood" along with his Black and queer identity.[109] As he lies in bed, "crickets and frogs and cicadas [chirp] the beating of a thousand tiny hearts."[110] Briefly, he's able to listen, and to feel himself a part of this communion: not nature as an inhuman, predatory power, and not queer Black life as ending inevitably in doom. His own life, quite simply, is a natural part of a larger rhythm.

The cornstalk, the woodchuck, the grass, the mist, the jonquils, the cicadas: these offer alternatives to the lynching tree, the family tree, and the sinister forest as monoliths in the great expanse of the southern, and more broadly the American, natural imaginary. The natural spaces that Kenan's characters occupy are often metaphorized and weaponized within familiar narratives of violence and exclusion. But Kenan also revises those stories, offering visions of natural spaces that offer protection, affirmation, beauty, and power for Black queer life, even if only briefly. Such an ecology suggests that Tims Creek, that former swamp, is a space that holds the potential for radical refuge.

Reorienting Home

The idea that queerness is a threat to the sanctity of the American home and national identity is not an unfamiliar one. As Lauren Berlant writes, "conservative ideology has convinced a citizenry that the core context of politics should be the sphere of private life," and that citizenship involves primarily "an intricate set of relations between economic, racial, and sexual processes."[111] In that the "right" American home is white, heteronormative, and well-classed; it is a descendent of the plantation. To "queer" that home, then, is a disruption not only of the domestic sphere, but of citizenship more broadly. In this sense, the Black American home is already antinormative, and certainly always already under threat from the nation's pervasive and perpetual anti-blackness.[112] As bell hooks writes, the "brutal harsh reality of racist oppression" from slavery onward made the Black home—the homeplace—fundamentally distinct in its "radical political dimension."[113] The homeplace was "the one site where one could freely confront the issue of humanization, where one could resist."[114] But the homeplace itself risks reinscribing oppressive gender and sexual norming as a defensive response to the violence of dehumanization.[115] The result is that the radical protective power of the homeplace, and its capacity to nurture, becomes aligned with constricting gender roles and heteronormativity—a dynamic that reinforces an opposition between domesticity and queerness.[116]

The queer Black homeplace, as many critics have theorized, resists this alignment, insisting on the possibility and the vitality of queer kinship. Dwight McBride and E. Patrick Johnson, for example, discuss homophobia within Black domestic spaces, but both critics also see homeplace as transformable and transformative, the "nexus that has to be rethought."[117] Home must serve as the "marginally safe place to critique oppression outside its confines" as well as "within homeplace itself."[118] It's this work of transforming the idea of the southern home, opening it to queer Black life—work that is always complicated, never completed—that takes shape through swampy readings across Kenan's work.

"Mamiwata" (2020) unfolds from the perspective of Mandy, a girl whose family lives in the camp the enslaved leader Pharaoh (familiar to us from Zeke's story in "Let the Dead Bury Their Dead") has organized in the swamp to escape the Cross plantation. Here, Zeke's words about Pharaoh's swamp community echo: They are "learning em to love themselves and the world around them."[119] When the softness of a rabbit's pelt leads Mandy into thoughts of the plantation, she remembers that former space not as one of domestic comfort and order, but as the scene of white luxury and violence inextricably intertwined, and "reckoned she liked it better" in the swamp; "she did not reckon, she knew."[120] Mandy is well taught by Pharaoh's warning that "you never know how far them dogs and catchers will come out here. . . . Always be ready to pick up and run deeper into the swamp," but she is also growing in the knowledge that although she should be careful, Pharaoh has no wish "to clip [her] wings."[121] Mobility and love are crucial elements of her understanding of home.

This kinetic, cooperative quality of the swamp home links liberation with more dynamic, fluid modes of nurture and domesticity. Out on an exploring expedition, Mandy sees a mysterious man bathing himself in the river. Claiming he is "standing watch," he catches her a catfish by drawing it magically from the river.[122] "Dog-sized," it jumps out of the water and lands with an abundant thud in front of Mandy.[123] Here, the slave-catcher's dog is transmuted into an almost Biblical miracle of food for the community. It floats mystically out of the water to hover above the river man's head, "cover[ing] the all of him like a great big oak bough full with leaves."[124] Just as the domesticated animal and agent of human cruelty turns to a wild animal and source of sustenance, the haunting/haunted tree of plantation violence turns to nurturing shade in the home of the swamp. When they hear dogs in the distance, Mandy joins the man in the river. The water's protection—and the riverman's—provide an almost womblike nurturance, invoking a traditionally feminine domesticity: "Warm like a belly full of hot chicken. Warm like a freshly picked ear of corn. Warm like a ripe tomato. Warm like Aunt Ines's hands."[125] And yet it is a distinctly masculine strength (the "man spread[ing] his big arms wide open") that provides this nurture, complicating gendered scripts.[126] Moreover, in ending on this mysterious note, the story refuses a heteronormative narrative equating progress with the child's growth up. It offers instead a conception of growth like a river: depth and lateral movement.[127]

Queerness, in this story, lies in the anticapitalist home, which reimagines the possibilities of childhood, gender roles, and domesticity. Sexual queerness doesn't enter explicitly into this swamp home, but it does linger in the epigraph to "Mamiwata," which cites to Phineas Cross, the queer son of Owen Cross, plantation owner, who ventures into the swamp looking for plant life. Phineas's threat to Pharaoh's and Mandy's home is apparent from his imperializing impulse to taxonomize and claim. This suggestion of destruction to the Black home, in the form of conquest bound up with white homosexuality, echoes in Dean's entrance into Ray Brown's "homeplace" in "Mourner." Like the camp in the swamp, this homeplace is hard to find, accessible only "down narrow back roads, through winding paths, alongside fields, into woods."[128] This maze protects "the bedroom where measles had been tended and babies created"—the place where Black life is beloved.[129] Ray has adapted his family homeplace as a space where he can take men during nights away from his upper-middle class home that he shares with his wife. Like the camp on the river, Ray's homeplace is located on the water, and it's here that Dean, as he reflects later, "unlearns . . . hate, fiery, blunt, brutal."[130] But of course, the homeplace is not meant for his learning experience (as Ray's ancestors, "screaming" in protest in Dean's imagination, would indicate), and the success of Dean's un-learning is called into question by his instrumental role in Percy Terrell's blackmail.[131] When Percy enters, he announces the end of the homeplace—it'll be swallowed up by his lucrative condominium project. But there is a glimmer of queer domesticity in Dean's memory of eating ice cream in bed with Ray, admiring the tulips outside. In these fleeting moments, the story begs the question: What would a queer homeplace look like that hasn't been limited to secretive nights under siege, one that *is* the family home, rather than a threatening (and white) outside influence?

We find an answer to some extent in "Resurrection Hardware." When Randall learns that his historical southern home was once a Quaker-run escape route for the enslaved, his revisioning of the space engenders a kind of temporal layering. First, he hears a man panting in terror, and finds him curled in the living room with "the light pour[ing] in."[132] He cares for the man—gives him a bed, covers him up—but when he returns with coffee, the man is gone. The mystery of the encounter, along with Randall's almost familial kindness to him, repeats when he finds the man sitting on the rocking chair on his porch. The man asks a question twice: "You live here?"[133] When Randall affirms this question by making the house his home, these guests-out-of-time appear en masse, roaming the grounds with lights and voices.

Randall's restoration of the house is the quotidian domestic kind, making an old and creaky house his own cozy place, but it also becomes a more radical project of caring for his out-of-time visitors and attending to his own history: inviting a series of far-flung friends, from different times in his life and of different backgrounds, for Thanksgiving dinner. This ritual codes both ghosts and friends as kin, family. His friend from the historical society has sage commentary on the nature of this kind of project: "These sorts of things are never complete, are they?"[134] Over Thanksgiving, as Randall reflects on his relationships, he ruminates on the impossible dream of completion. Just as a house renovation is never really finished, reunions never offer closure, but rather a reminder of incessant movement and change: "We expect some grand revelation. Revelations work on their own time, not ours. The beats beat on. The night beat on."[135] The "thing of pure joy" at Thanksgiving dinner is not only the goose that Randall describes, but the dynamic communion, the gentleness and care—homeplace in all its changeability—that reaches across time. "Resurrection" ends with Randall stepping outside to find that it's no longer late fall, but spring, the landscape bursting with flowers, and his antebellum guest is being ferried away—on a river Randall has never seen before—to freedom. The river, as in "Mamiwata," is part of the swampy home's protection, and in its unceasing motion, it allows for many forms of kinship and intimacy. Nurture, here, takes the form of a dynamic queer domesticity.

The spring flowers in both "Run, Mourner, Run" and "Resurrection Hardware" suggest changing seasons of queer life aligned with the delicate but vibrant possibilities of queer homeplace. These possibilities bloom more fully in "I Heard the Shuffle of Angels' Feet," a story in which the structures and possibilities of domestic life are, so to speak, shuffled. Cicero has been "dwelling—not really living—in too much house on the North Shore of Maryland" after his partner's death when he returns to Tims Creek.[136] Before going to see his uncle, Dax, he spends his evening catching up and reminiscing with his old friend Tony. Cicero thinks, quite self-consciously, in spatial terms, and so he conceives of himself and Tony as "time voyagers" who started from the same departure point in their innocent high school days, seeming now to find themselves baffled and adrift in their forties.[137]

The idea of voyaging through time is not just one of drift, but of agency: it suggests that "out of place" and "out of time"—spatial boundaries and temporal limitations—are changeable and changing constructions. Movement across time becomes, for Cicero, a way to understand space differently. In their reminiscences, Cicero and Tony bond over the catchphrase of their high school algebra teacher and track coach: "it is what it is."[138] Fitting, coming from this particular teacher, because the phrase is both an equation and a kind of circle—accompanied, for Cicero, by a syntactically similar revelation: "It wasn't enough to say you were coming back. Coming back was coming back."[139] He must turn the clock back and forward, voyaging out and back, to re-orient to the idea of home in the South.

Cicero's understanding of home changes as his intimacy with Tony develops. After spending the night on Tony's couch, Cicero and Tony have breakfast together and share a kiss, their bond carried forward by the unspoken memory of a brief but joyful sexual encounter in high school, the fleeting beauty of a season of hope: "Was it the spring air? The azaleas and the pollen and the fragrance of fresh-cut grass? . . . Unstoppable maleness?"[140] The memory is for Cicero "like time inside a beloved song with no grace note at the end, which lingers and lingers on."[141] And he does have a song in his head, one by the Temptations: "Just my imagination / Running away with me."[142] Queerness, in this musical conceit, is something that both stays in place and runs freely, enduring but impossible to grasp, like Randall's beat that "beats on," like the river in Mamiwata.

Much like for Randall, lover and home are equated for Cicero not only through a queer temporality, but through sustenance: Tony makes "eggs and bacon and coffee . . . and toast and grits. Lovely grits. How sweet the taste."[143] The sweetness of their high school memory and the intimacy of the present are joined in Cicero's adult gaze upon Tony as he stands cooking in the kitchen: "seeing his old buddy as if for the first time, that morning," in that April light.[144] It's the light of spring, once again, that expands the possibilities of a Black queer domesticity. Cicero's goodbye to Tony, however temporary, is "a heavy thing, a molten thing, a thing that drug down on him like the shackles of both their ancestors. He did not hesitate to kiss Tony full on the lips, and Tony responded as if with relief."[145] The ancestors, both as represented by Dax's homophobia and imagined by Dean in "Run, Mourner, Run" are fierce figures in protecting the homeplace for Black heteronormativity; but here, the heaviness is not queerness itself, nor is it the imperative to stay on constricting ancestral land. The heaviness is the leave-taking from queer domesticity. To stay, paradoxically, would be freedom, movement, and lightness for Cicero and Tony as well as their ancestors—a voyage through time that reaches back, once again, toward queer nurture and sustenance. Their kiss, rather than threatening the southern homeplace, strengthens it.

Reorienting Surveillance

The home, as a place where Black queer life might be fully and wholly expressed, is a site that escapes or refuses norming surveillance. The disciplinary gaze structures a geography; as Simone Browne writes, blackness has historically been "a key site through which surveillance is practiced, narrated, and enacted."[146] The plantation, the "earliest form of surveillance practiced in the Americas," becomes the "racial etiquette" of Jim Crow, demanding that "Blacks . . . stay in their designated, subordinate places in white-controlled public and private spheres," which in turn becomes the national surveillance of blackness in myriad contemporary forms.[147] The Black geography of resistance, then, is one structured by a counter-gaze—what Browne terms "dark sousveillance," an "imaginative place from which to mobilize a critique of racializing surveillance."[148] Her work offers a productive paradigm through which to chart how, in Kenan's fiction, a normative white southern geography is regularly upended by what Browne identifies as "anti-surveillance, counter-surveillance, and other freedom practices"; these are the queer freedom practices of the swamp.[149]

Percy Terrell's gentrification project wanders threateningly in and out of Tims Creek—but in "Now Why Come Is That" (2020), he is, finally, toppled by what is surely a counter-surveilling gaze. In this story, Percy Terrell's encounter with a hog dramatizes the destabilization of normative space. Like a plantation overseer, Percy Terrell moves about Tims Creek as the town's dominant white male authority. The heart of his kingdom is his office in the town's southern-style general store, complete with a rack of guns, a rattlesnake hide above the desk, and a gubernatorial citation hanging on the wall. This décor claims Percy's rightful position at the top of the food chain; he is the disciplinary agent of the state. And yet he's being followed around by a hog that appears suddenly one night in his office. The clack of hooves makes "ghostly" the formerly familiar "shadowscape" bathed in the red of emergency lights.[150] This sudden, "spooky" transformation of the room is accompanied by an enormous hog, described in ambivalent terms that evoke conflicted historical understandings of the humanity of enslaved and racialized people:[151] not a "human-being person," and yet with eyes "unhumanly human."[152]

What Percy would like to think of as meat turns its gaze onto *him*— performing the kind of "transformative" gaze that, as Browne writes, has the power to disrupt surveillance.[153] Just as the hog transforms Percy's office that first night into a newly unsolid shadowscape, it throws his "orderly" life in Tims Creek into "chaos."[154] The hog follows him everywhere, unseen by everyone but Percy, opening up a "void" in his mind.[155] This disbalance is accompanied by an atmospheric political shift perceptible even in this small southern town. Percy owes more taxes than he used to (which he finds calculating by hand, because he doesn't trust "the damn computers"), but, because of the "bleeding hearts," he can no longer hunt big game in Kenya the way he did in '52.[156] Things around him are changing in unpleasant ways, from globalization (the "compact Japanese-made piece of mess" he sees a woman filling up at the gas station), to gender roles (his son's wife, who commits the sin of confronting Percy when he gives her children candy against her wishes).[157] Rather than being sure of the territory that was his to surveil, solid ground is increasingly a nostalgic fantasy for Percy, like the cowboys of the "West that never existed" that bring him comfort on his flickering TV screen.[158] The hog's persistent gaze orients him newly in space: "Percy felt that he was not in Tims Creek, North Carolina. . . . He was a mere blip on some otherness, some twisted reality. He didn't know where he was."[159] The twisted reality in which Percy finds himself is like a Mobius strip, a non-orientable surface. The hog is both metaphor and real animal; Percy is both big man in Tims Creek and blip on an otherness. There is no knowing where he is.

To free himself from the hog's disorienting gaze, he finally visits Tabitha McElwaine, the Black woman whose great expanse of land inherited from her grandfather after the Civil War has been reduced, by the Terrell Corporation, to a mere five acres. Tabitha appears, in Percy's narrative, as a kind of witch, a Circean figure who has the sole power to banish the hog and return Percy to his rightful authority. Standing before the "witch," this "Weird Sister" in her grand house that "sparkles with light," he feels "febrile" with the strangeness of his need: "he wanted an old black woman to tell him, an old white man, what he must do to release himself."[160] She's the only one who can really see him, in his predicament, but the atonements (the reparations?) necessary to break the spell are, Tabitha informs him, beyond his grasp. She holds the gaze, and with it, power. With a look of "pity that quickly transform[s] into scorn," she informs Percy, "you ain't gone to be willing to do what you got to do to get rid of [the hog]."[161] Her gaze upon him is a powerful form of resistance: she looks "as if to say, *Boy, you don't know your asshole from your mouth, do you?*"[162] It renders Percy speechless. After this failed last gamble for resolution, he ends the story deeply "lonesome," unseen, mumbling like a child, reduced and lost in the disorientation of Tabitha's practices of dark sousveillance.[163]

Percy's story dramatizes how a transformative gaze can change an orientation to and experience of the world. His role across both story collections as head of the Terrell Corporation, always expanding his territory and identifying new victims, positions him as a direct descendent of the plantation system in all its exploitative, imperializing, and violent capitalist practices. Tabitha McElwaine's hold on her home as Terrell land encroaches is in parallel with Dax's insistence on keeping the family home and Pharaoh's camp in the swamp in "Mamiwata," resolute against slave-catchers who venture ever further in. But whereas the plantation system depends upon surveillance technologies that violently center blackness as object of spectacle and discipline, the swamp in "Mamiwata" offers the space of a Black subjectivity and a gaze of recognition, curiosity, and care. Although the story begins with an epigraph from Phineas's journals, the story circulates beyond his taxonomizing gaze. The swamp has not yet become Thames or Tims—it is simply "the swamp."

Mandy, the young girl at home in the swamp in "Mamiwata," orients to her landscape in a primarily visual way—her every mode of sensory knowing is transposed into sight. The result is a series of gazes that subverts a paradigm of predation. As she makes her way through the forest, even though "it was getting dark[,] . . . she could still see plenty."[164] The possibly ominous onset of darkness is unexpectedly lit by "a voice [that] grew and rose, and was the color of mint."[165] Mandy finds that its source is an unfamiliar man bathing himself in the water; he's no one from her camp. Her interactions with the man in the river are negotiations of seeing and being seen: She "walk[s] like a fawn," not prey to the hunter, but rather silent, interested watcher.[166] The man is "quite a sight. . . . His eyes seemed to flash."[167] And yet rather than capturing her with the camera,[168] as that description indicates, they "eye each other" in no hierarchy of power; he tells her that he is "standing watch," on the lookout not for Mandy but in protection of them both.[169] The second time Mandy returns to the river, she finds the man "star[ing] straight at her," offering up the "see-through" catfish that floats magically out of the river, which Mandy "peek[s] out to see."[170] After conquering her fear of this strange sight, she drags the giant fish proudly back to her family. The river man claims at their next encounter that the fish "was me."[171] The strange magic of their encounter lies in sustenance both visible and invisible—not only the fish, but the power of a gaze that gives rather than depletes. The focus on sight continues through to the end of the story, in which Mandy, after "peer[ing] into the woods to see what she could see," finally disappears into the protective water—becoming herself unseen—with the river man.[172] Safety, growth, and reality are all negotiated through modes of sight counter to the violent surveillance of the plantation. To be on the lookout is not only to escape the danger of the plantation, but to recognize landscapes of refuge.

This kind of geography of mutual care, oriented by a mode of sight beyond the surveilling gaze, seems always just out of reach in *A Visitation of Spirits*.[173] Like Percy's hog, Horace's ghosts disorient, but his shifting geography stops short of being truly transformative. Feeling both hypervisible and invisible in his blackness and his queerness, Horace attempts sorcery to turn himself into a hawk—an animal that can see over a great expanse but is not itself seen. He wants to become a great predator rather than easy prey. When he ventures to the library to research his transformation, Horace is aware that he has "no hall pass" except for his status as the "Great Black Hope," which comes with attendant freedoms and nascent powers within his tight-knit community—provided that he can "pass" as straight.[174] Especially given that Horace's school system, beginning in elementary school, has "a plantation-like grandeur," the hall pass suggests the slave pass—a powerful example of a surveillance technology.[175] To forge the pass or otherwise circumvent that technology in order to roam unseen and unmonitored is a form of resistance.[176] And surely to transform into a hawk is to rise above surveillance, becoming its agent rather than its object. But while the hawk's-eye view offers the potential to see a landscape in which boundaries and borders disappear—rising far above the school, seeing the forests of Tims Creek transitioning to highway and then, finally, to the vast freedom of the ocean—Horace can't quite leave his human geographies behind. Even as he fantasizes about being "unfettered, unbound, and free," his imagination is constricted to "perch[ing] on the ledge and watching the biology students."[177]

Horace's purest dream of hawkhood is caught within entrenched and racialized human dynamics. It's the accumulated voices of his community that surround Horace when his sorcery fails and spirits appear, leading him through Tims Creek and demanding that he gaze upon himself in a

Scrooge-like progression through the stages of his life. Like Mandy watching the catfish twirl in the air, or Percy waking up to the squalls of a hog in his bedroom, whether the "hobgoblins and sprites" that surround Horace are "really" there is less important than how they shift the geographies before his sight and therefore in his experience.[178] He walks around "baffled" and wondering what is "real."[179] But while this new multiplicity of sight is disorienting, it is, paradoxically, not disorienting enough. Horace's surveilling and norming gaze on himself stays stable, limiting his field of vision: "the voice said march, so he marched," while he misses "the low swooping owl or the scurrying wood rat."[180]

Unlike Mandy, Horace can't quite access the swampy gazes of reciprocal care. At one point in his journey, he watches a memory in which a group of boys (including Horace) lob insults at Gideon, a boy who fails (or doesn't try) to pass as straight. Horace is scrutinizing his younger self, who in turn is aware of being watched by the group of boys, waiting to see how he will respond to Gideon, and also watched by Gideon, who is "fix[ing] Horace with a gaze whose intensity frightened him."[181] There are three layers of surveillance here, three gazes onto his emerging masculinity. Horace's fear of being seen—by himself, by his peers, and by the object of his desire—becomes particularly intense in high school. Horace and Gideon bond over a science project on tropism and, ironically, begin to spend more time together in darkness, once kissing "in an unlighted and deeply recessed doorway" in an abandoned school hallway during a football game.[182] Although their relationship never comes to light in the community, so to speak, Horace's deepest fear is to be seen. He agonizes over the knowledge that his reputation at school and in his family is in Gideon's hands, and when he wants to tell Gideon he loves him, fear overtakes him as soon as he "looks into those brown eyes" that, however tender, recognize his most closely held secret.[183] From Horace's youngest years, the school is an institution of surveillance, threatening violence to those who practice the "wrong" kind of Black masculinity. Ultimately, it's a system that Horace internalizes so deeply that his relationship with Gideon paralyzed by Horace's anxiety around a surveilling and punishing gaze, and he can't imagine a different way of looking and being seen, finding an orientation outside of a framework of shame.[184]

The last memory of high school that Horace revisits is the painful scene of his break with Gideon, a rejection of the possibilities of queer intimacy. Gideon confronts him in the locker room to ask why Horace is ignoring him (he has joined the football team, and begun dating a girl), and Horace, in response to Gideon's teasing and persistence, punches him in the face. Before that final confrontation, Gideon reaches out in both lust and tenderness, "walk[ing] up behind Horace. His hands glided over the width of Horace's shoulders as though he were checking a wing span."[185] In linking queer touch with the power of flight, this small moment suggests a different way of imagining transformation, more aligned with Pharaoh's assurance to Mandy that he "doesn't want to clip [her] wings."[186] But the moment is shattered by fear and violence, and Horace leaves the space of memory and stumbles out to the football field to find a more threatening winged figure: a black, cloaked spectre with a scimitar, poised to deliver judgment, waiting to use his wings to deliver Horace to heaven or hell. It's in this moment of anticipation that Horace finds himself in the glare of truck headlights—white boys on the football field, peering at him "like a caught coon."[187] He is, once again, in the plantation's violent spotlight. The deathlike figure Horace has just seen vanishes, and he is left alone, "the object of a few things that would not simply be gone."[188] This understanding of himself, as the object of the surveilling gaze, shaped into abjection, is his final painful intractable vision.

Within the borders of what Horace's family will accept, his growth is distorted; he has no way of taking flight. In his memory of his time with Gideon, Horace thinks of their science project on tropism: "an orientation of an organism, usually by growth rather than movement, in response to an external stimulus."[189] Orientation here connotes not only sexuality, but a direction of growth that opens up a range of vision. Gideon, in this definition, takes the place of the sun, sustaining, nourishing, prompting upward and outward.[190] But so trained to see himself as "receptacle," it's that constraining, constricting structure that continues to enclose Horace and dictate the limited horizon he can see and orient toward. His only vision of the sun after his long night is in death, his eyes "rolled back, staking up, as though examining the sun through the canopy of tree limbs. In awe and respect."[191] Whether or not the demons are "real," their visibility to Horace leads to his death, undeniably true. As Holland writes, Horace, like a spirit, "appears naked and haunts our imaginative attempts to erase him from our fruitful landscapes and canons."[192]

Kenan insists on Horace's continued visibility to us as readers, and he also insists on Horace's lingering, loving gaze onto his home. The description of Horace's death is bookended by two odes to "remembering." One is a lyrical, nostalgic "requiem to tobacco" that revels in the fading rituals of traditional rural life, and the other is a deeply personal journey through Horace's memories, jumping from rural rituals that echo those in "requiem" to contemporary adolescent engrossments with Marvin Gaye, Batman, and *Lord of the Rings* as he struggles with his sexuality.[193] The ghostly alternative to Horace's death—that he might have oriented to the sun, and seen himself as other than the object of surveillance or its inhuman, predatory agent—lingers in both these modes of remembering. Kenan's work across texts, as across the novel's chapters in their dissonant styles, asks us, as readers, to revise our expectations of southernness, to reorient to it as a space of possibility for Black, queer resistance.

Coda: Forms

In focusing on the deviant space of the swamp, I'm conceptualizing queerness and southernness in terms of space and form: landscapes shaped by borders (however loose), planes of thought delimited by given rules. Form is also, of course, genre, rhyme, narrative structure—the space the text provides for the reader to dwell within.[194] Kenan plays with several generic forms and conventions across his works, not least of which is the pastoral "Requiem for Tobacco" in *Visitation*, its lyricism clanging sharply with the preceding account of Horace's death. Kenan's novel contains within it a series of dramatic dialogues, complete with stage directions, and characters across his works often place themselves imaginatively in the scenes of other familiar fictional worlds: the superhero origin story (Horace); the zombie thriller (Randall); and the Biblical myth (Maggie), to take a few examples.

Perhaps the starkest example of a character placing himself within a different form is Dean, who in "Run, Mourner, Run" compulsively condenses his world into the frames of nursery rhymes and folk tales. His "Bible" is Mother Goose, and this literary framework not only leads Dean into moral bankruptcy, but bleeds, through free indirect discourse, into the text the reader receives. "Percy the cunning, Percy the lay, Percy the conniving," fairy-tale villain, offers Dean a proposition that takes the shape of a fairy-tale plot: "Surely, he wasn't actually sitting in a truck with the richest white man in Tims Creek being asked to betray the richest black man in Tims Creek."[195] He is, and like the guileless child in the fairy tale, Dean agrees to Percy's plan, swayed by a familiar narrative arc. Percy promises Dean that, should he "do [his] bidding," he'll get a promotion and a raise at the Spinner Corporation, where Dean works making thread.[196] If he can thread the needle, if he can spin a yarn for Ray, he'll spin gold. The pressures of capitalism lead to rhymes in Dean's mind that are eerie and absurd, but nonetheless familiar to our ears in more ways than one. Little Miss Tuckett screams when she's confronted by a beast who wants her peaches and cream; Little Jack Horner is a good boy because he has his own plum pie, which he possessively guards alone in a corner.[197] Rhyme constricts, limits change, preserving old stories and foreclosing on new ones. When Percy Terrell and his boys burst into the bedroom where Dean and Ray are lying together, the intrusion "ricochet[s] in a cacophony in Dean's head," as if those rhymes of greed and acquisition are so close, so claustrophobic, that they incite chaos rather than comfort and control.[198]

Looking back, Dean wishes that he'd been warned away from the grinning wolf. "If he'd had some warning from a crow or woodchuck," he muses, "if he'd had a bad dream that night before that would."[199] Would what? (Could chuck wood?) Dean's thoughts are frequently incomplete fragments on the page. They don't fit together as neat couplets, reassuring him of a plotted, rhyming world, but rather trail off half-written, suggesting a thousand unspoken possibilities instead of the single, definitive answer. Queer expansiveness lingers in the uncompleted sentence, the split-open form— the possibility of refusing Percy and creating a real bond with Ray. But Dean's paralysis, as he sits swinging in the final pages, is one of being unable to fully exit the nursery rhyme. He trusts too much in a certain kind of story and accordingly becomes a character within it, betrayed by it. Dean provides a kind of cautionary tale (a fixture of the folk tale) for the reader: the mistake of clinging too closely to a stagnant narrative geography. Across Kenan's oeuvre, there is no single form or narrative, but rather an accrual of many, offering to the reader productive experiences of disorientation, entanglement, and bogginess. Many manifestations of queer southernness— both radical and reactionary—dwell in that swamp.

When stories do the work of reconceptualizing geographies, the ethical dimensions to their telling and hearing loom large. Does breaking out of a familiar form, revising a story, change what it means to actually live Black queerness in the South? At the intersection of race and sexuality, E. Patrick Johnson points out in *Sweet Tea*, "neglect on the part of historians of the south, black sexual dissidents' complicity of silence around issues of sexuality, and southerners' habitual taciturnity on things of a 'private nature,' all collude to keep the stories of southern black gay men's lives, like most taboo things in the south, 'hidden in plain sight'."[200] But space on the page can make geographical spaces more visible; Johnson reminds us, through Michel de Certeau, that "What the map cuts up, the story cuts across."[201] The production of space is actively shaped and reshaped by narrative. The

South needn't be only a story of migration North for queerness and blackness, but a story of powerful refuge. Johnson's storytelling is, by "giving name to [his] narrators' specific plights in history," seeking to "impact their material conditions."[202] The extent to which narrative has this kind of impact is never guaranteed. But Kenan's work seems to me heavy with that hope. As he writes in his letter to himself, "creation is the great healing thing."[203]

In "Let the Dead Bury Their Dead," the Reverend Greene documents Zeke's story, that afternoon with Ruth on the porch, of how the swamp community developed into a town called Tearshirt before it was Tims Creek: "Folks commenced to build. They got a post office."[204] There is, as Kain informs us in a brief footnote, "no such post office . . . on record."[205] But this *is* the record: Zeke's story, relayed through the Reverend Greene, published by Reginald Kain, in a story invented by Randall Kenan, influenced, as we are given to understand from the epigraphs, by Hobbes, Bakhtin, and Hurston. These interlocutors float above the story whispering of "dark and erroneous doctrines"; a "fantastic" built out of a "sense of the needs and possibilities of men"; and "lies above suspicion."[206] At each of these levels, it's the act of listening to a story that builds out the many overlapping geographies of Tearshirt. The swamp, post office and all, gives us the postage stamp(s) of native soil that we hold in our hands. We, in turn, are asked to pass it on.

3 Pornographies of History

Queer Southern Melancholy in the Works of Monique Truong and George Saunders

∙∙∙

Growing up in Alabama, I felt surrounded by the Civil War: in the form of bullet casings I was made to look at in class, the reenactments that my neighbors took part in, the silent forts I sometimes trooped through on hot field trips—all in the name of history. I also felt surrounded by the legacy of space exploration, given the presence of NASA in Huntsville, Alabama. But it wasn't until I left the South that I became aware that my city (any southern town) would usually be assumed to be—in some vague but essential way—more obsessed with the Lost Cause than the final frontier. The attendant affect of the Lost Cause—the mythology of a pleasant, or valuable, or at the very least endlessly fascinating Old South, one white southerners can never get over losing—is surely melancholy[1]: an enduring sense of failure, loss, alienation. But as apparent as this should be, it is still worth saying that the cultural icon of the Lost Cause, the Confederate flag, is not only a symbol of melancholic longing for some "South" that has become irretrievable, but effectively (and usually intentionally), also a threat, signaling an allegiance to a violent racial hierarchy.

The presence of the stars and bars is striking in photographs from the Capitol riots of January 6, 2021; the Confederate flag is hardly exclusively a southern symbol in our contemporary national life. In one photo, a man trails an enormous Confederate flag through the building, his long, confident step halfway between a portrait of Charles Sumner and one of John C. Calhoun.[2] In Freudian terms, the portraits might be said to represent an attempt at national mourning: the trauma and sectionalism of the Civil War years and all that they represent processed and accepted, converted into chaste, still portraits on the walls of a house that declares itself no longer divided. But that mourning is incomplete, unsuccessful. The man's flag is a symbol of violence and incitement—it signals an unreached, even unreachable, national unity. Violence is on full display in that photograph. But the flag, especially in its connection to the "Lost Cause" narrative, remains most often associated—especially in so-called southern literature and literary studies—with regional melancholy rather than national rage.[3]

Melancholy writ large (sometimes explicitly associated with the Lost Cause, sometimes not) is a familiar affective construction of southernness. But it is not a historically dominant affective framing of US nationalism: melancholy emphasizes loss rather than victory, stagnation rather than progress, the backward glance rather than the determined forward step. In the past few years, there has been a great deal of long overdue attention paid to the politics of remembering loss, particularly in the form of Civil War memorialization, as Confederate statues across the nation come down. But my focus is on the affect itself, rather than the memorialization it generates: the uses and effects of representing "the South" as a space characterized by a melancholic relation to history, and "southernness" as an identity constituted by melancholy.

Insofar as melancholy denotes a lingering attachment to a lost object, it has played a central role in discussions of southern culture and in the emergence of southern studies. Southern melancholy is not, of course, an affect belonging exclusively to white supremacy. Attachment to loss is at work in Lost Cause narratives, but also, as Minrose Gwin has written, in broader understandings of the South as a cultural space "grounded in removals and diasporas, forced unpaid labor, human interventions in family structures, and violent deeds and institutions."[4] But a melancholic white southernness, looking ever back toward the Civil War as a moment of rupture and loss, is a particularly iconic part of (even as it is held apart from) treasured national narratives.[5] White southern melancholy is a crucial ingredient, for example, in the mythology of southern literature; Allen Tate, in his 1945 "epilogue on the Southern novel," famously remarked that the "backward glance" the South gave as it "stepped over the border" into the modern world "gave us the Southern renascance, a literature conscious of the past in the present."[6] Faulkner's Quentin Compson is "a commonwealth . . . filled with stubborn back-looking ghosts."[7] The South is the region that looks back, so that the rest of the nation can look forward.

Accordingly, southern studies has long embraced melancholy as a crucial affect, worthy of exhaustive study.[8] But as Jon Smith points out, melancholy's popularity in the "new" southern studies is on the decline (we're all anxious to assert some distance from Allen Tate), while that downward trajectory is matched by an inverse trend in cultural studies. Judith Butler's afterword in the 2002 collection *Loss* "channel[s] William Faulkner," Smith writes, in its pleasurable/painful insistence that the past is not really past.[9]

As editors David Kazanjian and David Eng point out in their introduction to that collection, melancholy, as a "concept with a long and expansive pedigree," has a wide range of meanings—but in the broadest sense, the collection focuses on melancholy as any attachment to loss that exerts "creative, unpredictable, political aspects."[10] In its idealization of loss, melancholy figures a turn away from the hegemonic structures of the present, making it a useful affective tool for postcolonial studies, Black studies, and of course, queer studies.[11] Disturbingly, in my own childhood, the little I knew about the "Lost Cause"—that it was somehow organized around loss and impossibility—felt, on a basic level, romantic to me because, I think now, it chimed with my emerging queer attachments.

This chapter dwells on melancholy as an affective intersection of queerness and southernness. Although these two forms of melancholy don't share a lost object, and although their political projects are starkly opposed, I'm interested in what happens when we locate queerness in southern melancholy and southern attachments in queer melancholy. As I argue, queer and southern backward glances align in opposition to a treasured narrative of national progress. In this alignment, queer melancholy complicates a constricting formulation of southernness, and southernness lends a productively dissonant tone to a key affective register of queer kinship. Can this linkage evoke, rather than reactionary violence, alternative understandings of regional and national belonging? And to what extent does melancholy's disruption of dominant historical narratives possess the power to alter lived experiences and identities? To answer these questions, I explore three texts that employ shifting figurations of melancholy in the narrativizing of southern and national history and the formation of queer attachments: George Saunders's *Lincoln in the Bardo* (2017) and *CivilWarLand in Bad Decline*, (1996), and Monique Truong's *Bitter in the Mouth* (2010). In Truong's novel, melancholic attachments allow many, overlapping forms of southernness and queerness to manifest, making space for characters to narrativize their lives and communities in more inclusive ways. But in Saunders's work, the dream of this political project falls critically short.

Uses of Melancholy

Although melancholy seems to denote any constellation of affect emerging around loss, primary to modern theorizations of melancholy is Freud's essay "Mourning and Melancholia," in which mourning, the successful acceptance of a loss, is opposed to melancholy's continued, narcissistic (and for Freud, pathological) identification with the lost object. Melancholy sees the ghostly trace that loss leaves—what can't be integrated by the work of mourning—and insists on faithfulness to this remainder. But as Žižek remarks, "this story can be given a multitude of twists."[12] For Immanuel Kant, melancholy elides *loss* and *lack*: we transmute what we are fundamentally lacking into something that we had, and lost. Lacan reads this lack as a constitutive void, one that we must constantly obscure in order to build and bolster our stable reality. Melancholy, then, is the necessary elevation of some element of reality (the *objet petit a*) to a Lost Object that can stand in front of, and cover, the void. There is a hopeful quality in this—insisting on the idea that completion and fulfillment were at some time possible. In our attachment to the lost object, we in some way possess it (the most comfort we can find adjacent to the gaping void). This circular structure inheres in melancholy's temporality, as Giorgio Agamben theorized: it occupies both past and future, offering "the paradox of an intention to mourn that precedes and anticipates the loss of the object."[13]

These understandings help situate melancholy as an organizing affective and political structure for constellations of both queer and southern kinship. Queer theory has turned to melancholy in the past two decades as a way of grappling with loss—especially the staggering losses of the AIDS epidemic.[14] Amid historical erasure, melancholy attends to the absence of archives of queer life and, more broadly, to all the losses sustained within a heteronormative, capitalist state.[15] In Heather Love's influential study of queer melancholy, "backwardness," the insistent turn to the past, is "a key feature of queer culture," characterized by "feelings such as nostalgia, regret, shame, despair, ressentiment, passivity, escapism, self-hatred, withdrawal, bitterness, defeatism, and loneliness."[16] The need to progress forward, accompanied by the irresistible, Eurydice-like seduction of the turn back, structures queerness in Love's project: it is "both abject and exalted, a mixture of delicious and freak."[17] Where queerness is structured by affects attached to historical loss and trauma, a political impetus takes shape. Melancholy is not only seductive, "sensuous," in Butler's words, but ethically imperative.[18] It serves as a reminder of the dangers in forgetting history and its gaps, of becoming good neoliberal queer subjects, gazing always ahead into an idealized future, and vacating radical hope in exchange for full entry into the corrupt order of late capitalism.[19]

Within this revolutionary consciousness, queer melancholy describes not only an orientation to the past, but to a utopian futurity. As José Esteban Muñoz argues, "the *then* that disrupts the tyranny of the *now* is both past and future."[20] Feelings like melancholy mark "the affective disjuncture of being queer in straight time"; rather than linearity, "queer time" collapses past and future to offer "a path and a movement to a greater openness to the world"—utopia as hope, imagination, and resistance to the present order.[21] Given such openness, melancholy can be, perhaps counterintuitively, an affective counterpart of creativity. Jack Halberstam writes of the "art" of loss as one of the more generative aspects of queer "failure." Sara Ahmed speaks more specifically to narrative creativity: "queer use" is a way of "making connections between histories that might otherwise be assumed to be apart" amid personal and political grief—of "shatter[ing] under the weight of history."[22] In these formulations particularly, melancholy is crucial to the project of imagining a narrative that refuses nationalism and late capitalism.[23]

The anti-capitalist aspirations of queer melancholy are politically entirely distinct from white southern melancholy, not least because queer utopianism, in formulations like Muñoz's, depends upon imagining a world beyond white supremacy and Western imperialism. But Love's description of queerness as "delicious and freak," animated by a burning sense of alienation, sounds suspiciously southern. Queer and white southern melancholy are both deviant affects, refusing to partake in the optimism of a national progress narrative. Lost Cause mythology, as Niall Munro puts it, traffics in an embrace of failure and defeat, resistance to dominant cultural scripts, and a simultaneous pride and bitterness in feeling oneself an outsider and an anachronism.[24] This kind of southern melancholy also refuses a linear temporality, favoring instead "radical historical thinking that dismantles the idea that past/present/future are distinct periods."[25] In this collapse of past with present and future, Lost Cause melancholy is connected to that always-nebulous idealization of the "South" as a nationally unique space of cultural authenticity.[26]

However false the idea that folksy, temporally disjunctive community is what one could find exclusively and particularly in the South, the region's perceived estrangement from the structures of late capitalism chimes with the utopian note in queer theory's melancholy. As Martyn Bone points out, the Agrarians "conceived (or invented) their 'South' as a site of resistance to capitalism's destruction of 'place,'" and that imagined resistance has remained a treasured fantasy.[27] The endangered southern "place" becomes, in the cultural imagination, the site of the last bastion of "real" community in a nation that's lost its soul to strip malls. Lost Cause melancholy, it bears repeating, is built on anti-blackness. But it's also the case that there emerges, from the Lost Cause, a looser set of melancholic attachments to the South. As Smith puts it, "Southern studies has spent a long time asking whether, as a result of modernity's instability, we have not Lost Something Very Important" (the enjoyment, he concludes, is in the asking).[28] As Smith astutely remarks of the "cause" supposedly lost to the South, southern melancholy can be understood in some cases "not as the loss of white male privilege but as a free-floating Lacanian drive."[29]

In aligning southern and queer melancholy, my intention is not to set forth a bad-faith comparison of losses. Rather, in pointing out this overlap between southernness and queerness—a ghostly twinning of the backward turn—my aim is to open out a consideration of what these two kinds of melancholy do for and to one another. In this, my argument shares a methodology with Melanie Taylor, whose work on the Native South explores the ways in which both "the biracial US South and its Native American survivors . . . are haunted by their own private, separate histories of sweeping loss and crippling nostalgia[,] . . . echoing one another's voices and preoccupations in kindred, unmistakable intimacy."[30] Taylor acknowledges that what can seem like a "counterintuitive and perhaps counterproductive yoking" nevertheless takes up "threads running consistently between these stories and groups[,] . . . perhaps pointing us toward templates for a productive new kind of comparativism and solidarity in the age of globalization."[31] This solidarity—which for Taylor comes down to the reinvention of community within systems of toxic nationalism and global capitalism—demands a southernness that engages with but reaches beyond familiar scripts of Lost Cause melancholy. For our purposes, it demands a queerness willing to enter into dialogue with southernness, a consideration of how an overlap of melancholies, however dramatically distinct, might lead to a better understanding of the affect's possibilities as well as its limitations for both theoretical orientations and identity formations. Walter Benjamin's angel of history, who insists that striving after lost stories of the past is as important a task as it is an impossible one, surely serves as an appealing figure for both queer and southern loss: "His face is turned toward the past" while the storm of progress "irresistibly propels him into the future."[32]

Reading for Ghosts

When southernness and queerness are implicitly connected through melancholy, as I argue in my reading of Saunders's *Lincoln in the Bardo*, the linkage can serve to shore up a heteronormative national progress narrative.

Saunders's novel constructs the cemetery, its central setting, as a singular southern, queer melancholic space, one that must be left behind in the interest of the forward-looking nation-building project. And yet the novel's very form is melancholic, highlighting our attachment as readers to the Civil War as a moment of pivotal national rupture and cohesion, which, being impossible to remember or narrativize properly, is always over-present in its unavailability to us in contemporary national crisis. Learning From History is a battle we are always losing. Monique Truong's *Bitter in the Mouth* teases that desire for the sense-making power of history, using the affective power of melancholy to expand and complicate networks of queer and southern kinship. As I argue, Truong joins queer, southern, and racial forms of melancholy, attentive to their differences, to embrace the backward gaze as a means of creative expression—and to give voice to untold stories within familiar southern histories. In so doing, she mobilizes the affect to destabilize southern exceptionalism as well as nationalism. That being said, there are limits to the reparative powers of narrative in the face of global, national, and regional histories of violence. Amid claustrophobic late capitalism, the alternative futures available to the imagination are increasingly foreclosed. Ending with Saunders's *CivilWarLand in Bad Decline*, I grapple with the limitations of melancholy's power as an affect that might spur material change. Melancholy (as the affect of queerness) is not always politically radical, nor (as the affect of southernness) reprehensible. Rather, as an orientation, the backward glance is critically productive in its capacity to offer a panoramic view of many stories of southernness and queerness, making visible the complex interactions among those stories.

In all of these texts—as with Taylor's haunting histories, as with Benjamin's angel of history—melancholy's capacity to shape a historical narrative toward a utopian futurity is dependent on the power (or lack thereof) of ghosts. Ghosts in one form or another appear throughout this chapter—as the lingering souls of the departed, as intangible traces of experiences, memories, and relationships past, and as the more material, everyday work of historical narrativizing. As Patricia Yaeger writes, though ghosts are "notoriously hard to see[,] . . . the least act of speaking summons them" in the form of "scraps or remnants[,] . . . fragments, residues, or traces."[33] Through diverse archives and memorials, ghosts become visible to us and demand that we bear witness to stories of the past. Even the neurological phenomenon of synesthesia, so central to Truong's *Bitter in the Mouth*, is a form of ghostliness: as a perception that conflates two senses (a heard word with a taste, or a musical note experienced in color), it layers a "real" perception with one "unreal" but no less vividly present, capable of changing and enriching the way we see/hear/feel the world. In its gaze upon loss, melancholy is the affect that attunes us to the presence of ghosts.[34] The question is: what do our (queer, southern) ghosts do to us and for us? What power—if any—does ghostly visibility wield?

Lincoln in the Bardo: A More Perfect Child

The opposite of melancholy is surely hope: a face uplifted and turned toward a bright future. This figure, for whom nothing is yet lost or irretrievable, is the child. Kathryn Bond Stockton identifies our culturally favored child as white, middle or upper class, and pre-sexual, representing always "vertical movement upward . . . toward full stature, marriage, work, reproduction, and the loss of childishness."[35] This is the child of George Saunders's *Lincoln in the Bardo,* which revolves around the figure of Willie Lincoln. Saunders takes his early death in 1862 as a lens through which to consider the personal and national traumas of the Civil War years. This is a novel about mourning and integrating loss, turning away from melancholy toward the future—upholding, through the rejection of a southern and queer backward glance, a "straighter" genealogy of a national history. But it is also a novel that runs on melancholy's powerful current.

The 2017 winner of the Booker Prize, widely lauded as formally innovative and emotionally powerful, Saunders's novel reconstructs the story of the Lincoln family and the Civil War from an impressive number of historical sources, along with the dialogue of the many, many ghosts that Willie Lincoln finds himself residing among in Oak Hill Cemetery in Washington, DC, where he is buried at the age of eleven. The cemetery is what Saunders labels the bardo—the transitory space between life and death, housing those who refuse to let go of life. Willie's central problem, when he finds himself in the bardo, is that he is not ghostly enough. He is the beloved son of a doting mother and father. He has been a delightful, gentlemanly, reasonably mischievous child. He owns a suit. He is, in other words, a paragon of the American future—wealth, success, innocence, masculinity, energy—endangered by the "house divided." So full of promise, Willie can't remain a ghost, especially among the other spirits he finds in the bardo: perversely angry, confused, and melancholy misfits who insist on retelling the stories of their lives over and over, and frequently shouting desperate, quixotic inquiries to one another from their separate corners of history ("Do you know," one pleads, "what became of my pickle factory?").[36] Like Bruce Willis's character in *The Sixth Sense* (stop here if you haven't seen the movie), they don't know—or rather, refuse to accept—that they are dead. But the bardo residents are also accustomed to being abandoned by the living, and so are shocked when Abe Lincoln continues to return to the cemetery, attempting to hold Willie's body and sitting grieving him late into the night.

Unable to return to his father, Willie—rather than growing sideways, perhaps, among this collection of misfits—finds that the only way to grow up is to *go* up, spirited away to wherever ghosts go when they have accepted their deaths. In the novel's climax, Willie turns and stands before the others in the bardo, who are clinging to their past lives and having a kind of brawl. "Everyone, we are dead!" he cries, like Tiny Tim gone disturbingly off-script.[37] And then he—and, soon after, the others—allow themselves to be raptured up. Willie's leadership allows Lincoln to wrest himself from his own backward gaze, to look ahead to the future and lead the nation toward it with all the qualities that we most like to ascribe to him: steadfastness, kindness, moral courage. In Willie, we find the classic symbolic child of the future, despite the fact that he's dead. He insists on looking forward and cannot stay where his only choice is to look back. His father, sensing a supernatural shift, knows the same. Neither family nor nation can sustain itself on the backward glance, lingering on loss, trauma, and rupture—to look ahead is the only way to keep one's house together.

The ghosts in the bardo hardly belong to the same nation, considering that they can't agree on its president, let alone the layout of the Capital's streets. The closest relationship formed in the bardo is the surprising kinship between Hans Vollman and Roger Bevins III: Willie's introduction to the bardo, and the reader's, begins with Vollman, introducing the story of how he came to be in what he terms his "sick-box" in the "hospital-yard."[38] After marrying a much younger woman, and treating her kindly, as a friend, he one day learns that his affections are returned, and they make plans to consummate their relationship. But that very day, he's hit in his office by a falling beam. What he struggles to explain—that the so-called sick-box is "efficacious" treatment, that "all things may be borne"—is supplied by his friend Bevins.[39] Bevins's story comes next: finding the "quite natural and even wonderful . . . predilection" of his sexuality rejected by his community and then even his lover, Gilbert, he slits his wrists before realizing, too late, that he is "on the brink of squandering a wondrous gift."[40] Together, the two look back at the lives they can't let go of, the moment of rupture that they can't name. They find deep pleasure in helping one another tell the stories of the moments in which something might have been gained but instead was lost. Together, they look back to moments of sexual and romantic connection ever just out of reach.[41]

Vollman's and Bevins's embodied forms reflect their pivotal moments of longing and loss: Vollman is naked, his "member swollen to the size of—" as Willie delicately observes, and Bevins has "several sets" of eyes and noses, searching out, Whitman-like, the sensory delights of the spring season he left behind.[42] They stay in the bardo, queerly embodied, by dint of the intensity of their impossible wish for the "longed-for return to . . . green grass kind looks" (as another ghost, Elise Traynor, puts it).[43] Willie's experiences with these strange, wistful figures, the speaking dead, evoke a history of texts linking rural American communities with a grotesque backward glance and with death literal and figurative.[44]

This endless, sensuous (in Vollman's case, explicitly sexual) melancholy is not only figured as provincial, but specifically southern. Although that ideologically loaded word, "South," is used just once in Saunders's novel,[45] it looms over the bardo as a space of racial violence and stubborn stagnation. Even in this unembodied realm, racism is unquestionably present, with segregation structured by separate cemeteries and enforced by a ghost known as Lieutenant Stone—he makes it his work to continually push the Black ghosts he characterizes as "shards" past a dividing iron fence.[46] But what most links the bardo with the South is the military language that its residents employ to describe the forces operating *against* the backward glance. Every so often, groups of what seem to be angels beg the ghosts to come away with them and abandon the hope of returning to their earthly lives. As Vollman describes it, "a wall of water rushed in from the north, then divided itself with military precision into dozens of sub-streams."[47] Along with this water, the February trees bloom and bear fruit, but all this is "merely the advance guard . . . of what was coming."[48] In "lengthy procession" appear identical images of whomever the ghosts most want to see: country girls, beautiful young brides, and in Willie's case, his mother. The angels resemble, in other words, troops advancing, and the direction from which they approach makes this "military" conflict eerily reminiscent of the earthly one Lincoln leads. This Northern guard brings material abundance ("food . . . upon fine plates[,] . . . diamond tureens[,] . . . coffee, wine, whiskey") as well as the lure of spiritual fulfillment ("beautiful singing[,] . . . promise, reassurance, patience, deep fellow-feeling").[49] And yet the ghosts consider themselves "under siege," despite the fact that their lives in the bardo resemble, in Bevins's words, "eternal enslavement"— the political threat of the South's victory.[50] They regard the departure of a neighbor, evaporating in a "matterlightblooming phenomenon," with terror.[51] However beautiful, they see the rapturing-up as a "victory" of enemy forces. The backward glance is more appealing than fellow-feeling and a full plate—a southern ghostliness, indeed.

The veterans of the bardo are not only reminiscent of Confederate soldiers in this way, but a queer family. Willie becomes, briefly, a kind of adoptee, a way for Vollman and Bevins to fortify a kinship organized by longing. They are a close pair in the bardo, and an unusual one, in that their bond is formed after death rather than before. When the angels leave, they feel "a renewed affection for all who remained," who have the "resolve" that is lacking in those for whom "nothing matters *sufficiently*."[52] But the two are surprised and disturbed as much as pleased when they first discover that Willie has survived the attack. Although they take it upon themselves to care for him and show him the way of this new world where one's earthly family ceases to return, the presence of the child is also unsettling to them, feeling as they do that "young ones are not meant to tarry."[53] Finally, this queer family is tinged by a sense of itself as unethical, being devoid of a future. Vollman and Bevins have nothing to promise a child. Rather, their lives are organized by the backward glance—the "sterile, narcissistic enjoyments," as Edelman puts it, of non-reproductive queer pleasure.[54]

Finally, both this structural queerness and the perverse southern backward glance signal what must be left behind in pursuit of national wholeness. The role of the Civil War is to isolate the deviant South, the backward-gazing, ghostly South, the temporally dragging South.[55] When "the South" finally appears explicitly in the novel, it is at the very end, as Lincoln, gathering his strength from Willie's courage, considers what he's up against. Although Saunders is careful in his excerpted materials to record Union as well as Confederate opposition to the war, in these final scenes "the South," along with Europe, metonymizes perversity and obsolescence: "Across the sea fat kings watched and were gleeful, that something begun so well had now gone off the rails (as down South similar kings watched)."[56] The region becomes a foreign country, even as its integration into a cohesive nation remains the crucial project. The South is a useful tool for Lincoln: its imagined smugness that "the rabble cannot manage itself" is what leads him out of the bardo, and his determined resolution that "the thing would be won" is what finally convinces Vollman and Bevins, too, that they "must go on."[57] Having just seen Willie welcome the "matterlightblooming phenomenon," they consider, as a family, his rejection of the backward glance: "*Our* Willie would not wish us hobbled . . . by a vain and useless grief"

Pornographies of History 99

(emphasis mine).[58] Finally, they leave their grief—their sexual and romantic longing ever unfulfilled—behind, to follow after the child into the unknown future.

These departures mark a poignant ending to a poignant novel. Lincoln's decision to move toward the future, toward unity and progress, might be the right one, but it is no easy turn away from the queer, southern melancholy of the bardo. As many of the historians in Saunders's archive explore, Lincoln is widely noted for his melancholic character.[59] In the cemetery, that disposition takes the form of a richness and stubbornness of grief. Lincoln is unwilling either to return to the land of the living or relinquish Willie to the land of the dead, a position that appears strange to the cemetery watchman and even to the ghosts.[60] It makes Lincoln unusual; it makes him as queer as the ghosts who watch him with amazement.[61] His final departure from the cemetery, moving determinedly toward progress, is both a straightening out and a hollowing out. In relinquishing the backward glance, the powerful temptation to cling to the lost object, he is left with a void. It is just this hollowing that makes him available as metonym: the man becomes the nation. His knowledge that "the thing must be won" is also his knowledge that the thing must be one: e pluribus unum (as is engraved on his penny), the many in the one.

Becoming hollow in this way makes Lincoln available to Thomas Havens, the Black man who decides to accompany Lincoln out of the cemetery. "I felt a kinship," Havens explains, "And decided to stay a bit. Therein."[62] "Therein," its own solitary sentence, feels oddly euphemistic as a descriptor of Lincoln's body and how Havens penetrates it. This penetration is framed as a means of an atmospheric rather than a relational kinship: the sense of a space of roomy possibility, of welcome for all this nation's citizens, expanding ever "forward, past the sleeping houses of our countrymen."[63] But it is also quite clearly queer. The ghost of the Black man, entering the living body of the white man, evokes a history of anxiously conjoining raced male bodies in American letters and literature, as well as the unsettled subjectivity so characteristic of the Gothic.[64] Saunders's model of a straightened-out, forward-gazing Lincoln who rejects melancholy in the interest of national unity is, paradoxically, also the model of a Lincoln whose unification project is inseparable from the queerness of a ghostly (and southern) beyond.

While Saunders's novel attempts to confine the melancholic South to the bardo, it also expresses, in its very form, a different kind of melancholy. The narrative's amalgamation of voices suggests another loss: the belief that a singular, authoritative story, told in just the right way, would allow us, finally, to Learn from History, to understand from this iconic moment of national rupture and reunification how to bring about kinship with one's countrymen in our own time. That edifying story is intensely present in its absence—the way to make sense of our nation is ever just out of reach. The novel's archive functions like a jumble of puzzle pieces that fail to fit together, emphasizing the incompleteness of the Lincoln family narrative and its accompanying national narrative. In nineteenth-century and contemporary historical accounts, and in letters from wartime, a hazy picture emerges: Willie was dying of typhoid fever on the night that the Lincolns hosted a large party to boost spirits for the war effort. Abe and Mary Todd were devastated by his death. After his interment at Oak Hill, the president returned to visit his son. But what were things *really* like the night of Willie's death?

The archive's accreting effect is of a compulsively repeated backward glance that finds something different each time. The loss of history's knowability is inescapably present. The moon on the night of Willie's death is yellow, or it is gray. It is bright, or it is clouded. It is remarkable, or it is not there at all. This detail particularly emphasizes Saunders's postmodern approach to history; like the moon itself, the truth is never "whole" to our perception, as Timothy Parrish puts it, but is rather "always seen from a particular, and thus fallible, point of view."[65] But if postmodernism frames history as "a story, one that is well or not so well told, and thus . . . a way of perceiving the world that is also a fight to make the world over as one wants it to be," it is painfully clear from Saunders's extensive archive that the story of the Civil War, inevitably told in too many ways, by too many voices, cannot make the nation into something kinder, gentler, more just, more cohesive.[66] The fantasy that Thomas Havens and Abraham Lincoln could see out of the same eyes, mobilized by a unified perspective and a singular hope, is revealed as just that—a fantasy, painfully small beside the ever-unreachable complete story that might serve as a guide.

Bitter in the Mouth: Lost Legacies

If Saunders's novel expresses an ambivalent refusal of melancholic queerness and southernness in the interest of a longed-for national union (or at least the story of one), Monique Truong's *Bitter in the Mouth* joins disparate modes of melancholy as source materials out of which to imagine many possible stories of the past, present, and future—multiple queer, southern alternatives to a limited and limiting national mythology. In the novel's "family narrative," as it is described in the first chapter, the reader follows the narrator, Linda, from her childhood family life and friendships in Boiling Springs, North Carolina, where she feels distinctly othered, through college at Yale and a failed engagement in New York, back home to the South, where, finally, she decides to stay and (re)form a family.[67]

As in Saunders's novel, Truong takes a postmodern approach to national and personal history through her play with narrative form. Linda is constantly drawing attention to the potential or certain fictionality of the narratives she relates to point out how we are always drawn more to what she calls "pornographies of history"—stories that exploit history to serve various ends—than true histories (if such a thing is even possible). As a narrator, and an English major at Yale, Linda is well aware of the power of narrative: "history [is] in the missing details" and in the way the story is told.[68] In the first few pages of the novel, she cues her reader to the fallibility of the project of looking for a "true" story, and to her interest in playing with alternative narrative possibilities, by constructing a complicated relationship between narrator and reader: "I'll tell you the easy things first. I'll use simple sentences. So factual and flat, these statements will land in between us like playing cards on a table."[69] With the use of the second person, Linda invites her reader explicitly to consider the ethics of narrative. This first section's title—"Confession"—indicates the role of the reader in bearing witness. But quickly, she flips us completely out of this role and invites us into something different, more playful. Confession becomes con.

As Linda lays down the story of her life, Truong draws attention to the narrative ethics of bearing witness only to suggest something much slyer, replacing an earnest entreaty with a wink. "Once these cards have been thrown down," Linda tells us, "there are bound to be distorting overlaps, the head of the Queen of Spades on the body of the King of Clubs. . . . The only way to sort out the truth is to pick up the cards again, slowly, examining each one."[70] The simple statement of "I grew up in Boiling Springs, North Carolina. My parents were Thomas and DeAnne. My best friend was named Kelly," becomes, after these cards are thrown down, "I grew up in (Thomas and Kelly)."[71] As Michele Janette suggests, the card metaphor "teaches us . . . to read connections, interchanges" not only by picking up the cards individually but also "explor[ing] them as palimpsest, analyzing the pattern of overlap and reconfiguration created by their mixture and interaction."[72] "Mixture"—what would in most contexts be an imprecise word for the jumbling of playing cards—here is particularly apt. The trick of the game is that the cards, once thrown down, lose their discrete borders, and so to pick them back up again and examine "each one" as a stable object is an impossibility. It's a trick that relies on our belief in a stable and hegemonic archive, a retrievable history. But as Lisa Hinrichsen points out, "Truong is preoccupied with the inevitable erasures that result in making a particular social history recognizable or intelligible in narrative form."[73] The task Linda proposes—to sort out and recover a true story through the set of cards, to unweave threads and separate them into appropriately distinct categories, and thereby recover a single lost history—is a lost cause (so to speak) from the start.

Lost, to Linda, is not only the story of her past, but a "normal" way of seeing the world. She has the unusual neurological condition of synesthesia, through which she experiences words as tastes, and she is a Vietnamese child adopted by a white family, the Hammericks, at seven years old. In both her mode of perceiving the world and in the way she knows herself to be perceived, she is a radical outsider—a ghost among the living, not confined to the bardo, but trapped all the same by her status as "other." For that reason, she "confesses" early on, "During my four years at Yale, I would gravitate toward classes with the word 'dysfunction' featured prominently in the title."[74] But just as Linda plays with narrative form, she teases the reader with her disclosures of what constitutes her outsider status.

Linda's synesthesia is from the novel's opening in full view to the reader, represented typographically on the page so overtly as to be at times distracting ("Linda*mint* is from North*cheddarcheese* Carolina*cannedpeas*").[75] This gustatory bombardment is by no means composed of solely "southern" foods (like, for example, fried green tomatoes); it eludes categorization entirely. Her taste-word associations have no logical pattern and no clear origin. "Food and taste metaphors," Linda muses, "were of no use to me. They shed their figurative qualities, their diaphanous layers of meaning, and became concrete and explicit[;] . . . the word that made me taste peach cobbler, for example, was 'matricide'."[76] Linda's disorienting experience of the world and its bombardment of surprising connections, so relentlessly apparent on the page, is a "secret sense" throughout her childhood to everyone but her best friend Kelly—and, of course, the reader.[77] But our sense of being "in on it" is a red herring. The novel's formal emphasis on synesthesia takes precedence, for the novel's first section, over Linda's second "secret": that she is a Vietnamese adoptee.

Looking Asian in the South

By obscuring her ethnicity from the reader in the novel's first half, Linda dramatizes her status as somewhat ghostly: she isn't seen, not really. Although Linda withholds all but the subtlest physical descriptors and details of her life before her adoption at the age of seven, there isn't much else she withholds. Rather, she simply lets her reader make the wrong assumption, based on her southern family, based on the fact of Boiling Springs, North Carolina—until her Vietnamese heritage is revealed somewhat dramatically at the moment she walks across the stage at her college graduation: *Lindhao Nguyen Hammerick*.[78] As Linda looks ahead toward adulthood, Truong asks the reader to look back across the pages of her childhood, at what we missed and why we missed it. Somewhat jarringly, Linda's synesthesia refocuses into a larger frame of unexpected connections. Several critics have explored the link between Linda's synesthesia and her late-revealed ethnicity. As Sara Gabler Thomas writes, "taste . . . becomes more visible formally in the text than race"—a dynamic that Denise Cruz argues "critique[s] dynamics of visibility and invisibility that have become central to our understanding of racial formation."[79] In these analyses, the moment of the shift between visibility and invisibility is key: the palimpsest, the trace.[80]

Linda narrates, in the novel's second section, how her ghostliness has come into being—she is well aware of the structures by which she becomes invisible. As a transracial adoptee, Linda grows up with the uncomfortable experience of "looking Asian in the South" without claiming an Asian identity.[81] As the adopted child of successful white parents, Linda seems to embody the "logic of colorblindness," as David Eng puts it, which asserts "that racial difference has given way to an abstract US community of individualism and merit."[82] But as the adult Linda muses, the community of Boiling Springs "vowed to make themselves color-blind on my behalf. That didn't happen. What did happen was that I became a blind spot in their otherwise 20–20 field of vision."[83] Within the Hammerick household, there is more that must go unseen and unsaid. Linda's adoption fits uncomfortably into a long history, as Mark Jerng has explored, of "the sanctification of white fathers and mothers as benefactors to infantilized racial others."[84] The Hammericks have "made their money in cotton, which was another way of saying they had made their money in slaves."[85] The latter "way of saying," of course, can never be said. From childhood, Linda understands the impossibility of the demand placed on her to *"be one of us"* in a white southern family that either romanticizes or ignores the past.[86] Although she can never resemble them, how Linda "looks" in her family (both how she perceives the family, and how she is perceived—or not—within it) has high stakes for the stories available to her about what community, and nation, can and should mean.

If Linda is in a sense invisible, she is in another sense hyper-visible. Despite the apparent ethos of 1970s multiculturalism, Linda finds herself cast into various stereotypes of "Asian-ness" growing up in Boiling Springs; as an Asian immigrant in the US she becomes, as Lisa Lowe argues, "a phantasmic site, on which the nation projects a series of condensed, complicated anxieties regarding external and internal threats to the mutable coherence of the national body."[87] From an early age, Linda is the object of a generalized erotic fantasy that swirls around a mix of imperialism, desire, and violence. Her body is the site of Orientalist projections by peers ("there was also a rhyme that they recited that intertwined foreignness with an unclean and sexualized body. *Chinese, Japanese/Dirty knees,/Look at these!*").[88] For the grown men that ogle her, she imagines that her body evokes associations with the Vietnam war ("If they saw my unformed breasts[,] . . . the hands and feet small enough to fit inside their mouths, how many of the men would remember the young female bodies that they bought by the half hour while wearing their country's uniform?").[89] And surely, for the seemingly inexhaustible range of stereotypes of Asian women, the Vietnamese American is, in the late twentieth century, a particularly vexed figure in the US imagination. As Marguerite Nguyen writes, "Vietnam has become known as the war that never ends—a post-1960s benchmark for how we talk about, enact, and remember war."[90] To "look Asian" for Linda is not only to have her body Orientalized by peers and grown men, but to serve as a signifier of a contemporary military "lost cause."

Linda's racialized body also evokes specifically southern narratives that emerge around war, loss, and otherness. Her account of those Boiling Springs men who "wore their country's uniform" is an unusual moment in the novel, because the figure of the Vietnam veteran—and the Vietnam War more broadly—is rarely made visible in the novel as a cultural preoccupation.[91] Linda doesn't learn that she is Vietnamese until high school, when she finds a name similar to her own in her history book: "I learned that the war was still in progress in 1968, the year of my birth, and that it ended for the Vietnamese in 1975, the year of my second birth at the blue and gray ranch house. . . . All that I learned about Vietnam had to do with war and death and dying."[92] The "blue and gray ranch house" evokes another, further removed history of war and death and dying. As Gilman Owen points out, "In the early 1970s, four out of five Vietnam generals came from southern towns."[93] Owen suggests that southernness—in the sense of an Agrarian heritage, a la Allen Tate's "Ode to the Confederate Dead"—provided a distinct perspective on the Vietnam War, invoking a long cultural heritage of honor, violence, and the trauma of loss. And yet if southernness provides a long view of the effect of the war on the American psyche while furnishing a "warrior culture" to fight in that war, it also represents the fantasy of the opposing side: an exceptional, uncivilized, foreign land.[94] The Vietnam War, then, becomes a way of renegotiating the legacy of the Civil War as well as exploring the South's imagined place as a Gothic other. If "looking Asian in the South" signifies international conflict, it signifies, too, the South's lost fight, and even the Gothic South itself.

Linda's ghostliness is not relegated to Boiling Springs. In college, and once she has moved to New York, the question Linda receives frequently, about what it was like to grow up "Asian in the South," accomplishes two conflicting goals: it defines her according to a racial identity that she has not herself claimed, and it then confines racism, or at the least a preoccupation with race, to the South.[95] This is not only an irritating question for her, but a lonely one; it makes her feel isolated and objectified. She suspects that her long-term boyfriend, Leo, fell in love with her because she was "rare, probably one of a kind. My southern accent, my Vietnamese face[;] . . . the connoisseur in him found that difficult to resist."[96] Linda finds a parallel to Leo's regard for her "rarity" in a TV program on synesthesia. When she stumbles upon a PBS program devoted to her "secret sense," she instantly recognizes herself in the interviewees—and she recognizes, too, the way the interviewer ogles her subjects.

To be "unique," as Linda is, is to be without a narrative, unable to fit into any story. Her synesthesia and her "one of a kind" southern accent and Vietnamese face meet in her earliest memory, just before her adoption: of a "word that made me taste an unidentifiable bitter[,] . . . flames cutting through the seams of a trailer home, the sound of footsteps on gravel, then darkness."[97] By high school, the "bitterness" of this still-mysterious racialized violence has become the bitterness of a more generalized racial exclusion. Linda dyes all her clothes black in "mourning. . . . I decided that I might as well make my grief public."[98] She has "no role to play within the romances, the dramas, and the tragedies that my classmates' hormones were writing for them. . . . I watched it all from a distance, which . . . just made me lonely."[99] In her loneliness, her silence (the result partly of the flavorful "incomings" that conversation causes for her), and her darkness, the primary role that Linda plays is ghostliness.

In this way, Linda is intimately acquainted with melancholy. In experiencing herself as racialized from her southern childhood through her more metropolitan adulthood, either as a stereotype or as "one of a kind," she is both subject and object of a racial melancholy. As Anne Anlin Cheng writes, the racial "other" is the melancholic object to the American national ego in the Freudian sense that it must be always both excluded and retained in a push and pull that betrays a fundamental ambivalence: "the history of American national idealism has always been caught in this melancholic bind between incorporation and rejection."[100] And the racial other, a kind of "serviceable ghost," is herself a melancholic subject, having internalized this dynamic of discipline and rejection.[101] This is apparent from Linda's earliest memories in Boiling Springs; in her new home, she would coax herself to sleep by playing a game in which she "imagined not having different parts of [her] body.... The point of the game ... was to list the things that I could no longer do because of the missing part. Another point of the game was to rejoice in the things that I would again do, upon the reattachment."[102] Each night, she disappears herself and brings herself back into being.

Cheng's theorization is useful for understanding Linda's experience of racialization; but there is yet another kind of melancholy at work. Linda's insistence on the position of "looking Asian in the South" suggests that it is something different to *be* Asian in the South—to have a more constitutive racial identity. That identity, presumably, comes from stories and histories, even histories of trauma and loss. If she could find the word attached to the "bitter taste" that marks her earliest memory, she could piece together more of her history. But she grieves that "there were no photographs and no history, official or anecdotal. There was only my memory.... I have come close to identifying that taste of bitter, but close isn't good enough.... As for the word that triggered it, the usual trailhead of my memories, it remains lost to me."[103] Linda's lost object is her origin story, and in her melancholic attachment to that origin story, she keeps its indeterminacy ever aloft.

Synesthetic Melancholies

Indeterminacy is key to Linda's narrative approach; in presenting the story of her life, Linda is keenly aware that, without a "trailhead" to direct her or her reader, she might shape and reshape her history as she likes. What's more, in her backward glance she constructs a synesthetic linkage among southern, queer, and racial forms of melancholy. As Cheng points out, melancholy is presented in Freud's theorization as a mode of consumption, wherein "the melancholic eats the lost object—feeds on it, as it were," a kind of paradoxically nourishing self-impoverishment.[104] A significant component of that nourishing power, in many formulations, is the community that organizes around melancholic attachment.[105] Linda's vivid word-taste associations evoke the process of melancholic consumption; they speak to how she consumes stories and histories, and also to the surprising connections possible among different communities "feeding" on distinct lost objects. Linda's narrative style—her playful approach to storytelling, her inclusion of varied historical and literary narratives, her insistence that "history is in the missing details"[106]—also invokes her reader's consumption, begging the question: Which types of stories, which manifestations of melancholy, are we looking to consume?

Linda highlights her reader's consumption of melancholy, and forms links between southern and racial melancholy, by putting her narrative in dialogue with a classic southern literary canon, most notably Harper Lee's *To Kill a Mockingbird* (1960).[107] Linda cites several times to Lee's novel, comparing it to her own life; her Maycomb is Boiling Springs. She compares her father, a lawyer, to Atticus, invoking Scout as her own kin—and sharing, therefore, her place in a southern heritage. *To Kill A Mockingbird*, it is worth remembering, begins with what it means to claim a history. In discussing "the events that led up to [Jem's] accident," Scout and her brother—motherless children—can't agree on whether the story should begin with the Ewells, with Dill, or with their ancestor, Simon Finch, a slaveholder who "would have regarded with impotent fury the disturbance between North and South, as it left his descendants stripped of everything but their land."[108] This is a legacy that somehow links the Lost Cause narrative (the Civil War is not even a "War of Northern Aggression," but rather an uncouth "disturbance" here) with the most accurate way that Scout and Jem can find to tell their own story. In claiming this origin story, however arbitrary, Scout seizes the past's usefulness to her present. This southern bildungsroman is predicated on a look (way) back.

A southern literary heritage renders Linda familiar to her reader, but she unsettles that sense of familiarity even as she establishes it. Although Linda, looking back as an adult, evokes Scout as her literary kin, she also warns that she felt, in childhood, like an aberration in its original sense—a mirror that produces a warped image. (This is a definition that she learns in another fitting college course, "Alienation/Alien Nation").[109] This warp has partly to do with a changing region: The South of Linda's childhood in the 1970s isn't romantically isolated, but a typical example of Sunbelt suburbia. And the closest thing to the "War of Northern Aggression" is the tension in Linda's own home, the blue and gray ranch house, battleground for the chilly relationship between her parents. She is "little sparrow" to her grandmother Iris, again recalling Scout Finch, but the novel opens with the violent destruction of that bird: Iris promises, on her deathbed, that she "knows secrets . . . that would tear [Linda] apart."[110] Increasingly, the revelation of these secrets does tear her apart—or rather, she tears apart her own familiarity to the reader as the southern child of literary convention.

In the second section of the novel, Linda's affinity with Boo Radley, rather than Scout Finch, stands out: "Instead of invisibility, Boiling Springs made an open secret of me. . . . I was Boo Radley, not hidden away but in plain sight."[111] The discomfort of Linda's community is not only due to her Vietnamese heritage, but to the way she troubles the color line. In the wake of the Civil Rights movement, Linda embodies the uncertainties of integration, giving the lie to racial politics framed in black and white. As Leslie Bow writes, "the metaphor [of the color line] admits no middle, or interstitial, space."[112] Thus situated "between the terms," Linda becomes a site of uncomfortable perceptual negotiation to the community around her, impossible to miss and yet "unseeable" through established categories.[113] In aligning herself with Boo Radley, she suggests that this is the case not only in her diegetic world, but the metadiegetic—she nods to her own disorienting effect as a literary figure. As Jigna Desai and Khyati Joshi write, "Within the American imaginary, the Asian American as perpetual foreigner and alien is always seen as a recent immigrant, and therefore associated with contemporary times, while the South is perceived as an anachronistic and isolated region," rendering the two "mutually exclusive and incongruous," somehow monstrous in combination.[114] Linda offers a biting critique of that perception by bringing "monstrosity" into explicit terms for the reader, modeling how not only regional but national bias clings to the vicious labels assigned to the many diverse arrivals into her supposedly insular southern town: "Queers, Jews, Chinks, Japs, and Gooks came to Boiling Springs."[115]

Despite her incongruity, Linda attaches to a melancholic literary heritage that is both queer and southern. Fittingly, it's during her class "Dysfunctionalia: Novels of Misspent Southern Youths and Their Social Context" that Linda begins to grieve her grandmother (whose desire for a southern funeral complete with magnolias in February, it is worth noting, required a special floral shipment from South America).[116] Linda's tears are somewhat mysteriously connected not to a discussion about her own southern family, but to "the lesbian subtext in Carson McCullers's *The Member of the Wedding*."[117] Queer longing, an amorphous sense of loss, an experience of not fitting in anywhere: these are the affects of McCullers's work that seem to lead to Linda's regret at leaving her dying grandmother's bedside before "a little skeleton key might have fallen out of her mouth."[118] As a result, she understands the distance between her and her history as "immeasurable."[119] Linda's sense of loss is awakened, in this class, by both southern and queer melancholy.[120] Linda is perhaps drawn to McCullers's Frankie and Lee's Scout because the "misspent Southern youths" of her class's syllabus belong to a literary canon trafficking in ghosted and ghostly children.[121] McCullers's work, particularly, is emblematic of queer melancholy: a focus on loss, death, backwardness, and failure. The terms "dysfunction" and "misspent youth," after all, imply failure to progress, a backwardness or strangeness.

Linda's synesthetic attachment to McCullers's queer melancholy is closely connected to the melancholy of her very southern, queer great-uncle, "Baby" Harper. In name, he evokes Harper Lee and, in Linda's love for him, her first literary crush: Scout's neighbor Dill.[122] Described by their small-town community as "light in the loafers," Harper is Linda's closest family ally from early childhood.[123] Like her, he is ghostly in their community, in his case because of his sexuality: "the good folks of the greater Boiling Springs-Shelby area looked at my great-uncle and looked right past him."[124] Although Linda doesn't tell him about her synesthesia, he is the only family member to whom she conveys a more painful secret: at the age of eleven, she was sexually assaulted by an older neighborhood boy named Bobby, dead in a car accident soon after the event.[125] Linda confides in Harper because she trusts that he understands her, at least more so than anyone else in their family; as a queer man in the South, he has a sense of the way regional and national stories write themselves on the othered body. He is a kindred spirit as much as a mentor, and when they're together, they can turn their ghostliness into something joyful. He teaches Linda to dance when she is a small child: "forgetting" the body, they "bopped our nonexistent selves up and down and side to side."[126]

As a photographer, Harper's dearest project is to capture the fleeting moments already past as soon as they come under the camera's gaze. In a town photography contest, his photo "Ice Debutantes," of tree limbs under ice, suggests the movement of an antiquated southern custom now captured only in the stillness of photography.[127] It's this hobby that leads to his late-in-life career as a funeral photographer, and to his partner Cecil, a mortician who "posses[es] a profound empathy for the dead."[128] The domestic bliss between the two begins with, and is subsidized by, the backward gaze: one that beautifies the dead and that captures elegy with the permanence of the camera. Their relationship, as much as the *Baby* in front of Harper's name, would seem to embrace the "backwardness" that Heather Love identifies as a key feature of queer culture: "defiant refusals to grow up[,] . . . explorations of haunting and memory[,] . . . stubborn attachments to lost objects."[129] This "archive of feeling" reckons with the impossibility of documenting and historicizing intimacy.[130] And yet Harper and Cecil are, in addition to melancholic figures, savvy ones. There is a market for the backward gaze in their southern community, and they know how to use it to turn a profit for their travels in South America: places further South, so to speak, than Boiling Springs (an interest that begins, for Harper, in acquiring magnolias for his mother, which leads him to "think about places in the world even more southern than where he was born and raised").[131]

Baby Harper's love of travel southward expresses well his mode of reckoning with a "lost" southern identity. If, for the melancholic, the lost object is always over-present by means of his identification with it, Harper uses the structure of the backward glance to subvert its power. In his continued pursuit of the lost object, he draws aside the veil, showing the machinery of its perpetual retreat. Linda recalls him singing the Confederate state loyalty hymn, "Tar Heel," which for him is "all about fate."[132] The present tense in the song's lyrics—"*when I die, I'm a Tar Heel dead*"—suggests a South always already dead, as much as ever-present. In tying familiar understandings of the American South to the global South by way of Latin America, Baby Harper's travels express a different way of claiming regional identity. His literary tastes—works like *One Hundred Years of Solitude* and *The Hour of the Star*—allow for, in Cruz's words, a wider way to "imagine a literary South[,] . . . read]ing] the region in shifting scales of the transnational and global."[133]

To move toward "a different South" is to take the idea of a fated regional identity ever further toward its source (back, on the temporal axis, and down, on the geographic one), and find there the absence of the object of desire, as well as something completely new.[134] This is how Harper dies—on a plane headed south to Brazil with Cecil. He leaves to Linda a series of photographs in which he is pictured in South America, happily expressing an identity as a woman whom Linda has never seen in life.[135] As Cruz points out, "Baby Harper comes out for the reader formally . . . through the juxtaposition of the rural South with its links to a larger hemispheric South; these moments literally occur on facing pages."[136] For Linda, the photographs link her grief for the man she knew, with her introduction to the woman she didn't know, with the global South. To look at the South of Harper's photographs is to look back into unreachable lost territory.[137] Venturing there never locates an origin point, just as going back in time through this photographical archive can't help Linda locate Harper's original or "true" gender: she only finds, in looking back, his pleasure in performing the exploration of the absent origin.

Harper's legacy suggests the possibility of finding vital moments of kinship through a backward gaze that joins queerness and Lost Cause southernness. But even so, this utopian melancholy has no reparations to offer for the violence that a white southern melancholy—and larger structures of US imperialism—threaten to the racial "other." When Linda and Kelly enter Harper's bedroom for the first time, after his death, they find the "full ruffled-parasol bloom" of high camp a la *Gone with the Wind* in combination with a "drunken" red color palette expressive of his "love . . . for the other South."[138] The campiness of Harper's home surely parodies and queers a Lost Cause mythology: its aesthetic is, as Kelly puts it, "if Scarlett O'Hara and Carmen Miranda had been lesbian lovers and they had had a baby."[139] But there is little restitution in Harper's queer southernness, even as Linda recognizes that the red paint of his walls is the same that he used to paint the word RAPIST on Bobby's gravestone the night Linda told him about her assault. As Cruz writes, especially in light of the revelation of Linda's Vietnamese ethnicity, "this act of reinscription makes glaringly visible the unacknowledged ties between the US South and the global South, the lingering traumas of sexual violence in US domination, and how the repercussions of this violence have been forgotten or remained unquestioned."[140] The original inscription on Bobby's stone—BELOVED—also cites to Toni Morrison's novel, connecting the violence of imperialism and racial violence at multiple geographical scales. Baby Harper's parodic and drunken celebration of two registers of southernness does the work of making violent connections more apparent, but it also highlights the limitations of this work. Driving home from defacing Bobby's grave, Linda experiences the southern night, filled with the smell of honeysuckle, the sound of crickets, and moonlight, as "glow[ing] . . . less like stars and more like bleached bones."[141] War and death and dying, still, are all around.

Mix and Match Archives

The connections among southern, queer, and racial melancholy do not erase historical violence; but their surprising linkages do give Linda a way to adopt a creative orientation to narrative. Harper's practice of making imitative and iterative melancholic connections is important to Linda from her early childhood. One of her fondest memories is of leaving the family dinner table for the privacy of the bathroom in order to take solace in the repetition of a word she finds more appetizing than the food on her plate—"again," with its attendant flavor of pancake syrup. In iteration, even as she enacts the word's command, meaning is lost underneath the accrual of the sweetness of its sound. She links the moment, for the reader, to sexual self-discovery: "How old were you when you first touched yourself for the sake of pleasure?"[142] A spoken sentence, for Linda, has the capacity to elicit a vivid and surprising combination of flavors, pleasures and displeasures, desires and disavowals cast adrift from their usual significations. As a narrator, Linda asks her reader directly to reconsider their own systems of meaning: she argues that even if she found a "match" for her earliest memory, that bitter taste, it would "only allow me the illusion of communication and you the illusion of understanding."[143] Synesthetic connections are in some ways preferable to apparently solid meanings and linear narratives.

Recombination and recontextualization describe Linda's approaches to storytelling; in her refusal of linearity, she makes clear the impossibility of return, even as she longs for an origin story. Linda begins the second section of the novel with the absent origin point; she divides the mystery of her background into a concept crucial to theorizations of melancholy—the distinction between "the void and the missing," the "thing that was never there in the first place" versus the thing that "existed but was no longer present."[144] She frames her first memories in both terms. "Born to [her] father Thomas, fully formed," she woke in the blue and gray ranch house with "no memory of where [she] had been."[145] Her absence of an origin story inheres in her very name(s): "'Linda' was the void. 'Minh-Dao' was the missing."[146] These shadowy traces, evocative of the violence of war and racial terror, speak to unrepresentable trauma. That bitter taste of the novel's title is melancholic, but it also asks the reader to consider outright the fundamental problem of melancholy: the inevitable confusion between missing and void, the ways in which we demand impossible meanings from elevated lost objects. In this way, what's lost—the origin story—begins to lose its power, while Linda gains her own.

Because her backward glance can never locate an origin, Linda constructs one from a diverse variety of archives. Truong's novel is full of what we might call ephemeral or partial archival material, either referenced for or directly presented to the reader: Harper's photos, letters between Linda and Kelly, favorite childhood books, and, of course, word/taste pairings. Variously theorized, archives organize a historical narrative; they consolidate a community; they legitimize an identity. In Derrida's famous formulation, "archive fever" expresses a longing—aligned with the pleasure principle, against the death drive—to preserve the past as a way of securing the present and the future. As such, the archive is fundamentally political. Control of the archive is control of public memory and therefore the ongoing normative structure of public space.[147] But Truong refuses a singular archive through which to organize personal, regional, or national history; Linda's archives are as slippery as her stories. As Martin Manalansan argues, "mess, clutter, and muddled entanglements are the 'stuff' of queerness, historical memory, aberrant desires, and the archive."[148] Rather than giving us a single history, Linda's archives suggest the way that different narratives present themselves (with different implications for the future) with each reshuffling of the cards.

As a child, Linda's primary source for (re)constructing her history is the book she received as a child from her father: *North Carolina Parade*. This kid-friendly history of the Tar Heel state is "chock-full of children, well loved and well remembered"; yet it is the children "without a name and . . . without a future, who drew [Linda] in again and again."[149] As critics have observed, Linda sees in this text reflections of her own experience.[150] In these forgotten children—specifically, George Moses Horton and Virginia Dare—she is able to revalue loss, invisibility, and disappearance through the idea of transformation. Both "othered" figures in their own times, George Moses Horton and Virginia Dare become figures of unexpected kinship for Linda; as Michele Janette puts it, these figures allow her to "claim an affective rather than an ancestral lineage."[151] As a slave, seen only as property, George Moses is well-acquainted with invisibility. He recognizes his own name—given by his master—as a "shackle" just as powerful as the invisible plantation borders that constrict his movement.[152] But although his master "saw what he wanted to see" in George Moses, as Linda tells it, "war changed everything. . . . Property became men and women and children."[153] This transformation, of course, is epistemological. For

Linda, George Moses's story offers a way to negotiate and talk against the gaze that would transform her body into something *other*. Much like George Moses finds, as a poet, that he can "move [words] around in his head and create something new," Linda finds that she can rearrange George Moses's story as it's told in the children's book to create something new: a way of making this historical figure, as well as herself, more visible.[154]

As she gets older, Linda not only creates her own history through *North Carolina Parade*, she reads for stories that undermine the "official" narratives of North Carolina—as well as familiar national narratives. Her other favorite tale is that of Virginia Dare, "the ghost who haunted North Carolina."[155] According to Linda's book, Dare was transformed into a deer by an evil sorcerer and then back into a woman by her lover, with a magical arrow, at the same moment she was killed by a deadly arrow. Although *North Carolina Parade* is complicit, as Janette points out, in making Virginia Dare "into a symbol of racial purity and US Anglocentrism" through the tropes of the vulnerable white maiden and the noble savage, Linda reads the story through the lens of political satire, reframing Dare as a figure of "bawdy borderlands hybridity."[156] Reading the story of Virginia Dare's sexualization and death through the critic's ironic eye becomes a way for Linda to grapple with her own experience of racialized sexual violence.

In her engagement with this story, Linda seeks to transform Virginia Dare and to be, in turn, transformed by her: "There were the minutes right before death, unheralded and untold, when you had just fallen, your flesh half animal and half human. . . . In between, inchoate."[157] "Shoot me through the heart," Linda begs of Virginia Dare: "Transform and transfigure me."[158] Whereas Linda and Kelly see early on the phallocentric subtext of Virginia Dare's violent death, Linda demands of the legend an alternate ending, giving Virginia Dare a queer power by asking this protagonist to pierce and transform her. This longing can't rewrite her rapist's violent penetration, nor grant her wish to be inchoate, unclaimed, unwritten in the script of regional or national myths. But it does reveal starkly Linda's utopian longing for the backward gaze to enact material transformation. In emphasizing the fictionality of all origin stories, she uses the backward gaze to claim—and place her hope in—the power of authoring her own.

As such, the backward glance holds potential as a political impetus for imagining, even seizing (however transitory) the "then and there," in Muñoz's words, that offers alternatives to limited and oppressive hegemonies. If origin stories are always in some way fictional constructions, highlighting history as such, Linda's melancholy becomes a way to undermine conventional national and southern mythologies. When Linda finally returns to Boiling Springs after years spent in New York, she and Kelly reunite, settling on a park bench in the town square in a position of intimacy that could mark them as transgressors in this normative southern space: "Kelly reached for my hand. We are going to get arrested for sure, I thought. Open displays of same-gender, transracial affection was certainly a misdemeanor of some kind."[159] Sitting there for hours, grappling with their complicated shared childhood, they do not get arrested. In fact, Truong presents the space as a confused cluster of ideologies somewhat defanged by their collective incoherence and obvious performativity. Linda feels as though she is walking onto "a movie set," devoid of action in the quiet night, and moreover, apparently unable to produce an evocative film.[160] The "cupola, domes, and columns" of the courthouse, now a museum, "struck fear into no one now except visiting schoolchildren, who were less fearful and more bored by what they found inside."[161] Grand performances of "history" have little authoritative command here.

The courthouse square honors both Revolutionary and Civil (Confederate) War heroes, but the intended pride in the origins of the modern nation-state and reverence for the losses of the South are glaringly absent. Kelly and Linda sit on a bench facing a Confederate statue, lit as if on set by the "red and gold sign for a Thai restaurant across the street," his intended martial and masculine prowess diminished by our sense that he is a character, a prop even, in a fiction.[162] When Linda and Kelly "stare up at his tight britches, his rifle, and his hat," both of them thinking of their shared adolescent crushes on a boy named Wade, the statue becomes less a man than a boy—or rather, the fantasy of a boy.[163] Or rather, with his rifle recalling us to the arrows that struck Virginia Dare, less a fantasy of a boy than a painfully obvious phallocentric myth. Or rather, as the rifle and the suit take on a Redcoat-colored glow, less a myth of a Lost Cause than transparent imperialist propaganda. The Thai restaurant of Shelby also invokes a set of relations beyond the ones represented by this mess of a movie set: the Vietnamese refugees in Thailand during the novel's timeframe,[164] the Thai communities of the US South, and Linda, whose position amidst wars, identities, and modes of affinity and allegiance refuses the possibility that the memorial could represent anything but a confused fantasy.

The memorialization of the Confederate soldier belongs to what Linda calls the "pornography of history."[165] The phrase comes from her experience at Yale, where Linda belongs (through the name "Hammerick") to a long lineage. She enters into the same dorm as her "father and his forefathers," and like the blue-and-gray ranch house, Pierson's complicated national heritage inheres in its name—it's a colonial.[166] As part of a (primarily male) colonial legacy, Linda inherits both privilege and fantasy. The Pierson house includes a plaque noting its historical "Slave Quarters," supposedly once used by antebellum southern students—except that the dorm wasn't built until 1933. Linda understands that the skewed timeline points to a disturbing truth—that although nineteenth-century slave quarters "could be understood as the bones of history, reluctantly preserved," those built long after slavery ended represent "a pornography of history."[167] But this "incomprehensible" temporal disjuncture is anything but. Relocating slavery and racism to the South serves as a historical fantasy that exonerates the nation: the first decades of the twentieth century saw a proliferation of Confederate memorials, serving less to recognize the history of a past war than to secure a racially segregated future.[168] There are no "bones" to be found here—no historical body bound to a linear temporality and an origin point. Rather, there is only the "pornography": the fictional, the ideological, the endlessly reproducible conventions of genre. But whereas southern melancholy is a pornography of history in the service of an elite Northern institution, Linda knows, through her own approach to archives, that the recognition of history as performative and apocryphal can also hold queer, subversive potential. That knowledge gives her the power to create, so to speak, more ethical porn.

Nation, Region, Origin

Like Yale's slave quarters, Thanksgiving traditions traffic in national fantasies that Linda reveals as confused mythologies. During her time in New York, she spends every Thanksgiving with Leo, who belongs to revere(d) New England stock—the Benton Thanksgiving sauceboat belonged to Paul Revere. Linda learns this fact after complimenting it as a gravy boat: she "pick[s] out that vessel for commendation because 'Benton' tasted of gravy, not the under-salted, defatted turkey gravy that Goody Benton served every year, but the milk gravy thick with crumbled pork sausages that southerners poured over our biscuits."[169] The compliment falls flat: Leo informs her that the dish is not a gravy boat, but a sauceboat. Nevertheless, the synesthetic connection between "Benton" and southern gravy contains southernness inside the heirloom, muddying an apparently significant regional and semantic difference, just as Linda's sly comments interrupt the austerity of foundational national myths.

Pornographies of History 117

While Linda steels herself for under-salted fare each year, Baby Harper invites her to "fly South"—to return home and to a seat at the table of queer kinship. Linda's decision to spend Thanksgivings with Leo would seem to suggest the repeated victory of heteronormativity over queerness as much as nationalism over southernness. And yet Linda's descriptions of Harper's invitations, sent every year in the form of Hallmark cards, emphasize Harper's playfulness and interrupt the primacy of the Bentons' self-satisfied tradition. Harper's cards are campy: they feature "overflowing cornucopias, dimpled pumpkins, nonchalant turkeys[,] . . . a pudgy, round-faced little Native American girl holding hands with a pudgy, round-faced little Pilgrim boy."[170] In Linda's evocation of the cartoonishness of these iconic and commercialized images—representing, respectively, uncomplicated abundance, the idyllic autumnal scene, willing sacrifice, and a romanticization that erases settler colonialism—the Bentons' WASPy, sauceboat-founding-father version of this holiday comes to look equally ridiculous, and equally ideological.

But for all the playfulness in Linda's subversion of historical narratives, melancholy remains the somber affective structure organizing the southern community to which she finally returns—a community of longing, where the dead confer with living ghosts. Linda comes back to Boiling Springs after years away to help her mother, DeAnne, organize Baby Harper's funeral; he constitutes the center of a much wider sphere of grief. The sense of loss that encircles their family is "composed of many shattered things."[171] Linda hasn't spoken with her mother in years, their relationship broken by the mysteries of her past and by DeAnne's failure to protect her from sexual assault. Both she and her mother are still reeling from the loss of Linda's father, who died suddenly when Linda was a teenager. Her relationship with Kelly is strained and delicate from the radical divergence of their paths in high school, when Kelly became pregnant, moved away, and gave up her baby for adoption. And Linda herself is recovering from a hysterectomy after ovarian cancer and a broken engagement. All these losses inhere in the melancholic archive that Harper leaves behind: his photographs, each a testament to "the longing of his gaze," and "his collection of mourning embroideries[,] . . . faded, silk-flossed scenes of weeping-willow trees, Grecian urns, and young ladies draped upon them in grief."[172] These are manifestations of a powerful backward gaze.

The league of longing in which Linda finds herself, as she well knows, is one that her father would have shunned. In his opinion, "Lot's wife was Exhibit A of the consequences of clinging to a catastrophic past and the dire repercussions of regret."[173] But this turn to what's behind her does not freeze Linda; rather, it connects her to a new understanding of family and opens possible paths forward. In the novel's final scene, Linda sits down with her mother and Kelly over a bottle of bourbon, and together they look back, constructing an origin story for Linda together even as they remain resigned to their various losses—of histories, loved ones, and dreams. Linda's placement across the table from her mother recalls her early game with the reader: sorting out the "real" truth its always impossible. This time, Linda's metaphor is of a spiderweb. You pick a place to start tracing the thread of a story, but it can hardly be called the true starting place. As Linda lets the reader into her history, her words are precisely chosen: "The story of my life, *according* to DWH, began . . ." (emphasis mine).[174] DeAnne tells of Thomas's emotional affair in law school with a Vietnamese woman named Mai Dao, his attempt to help her family once they'd resettled in Chapel Hill after the fall of Saigon, and his and DeAnne's strained marriage before and after he brought home Linda, the only survivor of the mysterious trailer fire that killed Mai Dao and her husband. DeAnne's limited knowledge of this history comes from letters between Thomas and Mai Dao, carefully archived by Baby Harper after Thomas's death and now awaiting DeAnne and Linda.

Through this framed tale, it becomes apparent that DeAnne is constructing a narrative through a very limited archive, which Linda, in turn, is highly embellishing for the reader. The fact that Thomas and Mai Dao met at Columbia, for example, turns into the romantic scene of falling "in love right there on the steps to Low Memorial Library, while the corridor of trees . . . turned colors."[175] In Linda's retelling, Thomas and Mai Dao bond over their shared roots in "the South": "Well, I would have never known; you don't have even a trace of a southern accent," Linda imagines Thomas drawling.[176] And the rescue of this southern woman becomes Thomas's primary way of engaging with the war. It is "Mai Dao's country" that becomes "a household word even in Boiling Springs," "her country's civil war" that causes the violence he watches on television, and her family that he seeks to save and settle comfortably in North Carolina with his privileges and resources.[177] Through their letters, the histories of two Souths blend. DeAnne, grudging southern matriarch, has nothing on Linda, who, as she grows to "look more and more like the young Vietnamese woman her husband had loved," comes to embody two feminized Souths, both lost.[178] Given that this is something of a Cinderella moment, DeAnne's storytelling mirrors Thomas's first acts in his "sudden dash toward fatherhood," from which DeAnne was notably absent—reading Linda fairy tales.[179]

Pornographies of History   119

Whereas DeAnne refused motherhood in those early days with Linda, there is, in this scene, a proliferation of mothers joined by grief and by their capacity for the creation of story—and through it, community. Kelly and Linda are both "thinking about this idea of our bodies grieving," Kelly after her separation from her son and Linda after her surgery: "Kelly thought about the absence. I thought about the void."[180] DeAnne is grieving her deepened solitude, at the death of Baby Harper after that of her husband and mother, and her estrangement from Linda. But aided by bourbon and lemon icebox cake, she begins for the first time to tell Linda "the story of [her] life," and in doing so gives her a form of mothering she did not or could not during Linda's childhood.[181] The difficulty of the labor of DeAnne's storytelling, once it is over, is conveyed in terms that suggest the marveling at the end of childbirth: "We didn't break into two or three or four pieces. Our limbs were all accounted for. Our internal organs were pumping and filtering."[182] Linda, too, is laboring: She understands her role as listener to DeAnne be that of "bear[ing] witness"—seeing, recognizing, and therefore creating the both of them.[183] To bear witness, then, is not so distinct from bearing a child. The two of them together bring Linda's biological mother, Mai Dao, into the room. If "all families are an invention," she is invented right there—in the cue to the reader that Mai Dao lingers in Linda's features, and in the way her voice is ventriloquized through DeAnne's recitation of her letters to Thomas.[184] Kelly, providing the bourbon as an agent of incomings-alleviation, facilitates this scene of becoming. The kitchen table is both a hopeful and melancholic gathering space of the novel's failed, absent, and would-be mothers: women grappling with the missing and the void. Rather than tracing a lineage, this scene of storytelling creates an iterative, queer, and non-linear consolidation of kinship.

Finally, what Linda gives the reader is not the comfort of the "true" origin story, a backward glance that locates its longed-for object and validates a historical archive, redeeming Linda from her "ghostly" status, but a recognition and even a celebration of the power of melancholy and the creative potential to be found in loss. A backward glance that layers southern and Vietnamese histories in the queer gaze—Baby Harper as the documentarian and custodian of longing—allows Linda to imagine new modes of belonging. After she has concluded retelling DeAnne's story for the reader, Linda points to the limitations of DeAnne's memory and her own biases. The truth of the story is subsumed to its demands: "We all need a story of where we came from and how we got here."[185] As Begoña Simal-González puts it, ultimately Linda "is prepared to live with the radical unknowability, even the impossibility of origins."[186] To reshuffle the cards is to reimagine the kinship, and the possibility, to be found in loss. When Linda models readerly transformations for her reader, we see lineages with which we're familiar, and we're also asked to scramble those lineages and make new connections. Linda's narrative doesn't leave "the South" behind. She uses her origin story to "put down roots," to claim a home made up of many Souths and the complicated connections of her invented family: DeAnne, Kelly, the ghost of Baby Harper. Finally, "Hammerick," which tastes like Dr. Pepper, evokes both her adoptive grandmother's nighttime drives across North Carolina county lines for a nighttime bourbon-and-Dr. Pepper, as well as her birth mother's memory of a soft drink in Vietnam "exactly like" it.[187] The blue and gray ranch house becomes, rather than a familiar house divided, the home of a queerer and more expansive southern kinship.

"CivilWarLand in Bad Decline": Getting Our Money's Worth

In Truong's novel, the many facets of queer, southern melancholy change our field of vision, insisting on the power of the backward glance to write a better future. That power, though, is limited; Linda's decision to stay in Boiling Springs does not in itself transform the traumas of the past or nullify the threats of the present. Recently, I was teaching Percival Everett's 1996 short story "Appropriation of Cultures," in which the main character Daniel, a Black man, decides to reclaim the song "Dixie," and then the Confederate flag, for his own in his hometown of Columbia, South Carolina. In the story, the Confederate flag eventually becomes a symbol of Black power, and—as it now disturbs the white southerners—is removed from the state house. My students were eager to point out that such a sequence of events was unrealistic. On the one hand, they hoped that this change might be what Daniel's American Studies degree earns him—theory making good in the real world. But this was not, they pointed out, the real world: this was a Columbia in which Lost Cause melancholy was too easily alchemized into a better future for Black lives. Like Everett, Truong and Saunders, although ambivalent in their approaches, share the wish that melancholy might be used as a source material in the building of a more inclusive community. However unrealistic (when the real world is too often a toxic mix of profit and violence), that alchemy is appealing. In closing, I'll briefly highlight the pull of this dynamic in Saunders's *CivilWarLand in Bad Decline*, in which the dramatic absence of melancholy presents as a symptom of a wholly commodified nation—a dystopia in which the lack of a backward gaze constricts the narratives available to the imagination so much that social transformation for the future appears completely impossible.

The ways *Bitter in the Mouth* and *Lincoln in the Bardo* approach historical imagination tie in to the stories we like to tell about their respective historical moments: Truong's novel in 2010 (a time when a nation's progressive diversity shines so brightly that we can face our fear of the monsters down below the Mason Dixon line) and Saunders's in 2017 (when the Lost Cause South is appearing to overtake the entire nation).[188] These texts ask their reader to buy into the hope that history—even or perhaps especially understood through a postmodern lens—can make our lives more livable. But history has always been available to capitalism, and uncomfortably close to our wish for meaning is a fear that what we get for our "buy in" is only a brief sense of hope or satisfaction from what is in fact a cheap, flattened, and endlessly replicating version of history—Lincoln's face stamped on a penny. In Jean Baudrillard's terms, "the real becomes a theme park."[189] This is the condition of Saunders's *CivilWarLand in Bad Decline*. Here, we have in microcosm a nation devoid of melancholy (no southernness, no queerness) and a nation on the verge of collapse.

As a theme park, the preoccupations of *CivilWarLand* are both as specific and as vague as its name suggests. Nation, region, progress, the backward glance—all of these are crowded into a single incoherent and violent conglomerate. The idea of a Civil War theme park is specifically evocative of the South; states in this area of the country have long held a disproportionate fondness for all things Civil War when it comes to tourism and entertainment.[190] Confederate flags, a Jefferson Davis hologram, and an "O'Toole Gazebo," in Saunders's novella, suggest the profitability of southern cultural and literary icons.[191] As Romine argues, even after the South can no longer possibly be imagined as an insular cultural space, it nevertheless "continues to be offered, referenced, located, used" in the service of (often vague) ideas of "tradition, heritage, culture, and identity."[192] *CivilWarLand* offers a South built upon a corporatized "land" that is everywhere and nowhere; it is representative less of any "real" South than a broader nation organized by late-capitalist multiculturalism. Although the park arose out of "one Union costume," historical tour leaders now "distribute the slave and Native American roles equitably among racial groups," making sure "anyone is free to request a different identity at any time."[193] After the tour, one might visit the "Burn 'n' Learn," a national chain that involves tanning while young women on roller skates bring you history books.[194]

History serves not to solidify or reimagine a community or identity through loss, nor to tell us an edifying story, but to make a buck. As the nameless protagonist's boss tells him, "All I wanted to do was give the public a meaningful perspective on a historical niche I've always found personally fascinating."[195] His phrasing suggests history as a market that can be divided into lucrative segments—and, surely, it can. Employee meetings involve going over Verisimilitude Irregularity Lists for errors that might cause Revenue Impacting Events.[196] Overworked "Historical Reconstruction Associates" lead Old Tyme Skills Seminars in the Blacksmith Shoppe (a concept perhaps too familiar to anyone who has visited, say, Gatlinburg, Tennessee).[197] Saunders's superabundance of depressing corporate invention drives his point home again and again. In late capitalism, everything is a product, available in a Store Near You. So what's left to long for?

There is no melancholic southern backward glance, and neither is there a queer utopian one. The queer archive sees its negative (and its curator) in the form of Sylvia Loomis, the "queen of info" who works in Security and "has access to all records."[198] Sylvia is characterized by her apparently nonnormative sexuality—she is "an S&M buff in training"—but this, too, is absorbed by the casual language of commodity, wholly devoid of desire or connection: "she parties at the Make Me Club on Airport Road[,] . . . walking around talking mean while wearing kiddie handcuffs."[199] Her archive is available, at a cost, to be shaped into any given narrative: "I ask can she identify current employees with a history of violence. She says she can if I buy her lunch."[200] The narrator uses Sylvia's intel to look for violent employees in order to find someone who can resist the "gangs" of teenagers who periodically ravage the park.[201] Given the park's precarious financial state, they're willing to try anything. Samuel, an employee who "looks so Civil War" and was apparently "kicked out of Vietnam for participating in a bloodbath," is just the man for the job.[202] The connection between these wars unacknowledged, the implications of ramping up sectionalist conflict unconsidered, Samuel's retributive violence spins quickly out of control—the park descends into complete chaos, the space as bankrupt ethically as it is financially. If there's no melancholy in *CivilWarLand*, neither is there hope. So unmoored, the park becomes a space of nihilistic violence.

Even the McKinnons, a family of real Civil-War era ghosts who resided in life near what is now the Information Hoedown, are interpellated by capitalism. The narrator, who can inexplicably see and communicate with these ghosts, thinks of them in terms of profit, as a potential "gold mine of war info"; he gives "the Mrs." a Rubik's Cube in exchange for teaching him "a few obscure 1800s ballads" he can use for the park's Individual Achievement Awards.[203] The ghosts are indistinguishable, even to themselves, from park property. "The Mr.," a veteran who fought at Antietam, spends hours yelling at a hologram of Jefferson Davis. As *CivilWarLand* goes up in flames (literally: the proprietor "torch[es] this shithole for insurance purposes"), the narrator sees Mr. McKinnon, when he gets too close to his death spot, compulsively replicate the murder of his family with a scythe, followed by his own suicide.[204] Quickly thereafter, Samuel kills the narrator, who "knows a few things" too many, by stabbing him to death.[205] The narrator's own death echoes the McKinnons', making it all too clear that what he didn't know (because it wasn't profitable) could and did kill him: Mr. McKinnnon's lament, as he runs after his fleeing family, is that "hatred and war made him nuts."[206]

It's only in the narrator's death that the story's tone shifts to melancholy. As he's being murdered, the narrator acquires a panoramic view of his life, newly aware of the possibility of a world "keen with love" but unable to impart that knowledge to Sam, no matter how desperately he attempts to "sweep through Sam's body."[207] Unlike Thomas Havens, he cannot situate himself "therein." The narrator's shift from mindless investment in an empty futurity (concern for his "sweet" children in their "fairly expensive sleepers") to an obsessive engagement with loss and failure (relentless hope in this hopeless man, made "nuts," like Mr. McKinnon, by war)—is a scene of both southern and queer melancholy.[208] Sam, in his "so completely Civil War" looks and his insistence on scavenging for berries rather than dining on sandwiches, is also a melancholic subject, perversely attached to a bygone world.[209] And with his hate "as solid as stone," he is moreover that classic Lost Cause melancholic object: the war memorial, layering conflicts as much as the statue that Linda and Kelly gaze upon.[210]

The tonal shift of the story's ending is something of a relief: the plaintive poignancy of the narrator's final experience (finding only hate and hate) provides an alternative to an emotionally voided late-capitalist hellscape. After the story's relentless comic irony, the narrator's melancholy feels refreshingly earnest, a way of engaging in what Muñoz calls the "haunting and haunted cultural work" that "remember[s] and long[s] for a moment outside of this current state of siege."[211] But for all its earnestness, melancholy does not offer change.[212] As cathartic as the story's final scene is, it suggests no alternative structure to a nation that is itself a theme park. In this landscape, there is no historical narrative that isn't already a commodity, and no ghosts powerful enough to move us. Saunders's story dramatizes the limitations of melancholy as much as it makes us feel its importance—the backward gaze, the haunting and hauntedness that Muñoz describes as so crucial to queerness, may not move us anywhere politically.

Still, in a place as bleak as *CivilWarLand*, what option is there but to try? Whether southern and queer melancholy function as twinned forces that shore up a treasured national progress narrative, or whether their connection gives rise to more creative, fluid ways of narrativizing kinship structures, the backward glance holds an undeniable attraction. But I am compelled by Smith's critique of melancholy: that it runs the risk of obscuring the mundane truth that "most of us muddle through a very complex present," neither oriented wholly toward "future militancies" nor the sense of being "pathologically bereft."[213] Žižek, too, laments melancholy's "conceptual and ethical primacy" in scholarship.[214] But this primacy surely indicates the affect's strong and enduring appeal in theorizing alternative forms of community within and beyond national configurations. As long as that's the case, the magnetism between southern and queer melancholy is valuable to better understanding that appeal and navigating its political implications. The backward gaze continues to bestow some power onto the ghosts in our midst.

4 Southern Gothic Hospitality

Or, Inviting in the Queer Vampires of Poppy Z. Brite, George R. R. Martin, and Jewelle Gomez

....

In 2020, the popular author Grady Hendrix published *The Southern Book Club's Guide to Slaying Vampires*. The novel was billed as a cross between *Steel Magnolias* and *Dracula*, and quickly made bestseller lists. But although the book jacket features an illustration of peaches pierced by red toothmarks, the narrative includes no peaches, fried green tomatoes, or even biscuits. Still, that image conjures a host of associations. Just underneath the slightly fuzzed surface of this southern space, where everything should be just peachy (and suggestively feminized) is a dangerous monstrosity.[1] The novel's protagonist is Patricia, a white woman in 1990s Charleston who joins a "ladies' book club" only to find it infiltrated by a real-life vampire. Hendrix is self-conscious about genre: at one point, hiding from her bored children in the privacy of her bedroom, Patricia rereads *Dracula*, this time not as literature but as an anthropological text; only then does she realize her fatal error in inviting the handsome stranger inside to return the casserole dish she left with him.

The book club tends to gravitate toward real-life crime stories, but the ladies in the novel very well could have put together a book club not only of vampire stories, but *southern* vampire stories. Anne Rice, of course, leads off the syllabus with her 1976 classic *Interview with the Vampire* and its sequels. But from the eighties to the present, the southern vampire doesn't seem to be slowing in its propulsion of book sales.[2] And why? The vampire can find a comfortable home in the South. Not only is he (apparently) likely to be invited in for ice cream, but the terms that have often been applied to the South apply to him as well: Gothic, grotesque.[3] Other literary landscapes might equal the South in atmospheric spookiness,[4] but none seem to equal its reputation for monstrous perversion.

That monstrosity bears defining; it is, in Judith Butler's words, that which we "cannot bear to see"; Jeffrey Jerome Cohen defines the monster as "pure culture . . . [a body] quite literally incorporat[ing] fear, desire, anxiety, and fantasy."[5] It follows, then, that southernness is composed of the monsters that stalk US history: figures emerging from scenes of antebellum decadence, slavery, war, extreme poverty and neglect, cruelty pulsing underneath genteel manners. As the introduction to the collection *Undead Souths* puts it, "Southbound specters become holograms of an otherwise inarticulate, often distressing past."[6] This kind of southernness is so deviant as to become frightening; it troubles conceptions of what constitutes our humanity, as is evident from the strange figures that fill the pages and frames of the southern gothic.[7] In such a South, the vampire has little trouble fitting in.[8]

And yet the vampire is, by nature, a crosser and a dissolver of borders. He doesn't "fit in" to spaces, he obliterates them. The vampire assures us that boundaries between bodies are not so firm as we think, and that no space can be securely cordoned off—he might climb the walls, or fly in through the window as a bat, or trick you into inviting him in. Perhaps even more disturbingly, the vampire has over the years (as in Hendrix's novel) exceeded the bounds of genre. He is aware of himself as convention, cites to other texts—he shows us the puncture marks from which the diegetic world bleeds. So while the vampire seems on the one hand to belong in the South, he also unsettles its borders so much that we can hardly figure ourselves "in" or "out" of it at all. This skill at unsettling boundaries is one of many qualities making the vampire a notoriously queer figure. As Halberstam writes, "the danger of . . . the perverse sexuality within the form of the vampire" is a key example of how the Gothic "consolidates normal sexuality by defining it in contrast to its monstrous manifestations."[9] Queerness as monstrosity can be understood in terms of sexual or gender deviance, but it also speaks to a wider range of othered bodies, and as such has been useful to a queer of color critique. Ulrika Dahl argues that "the monster is the embodiment of what does not fit, what is queer and differently abled . . . deeply entangled in kinship and reproduction, and thus with the creation of gender, sexuality, and race."[10] Monsters like the vampire may be figured as solitary figures, but they elicit fear in part because they apparently beget new monsters—the replication of the queerly antinormative body.

The novels that I'll explore in this chapter focus on the vampire as a monstrous—and generically familiar—meeting place of southernness and queerness. As such, the vampire not only represents deviance and perversion, but threatens the spread of that perversion through embodied transformation and through story. I argue that Hendrix's *Southern Book Club,* along with George R. R. Martin's *Fevre Dream,* ultimately contain the monstrosity of queerness/Southernness and reassert a humanity organized by a white, heteronormative family structure and a firm boundary between modern nation and Gothic region. The vampire protagonists of Poppy Z. Brite's *Lost Souls* and Jewelle Gomez's *The Gilda Stories*, on the other hand, revise this familiar narrative arc to engage the radical possibilities in formations of queerness and southernness that trouble every border, from those organizing selfhood to nationhood. In these two novels, monstrosity's unchecked spread calls Western humanism into question. And across these works, disparate visions of the vampire—in terms of its relationality, its temporality, and its racialization—organize a multiplicity of constructions of southernness and queerness with a range of cultural and political implications. To travel with the vampire is to dwell critically in these overlapping and conflicting spaces.

Back to the Gothic

To survey the literary and critical history of the vampire is a daunting task, but for the purposes of this chapter, his geographical origins are relevant. As Halberstam writes, he is uncanny, by Freud's definition, because he "has no home and wants no home."[11] Even so, the fame of *Dracula* is such that the vampire writ large now carries a strong association with mysterious Eastern European lands and the accent of Bela Lugosi. But as Giselle Liza Anatol points out in her work on the Afro-Caribbean figure of the soucouyant, Bram Stoker tends to receive too much credit for inventing the figure of the vampire, despite the fact that a "wide array of vampire novels and short stories . . . preceded *Dracula*, as well as . . . myriad vampire tales from cultures outside of Europe."[12] As she discusses, even *Dracula* gestures toward a world far beyond Transylvania: "The bite marks on victimized children's necks are initially attributed to a bat[,] . . . 'some wild specimen from the South of a more malignant species'" that points to the "centuries-long British preoccupation with the West Indies."[13] Whether as critics, readers, or characters of these novels, we anxiously search out the vampire's origins, and it might lead us to the ambivalent colonial histories of a Global South—to those lands figured by European empires as exotic, dangerous, "wild," their influence too close for comfort.[14] To dig into the mythology of the vampire is to find patterns of global exchange.

Still, that Halloween icon—pale skin, fangs, and a black cape—is most firmly linked in the popular imagination to *Dracula*, and therefore to the Victorian Gothic, frequently read in form and narrative as a means of grappling with a changing society. This framework has been used to consider industrialization, imperialism, and especially shifting dynamics of gender and sexuality. Eve Sedgwick, at the forefront of a legion of critics, notes that "the Gothic was the first novelistic form in England to have close, relatively visible links to male homosexuality."[15] But the titillating appeal of the form is hardly limited to male homosexuality. As William Hughes and Andrew Smith put it, "the queer thing about Gothic is that it refuses to be exclusively queer in the sexual sense, and the queerness of the Gothic is such that its main function is to demonstrate the relationship between the marginal and the mainstream. . . . It mobilise[s] unpalatable if not actually taboo issues . . . even where a fearful publishing industry demands that these troubling things should be contained by the eventual triumph of a familiar morality."[16] Crumbling castles, stormy nights, and monsters tease what might happen at the dark. The Gothic raises the specter of a society's "unspeakable" fears, and then sanitizes them. In all this, the thrill of perversity which the Gothic invokes, the pleasure of measuring dutiful progress against decadent *wrongness*, lends itself well to southern gothic.

The crumbling castle does for the nineteenth-century English reader perhaps what the Compson homestead does for the twentieth-century American reader—invokes a strange and decadent past that might shore up confidence in a present nation. As Brasell puts it, the southern gothic was (and is) "a generic site that allows the nation to discuss its many ills under the guise of a regional problem, thereby providing the emotional distance necessary to engage constructively with issues considered by American society as deviations from the (supposed) normal."[17] These deviations—taking the form of bodies othered by gender, sexuality, race, or disability, in plantation houses haunted by history, sharecropper shacks haunted by poverty—borrow from and capitalize on all that the Gothic monster has to offer. Even in Faulkner's case, as Jay Watson argues, the southern gothic is not just an aesthetic, "setting mood, creating suspense, or evoking southern decadence and moral darkness," but an already-familiar script, an intradiegetic narrative strategy for characters "who create and circulate their own gothic stories . . . to make sense of their world and navigate its challenges, including . . . important challenges posed by modernity."[18] In this way, monstrous deviance can be a form of creative potential.

That creative potential has had a long shelf life. Ellen Glasgow famously coined the term "southern gothic" in 1935 to describe Faulkner and Caldwell and similar writers obsessed by the "tedious mass production of degeneracy[,] . . . a literary gospel of futility and despair" for a region struggling deeply, economically, and morally, in the early twentieth century.[19] Of course, even before that the South was well-marketed as a Gothic space, perhaps most iconically with Poe's "The Fall of the House of Usher." If Glasgow already considered all this degeneracy tedious in the 1930s, before Welty, before O'Connor, before a whole line of writers, the "tradition" should be even dustier today. Driving its broad circulation is "the gospel of [regional] futility" that provides a foil to a cherished American exceptionalism, as well as the continued relevance and pleasure to be found in the dizzying boundary-crossings that Sedgwick and Halberstam identify as hallmarks of the Gothic more broadly. In other words, the southern gothic, like its eighteenth- and nineteenth-century British predecessors, can function either to reassert or subvert the normative. The crime fiction writer S. A. Cosby, in a recent interview on the *New York Times Book Review* podcast, defined southern gothic as a "holy trinity" of "race, class, and sex."[20] Writers of the "new" southern gothic, Cosby argues, "take the traditions" of the genre to "examine the intersectionality between race, sexuality, gender identity, LGBTQ rights, indigenous rights, class, and so on and so forth."[21] Ultimately, the "traditions," as Brasell points out, depend not on "fidelity to a list of prescribed criteria but the assignment of the label to it by its users."[22] Given the enduring popularity of the term, the Gothic remains useful to us as a means of grappling with southern history.

In the southern gothic generally, and in the figure of the vampire particularly, the specter of slavery mobilizes metaphor. Trauma beyond representation hovers just beyond the conventions of genre. As Teresa Goddu argues, "the gothic's role in generating racial discourse and its production from the context of slavery . . . require[s] examination," especially when "the conjunction of morality and monstrosity" concentrates in "the Bible belt vampire."[23] Just as that blend of morality and monstrosity lurks behind Faulkner's southern gothic, it lurks behind the proliferation of southern vampires. Slavery is a vampiric system in that it drains lifeblood through forced labor. Sarah Kent, citing Frederick Douglass's description of slavery as a "bloody transaction," writes that "with the blood stains that linger from the legacies of slavery, envisioning vampirism's bloody transactions in relation to slavery is semiotically valuable."[24] A Lost Cause psychopathology, with its "undead" allegiance to a fantasy of a plantation South that relies on Black labor, is similarly vampiric.[25] And the metaphor also applies when flipped, as Kent points out: "Both 'slave' and 'vampire' struggle between the competing directions of human and other-than-human and are forced to occupy the liminal space in-between."[26] Like the vampire, the Black body is undead, the walking vision of social death.[27] Whether the vampire is envisioned as the slaveholder or the enslaved, humanity hinges on blood: who gives it, who takes it, and what it does to the body in which it circulates. But although there is perhaps no Gothic monster better suited to the South, the vampire's metaphorical resonance extends beyond its connection to slavery. This figure is perhaps most remarkable in its evasion of a single coherent metaphor, its multiplicity of meaning.

Dracula, who has inspired tomes of criticism, serves as a good example of the vampire's symbolic flexibility. He is himself an imperialist, as a conspicuously "pale" aristocrat seeking to extend his realm of cruel power, but he's also a racial other, a foreigner who introduces racial impurity and destabilizes our good English subject, Jonathan Harker.[28] So, too, the South, alternately figured as colonizer and colonized.[29] Dracula is both masculine and feminine; he penetrates the women who become his victims, but he is also maternal, giving his victims vampiric life by urging them to feed at his breast.[30] So, too, the South: patriarchal and paternalistic, and yet symbolically feminized.[31] Dracula is dead and not dead, and as such an apt figure for capital's relentless growth.[32] So, too, the South, as site of the enslaved labor force on which modern capitalism expands.[33] As Halberstam argues, this monster is "remarkably mobile, permeable, an infinitely interpretable body . . . a meaning machine."[34] He is, always, "open to numerous interpretations."[35] So, too, the South.

Just as the vampire exceeds the body, uncannily joining the monstrous and the human in the fluidity of blood, it exceeds symbolic containment—it is metaphorically over-available, a site of, in Halberstam's words, "vertiginous excess."[36] Although the twentieth-century vampire enters the South heavy with meaning, that meaning inevitably spills over and changes direction as interpretive frameworks come into conflict. Rice's vampires are not the first to enter the region, although *Interview*, with the dandyish Louis skulking about the plantation, is certainly an urtext for the southern vampire novel. As early as 1943, in the film *Son of Dracula*, the foreigner Count Alucard arrives in New Orleans to marry Katherine, a young woman inheriting a grand old plantation house.[37] He likes the swampland, likes the "young and vital race" he finds there, likes the Colonel's daughter, who is, the film takes pains to convey to us, far too domineering when it comes to her hapless fiancé, Frank. Despite the film's atmospheric southern gothic (the old plantation house; the shadowy swamp) and its temporal unmooring (it makes no reference to the ongoing Second World War), the film doesn't have the coherence to support any single ideological project in constructing an imagined South for the twentieth century. On the contrary,

Dracula is a liability, a stark figure of instability, his infamous story pointing too many directions at once.[38]

The same might be said of the much more recent swampy southern vampires of *True Blood*. As Hagood has pointed out, vampires in *True Blood* "tend to stand in for all kinds of things of varying and even clashing sociopolitical motivations that refuse to expire, whether Neo-Confederate platforms, conservative Christian ones, civil rights of a distinctly 1960s African American variety, or gay culture and the fight for its promotion."[39] The vampires and the show's swampy Louisiana setting both deny us firm metaphorical ground. I concur with Hagood's conclusion that the "heaping" (and, I would add, confused) "force of southernness" in the show ultimately makes *True Blood* visible as "a performance of people playing within the postsouthern plane of surfaces."[40] The redeployment of tropes, constructions, and "senses of place" of southernness, in other words, allow the vampires of *True Blood* to be metaphorically shifty figures. In *True Blood*, the tension between southern "authenticity" and the inescapability of generic convention is hovering always just outside the frame.[41]

This is true generally of the postmodern vampire text: not only does the southern vampire refuse a singular interpretive model, but he also regularly gestures to an enormous library of vampire texts, and by doing so, lives always at the edge of the diegetic world. James Harris, the vampire in Hendrix's novel, is of course familiar with *Dracula*, and can list a whole set of generic conventions from which he departs. As Nina Auerbach writes in the delightfully named *Our Vampires, Ourselves*, "there are many Draculas—and still more vampires who refuse to be Dracula or to play him," and each "feeds on his age instinctively because he embodies that age."[42] Louis, in Rice's novel, is the vampire of the modern age because he's stricken with an interminable existential crisis; he must search endlessly for meaning. But the vampires who come after Louis, those of the postmodern age, are wary even of the possibility of meaning. Their blood is saturated with irony; they are painfully aware of themselves as conventions. In southern vampire novels of the past few decades, then, the vampire in the South, no matter how comfortable he finds it as a home, always threatens to exceed it, just as he illuminates the ways in which southern space, too crowded with meaning, exceeds itself.

Given this hall of mirrors, the vampire and the South deploy convention to mobilize one another in complex ways. In Hendrix's novel, for example, the vampire is a foreigner, invading a familiar conception of the southern tight-knit community. But he is also, in his appetites and his table manners, the embodiment of southern monstrosity: perverse desires, racialized violence, haunted histories. What he threatens is the spread of monstrosity, though its direction is ambivalent: is he the stranger who invades the South, or the South itself, replicating dangerously out of control?

Insofar as Hendrix's is a horror novel, the threat is, essentially, that of infection. The vampire, after all, fits very well into what Patricia Wald has termed an outbreak narrative: a "formulaic plot that begins with the identification of an emerging infection, includes discussion of the global networks through which it travels, and chronicles the epidemiological work that ends with its containment," after "catalog[ing] the spaces and interactions of global modernity."[43] Although not as evocative of contagion as the zombie, the vampire is usually a stranger, a figure who comes into our space looking much like we do, but turns out to be a "carrier" of radical difference. Once that difference is discovered, the "intrigue and possibility as well as the anxiety" in the vampire story, like the outbreak narrative, is of communicability: the solvency of any border.[44] And, as Wald writes, whereas the outbreak narrative highlights global networks, it also "make[s] the act of imagining the [local] community a central (rather than obscured) feature of its preservation . . . from its fragility—its tenuousness—it also derives power."[45] The banishment of a vampire reasserts, or at least expresses the wish for, local insulation over global communicability.

"The South" into which the vampire arrives or emerges is a space figured in contradictions: it is both deeply insulated and broadly mobilized by the slave trade, the scene of both stagnancy and sweeping transformation. The vampire is patient zero of a frightening contagion—not only of vampirism itself or a vampire-caused illness, but of a region whose perversities ripple ever outward, *as well as* a morally corrupt modern world that infects the idyllic, quiet hamlet. Hendrix's *The Southern Book Club's Guide to Slaying Vampires* and Martin's *Fevre Dream* take conservative positions, ultimately replacing the vampire's border-crossing power with the reassurance of containment, even as the terms shift as to what, exactly, is being contained. In Hendrix's novel, there is monstrosity in the vampire intruding on the insular southern community and in the white southern mother making her way outward into the modern world. In Martin's novel, the South, figured as a space of global exchange, contagious in its spread of slavery, must be contained and then recast as an isolated, pastoral American haven. My second set of readings, Poppy Z. Brite's *Lost Souls* and Jewelle Gomez's *The Gilda Stories*, take a more exploratory approach to the spread of both vampirism and southernness, relying less on an outbreak narrative than on the radical possibilities that inhere in the vampire's ability to cross and dissolve national, regional, and epistemological borders. As with southernness, the queerness of monstrosity, across these works, is filled with contradictions: in radical deviance, the vampire is an agent of surprising kinship networks as well as self-shattering jouissance, his perverse pleasures the source of creation as well as destruction.

Read to Death

The Southern Book Club's Guide to Slaying Vampires begins with a preface: Hendrix writes that "[the vampire] is that iconic American archetype of the rambling man[,] . . . no past, and no ties. . . . Vampires are the original serial killers, stripped of everything that makes us human. They have no . . . roots, no family[,] . . . no children. . . . All they have is hunger. . . . In this book, I wanted to pit a man freed from all responsibilities except his appetites against women whose lives are shaped by their endless responsibilities. I wanted to pit Dracula against my mom."[46] In this odd face-off, Hendrix constructs the vampire as masculine, itinerant, sexual, and without obligations, and therefore the opposite of moms. But what this suggests is that without their "endless responsibilities" in their settled lives in their Southern town, their children, their constant focus on caretaking, their pearls and dresses, these women begin to inch toward the line that divides the binary: they become just a little more like Dracula.

Hendrix is well aware of the genre conventions he must negotiate. Even before the vampire, James Harris, comes on the scene, Hendrix's Charleston setting has the ingredients for southern gothic: a city with a disturbing historical role in the slave trade and fraught relations, in the present, between the Black and white neighborhoods. When James Harris first knocks on Patricia's door, he is already welcome before he's invited inside. He's a handsome, successful-looking white man, and Patricia is a lonely housewife, naïve and hungry for novelty. Her husband is already somewhat vampiric, ever demanding more labor (of all kinds) from her and from their Black housekeeper, Mrs. Greene. James knows that southern hospitality will serve him well, and he aims to take advantage of the fact that the South is just a bit *backward*, lagging behind the rest of the nation's development in all the familiar ways. In his last villainous speech, James Harris expresses his belief that a southern town, where the women would be hospitable and the men would be taken in by any white man with money, would be the safest place for a vampire in this modernizing world of "computers coming and all these new IDs."[47]

Patricia's book club tends toward true-crime stories, but when the familiar conventions all point in the same direction with James (drinks blood? Check. Can't go out in the day? Check. Has the power to bring on a plague of rats? Check.), they draw their knowledge of how to vanquish the vampire from literature. The Yankee of the group, Mary Ellen, takes a lot of convincing: "We're a book club," she protests. "What are we supposed to do? Read him to death?"[48] Of course, this is exactly right. The vampire is a tired genre, read to death and beyond, and so their knowledge of how to kill him must be generic knowledge. When the women confront James and prepare to destroy him, he protests that he is exceptionally unique, invaluable, and what they're doing is like "burning a library of books."[49] But the Gothic novel is the book that burns itself: it creates *and* disavows its lurid content. These women have invited the vampire in, and having done so, they must disavow him. Their plan, given that the vampire is notoriously hard to kill, is to hack James into bits. They do so, but gruesomely, each disembodied limb continues to move; the women have literalized the vampire's multiplicity, his incoherence as a singular body of meaning. All the things the monster could represent, all the threats he suggests, must be teased out and then disposed of.

But although the novel's principal arc is the "slaying" of vampires, its subterranean anxiety is in the blurring of the line between vampire and white southern woman—through predation and desire. After all, as ubiquitous as vampires are in the Gothic canon, they can't ever truly be killed. Patricia knows definitively that James is a monster when she discovers, in his attic, the dry and desiccated body of his housekeeper, a Black woman named Francine. In Patricia's prim, white (patrician) parlance, Francine "did for" James, just as Mrs. Greene does for her.[50] Although Hendrix's novel for the most part dances confusedly around the issue of race, the implication here is clear. Slavery and its legacy, the endless forms of labor slotted into that ominous blank space between "do" and "for," has sucked the lifeblood out of this Black woman. But despite her awareness of James's regular predation on the Black community, Patricia isn't ready to act until he has "seduced" her husband—with money, that is—and then, sexually, her daughter.[51] He's "grooming" her children, and rapes her best friend, Slick.[52] In the sense that his desires are unspeakable, fluid, and insatiable, James teases the vampire's queer potential. When the women finally commit themselves to killing James, they must first find a way to distract him—and Patricia offers herself up as bait. Her seduction of the vampire is a ploy, but in a narrative in which Patricia's sexuality is otherwise unmentioned, her mingled repulsion and sharp desire in response to James is a consistent thread, and one that suggests her own queer desire.[53] He directs her to the bed and, in a grotesque parody of oral sex, bites and begins to drink from her inner thigh, a cut that Patricia experiences as "the worst pain she'd ever experienced. Followed by the greatest pleasure."[54]

To kill the vampire, the southern woman not only gives herself up to him; she proves that they already share an intimate bond. The significance of white southern femininity comes to a pitch during the novel's vampire-slaying climax, piling on convention as the monster comes apart. The women are intent on disproving James's accusation of their harmlessness ("there's nothing nice about southern ladies," Slick says), and they dispense with him, tearing him limb from limb (using hunting knives, pretending to be dressing a deer) in the time it takes for Clemson to play USC.[55] Yankee Mary Ellen is noticeably less capable than her southern-identifying neighbors: she wets herself and stands frozen with shock during the scuffle. After it's all over, the women claim that they've been able to vanquish him because they value community and he is a wanderer, "all alone."[56] But more than that, they succeed because they are able, like he is, to stomach grotesque violence.

Although Hendrix's project is purportedly to hold up Moms victorious against Vampires, finally the two are too close for (southern) comfort. James has impregnated Slick; the vampire has breached the border of her body, and this is killing her. The neighbors believe she has AIDS. Her hospital visitors wear full hazmat suits. In her encounter with the vampire, she has become an agent of infectious evil, the containment of which is the conventional concluding chapter of the outbreak narrative.[57] If the vampire is "read to death," so must be the southern housewife. This tight little logic—to read the vampire is to invoke and disavow the Gothic South, all in the heady context of a notorious (and notoriously "queer") blood-borne global epidemic—is captured most neatly in the novel's last pages, in which Slick passes away. As her own infected blood ceases to circulate, Kitty is reading to her from Capote's *In Cold Blood*, quietly, like a lullaby or incantation.[58]

By setting his novel in the 1990s, Hendrix invokes a world on the eve of change—a new millennium of interconnectedness. The reviews of Hendrix's novel, oddly, by turns praise its "heady 1990s nostalgia" and its success at "recreat[ing] a time and place without the dangerous, distortive lens of nostalgia."[59] So which is it? To my reading, this is a novel nostalgic for the possibility of containing the fantastical, monstrous region spilling out over its borders—as well as a monstrous modernity encroaching on the insular community—at a historical moment (of those pesky "computers and IDs") in which this kind of border-policing is ceasing to look possible.[60]

The same could be said of *True Blood*. Although the show ostensibly takes place in the present day, the fictional Bon Temps, Louisiana, is remarkable for its lack of contemporary technologies and its old-fashioned aesthetic. (Compare this show, for instance, to the contemporaneous *Gossip Girl*: in the first scenes, the titular "gossip" spreads rapidly via cell phone cameras and text messages as a train arrives at Union station; then the camera pans out to give us an aerial view of Manhattan.) In the homes of Bon Temps, appliances appear to be decades old, as does the floral wallpaper. No one is using a computer or carrying a cellphone. When a waitress at the local bar is murdered, everyone congregates outside their homes, whispering to one another (in person!) about what might have happened. "I feel just like a cat on a hot tin roof[;] . . . that's from a play," one woman whispers to her neighbor, fanning herself.[61] The effect of this gratuitous Tennessee Williams citation is to place us associatively in a southern gothic world, a world that would be rudely interrupted by the existence of Google. We're asked to imagine the South as isolated in time and space—lurking somewhere in the past, solitary in its monstrosity, at least for a time.[62]

Fevered Thirsts

To contain some monstrosity and isolate the queer South, Hendrix looks back to the 1990s; George R. R. Martin looks all the way back to the nineteenth century. Published in the 1980s, before his *A Song of Ice and Fire* series spawned the lucrative television show *Game of Thrones*, Martin's *Fevre Dream* takes up themes that Rice touches on more lightly in *Interview with the Vampire*. Taking place along the Mississippi River (with important stops in New Orleans),[63] Martin's novel is concerned with "the red thirst" of its vampires and of the slave trade in the antebellum South. Like Hendrix's novel, *Fevre Dream* is billed as a crossover: between the horror of Stephen King and the more picaresque southern fare of Mark Twain. The narrative takes a folksy river captain, Abner Marsh, and pairs him with an idealistic vampire, Joshua York. Traveling South along the Mississippi shifts quickly from the thrill of adventure to terror for Marsh as York reveals to him the existence of vampires: York himself is a vampire, and he's fighting a more predatory vampire crowd. When he discovers these vampires, Marsh opens his eyes to the sins of humanity. *Fevre Dream* begins in 1857 and progresses to 1870, spanning St. Louis to New Orleans, ranging over the course of Marsh's partnership with York, the approach and denouement of the Civil War, and through the height to the fall of the steamboat industry.

The first encounter between Marsh and York establishes the vampire as a figure in queer opposition to an all-American masculinity. In the novel's first scene, York recruits Marsh to copilot a steamboat with him on the lower Mississippi. Marsh is a "massive man . . . [with] a red face and a full black beard" who easily puts away "a couple roast chickens with taters and stuff" at the dinner table.[64] He doesn't have any manners, but he's a hard-working man, "been a pilot and a mate and a striker, even a mud clerk."[65] York, on the other hand, wears clothes that "made it clear he was not a riverman."[66] He has no beard, but rather a "boyish aspect"—except for his hands, which are like those of a woman, in Marsh's view.[67] But before they even head southward, Marsh's own masculinity is diminished by York's sublime charisma: "Whatever thoughts he had had, whatever plans he had made, were sucked up in the maelstrom of York's eyes. . . . There was only York, the man himself, the power of him, the dream, the intensity."[68]

As Marsh soon learns, this dreamlike charm is a quality of a vampire "bloodmaster." As York explains to Marsh, the vampire's "red thirst" is akin to human sexual drive, but York has endeavored resolutely to conquer his destructive vampiric cravings through the creation of a synthetic blood cocktail.[69] Another powerful bloodmaster, Damon Julian, is less ethical, having taken to residing comfortably on a plantation in New Orleans, feasting on his neighbors and his slaves. His dissipated life there looks like a queer, polyamorous kink scene: Dandyish men and strange women kneel to suck at his wrist and call him master. The red thirst has overpowered Julian's every other impulse, such that he is, in York's words, "mad," morally vacant, "court[ing] destruction."[70]

Queer desire, in the form of vampirism, is monstrous, its practitioners' embodiments of the death drive.[71] New Orleans is home not only to this monstrous scene, but a monstrous rejection of humanist ideals more generally. The red thirst is desire untamed by ethical systems; as Julian puts it in a villainous speech, "there is no good and evil, only strength and weakness, masters and slaves."[72] For him, humans are "cattle."[73] As York explains, though vampires originated in "the dark winters of Northern Europe," the savage human and natural conditions of New Orleans "promise easy prey" for vampires such as Damon Julian.[74] "Down there in slave country," humans play at mastering other humans, distracted when what is truly a "superior" race creeps in. And then, "via the Mississippi, the whole continent would be open to them."[75] The South, both by its hot, humid natural climate and its unnatural failures of humanity, has become vulnerable to a (queer) apex predator.

New Orleans is described in ways that combine unnatural queer desire and uncivilized predatory impulses into a single space of miasmic monstrosity. The slave trade, and the dissipated opulence it brings, is on full display. Even at the height of the city's wealth, it is already defined by a notably cosmopolitan decay as steamboats and people pass through.[76] As York describes it, New Orleans is a city "very alive . . . but rotted with sickness. . . . You savor the rich sauces and the spices of the food, and then you learn that the spices are intended to disguise the fact that the meat is going bad. . . . Pestilence hangs over this beautiful city like a pall."[77] This "pall" extends to the extravagances of a New Orleans bar and brothel at which York is briefly employed. The city is decadent and brazen in its sin. It exploits, consumes, revels. It is death itself made beautiful, a force that dissolves discrete borders: between this place and the next, between bodies, between the human and the nonhuman. The city is, in other words, itself a vampire.

Martin's novel shifts the terms of our fear—the primary figure of unstable borders is not the vampire, but the southern port city. Via the Mississippi, New Orleans is geographically unbound, spreading its evil wildly and infecting men all over the nation with the "red thirst" of slavery. In the novel's repeated descriptions of the city as "hot," "damp," and "fevered," New Orleans becomes an associative port to Victorian discourses of the global South.[78] In the city's "pestilence" hangs the specter of contagion; disease is impervious to both regional and national borders. When the passengers on the *Fevre Dream* see the body of one of Julian's victims, they're convinced it's the "Bronze John," or yellow fever, that periodically sweeps through the city. By way of the Mississippi, that key new mode of transportation for vampires and humans, New Orleans spreads slavery, sexual excess, and fever, infecting the national body with the physical and metaphorical diseases of a wild southern otherness.

The vampires in Martin's novel are not themselves figures of contagion—they are only ever born through the paternal line, never made—but they do suggest the way stories spread and mutate like viruses. After York tells Marsh the origin of the "night people," he warns Abner of false stories: of "undead" who "sleep in coffins filled with their native earth[,] . . . shape changers. . . . Their victims become vampires themselves[;] . . . they cannot enter a house where they have not been invited. . . . A cross will send them fleeing, garlic can bar them, and they cannot cross running water. . . . [They] are not reflected in mirrors."[79] Like the story of a sleepwalker, which eventually becomes the story of the walking dead, time and the telling will distort any story, as York warns Marsh. Ahead of his time in the nineteenth century, Joshua York is the postmodern vampire par excellence: ambivalent about his condition, eager to tell his story, and aware that he must acknowledge (and subvert) his own genre to avoid appearing suspiciously predictable. In the mirrored grand ballroom of the *Fevre Dream*, "each night a thousand Joshua Yorks walk," but in a shipmate's later retelling, "them mirrors is always empty, even though she's got lots of folks aboard her, pale-looking folks."[80]

As a generic text, the vampire is both endlessly reproducible and empty of a single image; his meaning is everywhere and nowhere. York and his vampire kin teach us to read for the ways stories mutate as they spread. They teach us to distrust the apparent stability of convention. Julian's human overseer, Sour Billy, trusts convention to his peril. He is convinced, by vampire stories, that Julian can "turn" him, but his consumption of human blood only wastes away his humanity and his body. Faith in vampiric power, like power itself, not only misleads, but corrupts. Sour Billy believes that he can become monstrously powerful, and the men around him believe that monsters appear only under one visage. When Marsh asks around little port towns to learn more about vampires, he finds people who "seemed to know considerable about vampires, though none of the stories had a damn thing to do with the Mississippi."[81] The irony, of course, is that being on the route of the slave trade, they are surrounded by vampirism. Sour Billy, despite his mortal human body, is already, as an overseer, effectively a vampire.

Over the course of the novel, the red thirst originating down South finally captures the whole nation. As Marsh reflects, "He was an upper river man; it had been a terrible mistake ever to go down to New Orleans. His dream had turned into a nightmare down there in slave country, in the hot fevered south."[82] But finally, the fever that rages across the nation by way of the Mississippi is contained. When Damon Julian and his crew take over the *Fevre Dream*, keeping York aboard as a kind of prisoner, they run the steamboat on human corpses, and she falls into abject decay. York, accordingly, renames her the *Ozymandias*. By 1870, New Orleans has fallen in economic favor,[83] the nation has conquered the "red thirst" (by one metric, at least) and the *Ozymandias* is rotting in an indigo plantation somewhere outside the city. Damon Julian and his crew are still living there, stationary, in dissipated decadence—the steamer is a microcosm of the declining South.

Look on my works, ye mighty: like a vampire, like empire, the steamer's consumption of blood for energy—what once apparently strengthened it—has poisoned it. It's in this state that Marsh and York finally conquer Damon Julian and his crew. By this time, York has impregnated a female vampire, finding himself possessed of a "cleaner" heteronormative (rather than bloodthirsty and queer) desire after enough time on his diet of synthetic blood.[84] York has asserted his humanity by way of a reproductive masculinity, and the country, too, has turned away from queer southern bloodlust, toward more wholesome ideals.

When Marsh dies, he is buried by the river—whereas once it "swarmed" with steamboats, now it is tranquil and still.[85] On Marsh's tombstone is engraved a line from Byron, functioning as cautionary tale: "So we'll go no more a roving."[86] *Fevre Dream* is, as its name suggests, an outbreak narrative: disease, in all its terrifying mobility, spreads and is then contained. The reassurance that the novel's conclusion offers is that of an isolated South, whether as the variation on the grand and decaying plantation house, or the peaceful field of dead men whose time has passed. Even the immortal York appears somewhat contained by the gravitational pull of this pastoral space (and, presumably, by the obligations of fatherhood): he visits the site of Marsh's grave "often."[87] But although we are left at last with both the decayed and the idyllic isolated region, York and his brethren have taught us to be wary of the ways in which dangerous stories—and a monstrous southernness—might spread.

Runaway Dreams

In contrast to the southern vampire novel that stages a kind of outbreak narrative, the explicitly queer southern vampire story might make its project to engage with the dissolution of borders—of bodies, of conventions and norms, and of geographical fantasy—with an approach that defies generic expectations of horror and ultimate containment. Poppy Z. Brite's *Lost Souls* (1992) and Jewelle Gomez's *The Gilda Stories* (1991) take on this project.[88] Both novels embrace monstrosity, playing with what it means to occupy positions of queerness and southernness through the vampire's generic capaciousness. In the posthumanist orientation of these novels, they stage a debate over queer relationality: What are the ethical stakes of becoming a vampire?[89] Is it possible to form a "monstrous" community?

Despite their similarities, these novels approach this question from starkly opposing poles. Brite's vampires, like Martin's, are white men, born through the paternal line, never made. Their fundamental concern is the pursuit of pleasure, and this pursuit demands that they live wholly in the present. Gilda, Gomez's titular vampire, is a Black woman, transformed and cared for by another female vampire. She is deeply attuned to societal responsibility, and, accordingly, lives through history and dreams of the future and past as much as the present. But by claiming "the South" (quotation marks and all), both sets of vampires set forth the terms by which they imagine a form of family radically unconstrained by normative structures that would imprison, dull, marginalize, enslave, and gender them. In *Lost Souls*, I'll argue, this is ultimately a lost cause, but *Gilda* clings tenaciously to the dream of a growing vampire family, even at the end of the world.

Into the Kudzu

If Martin's novel expresses an anxiety about containing the South, Poppy Z. Brite's *Lost Souls* plays with the idea of the South's—and the vampire's—endless replicability. Brite's vampires look very familiar in that they are white, male, and beautiful: one could imagine them as direct descendants of Dracula. But over the generations, their vampire blood has been diluted. There are not, any longer, "pure" or original vampires. They are vampires of the late twentieth century, and as such, ones who have "progressively become associated both with the physicality of homosexual practices and with the expression of a specifically gay identity," as William Hughes puts it.[90] As reviews caution, the tale is "not for the weak of stomach[,] . . . graphic in its presentation of kinky sex mixed with vampirism."[91] Brite's novel tells the story of Jason, or "Nothing," a queer teenager who runs away from his adoptive parents and suburban Maryland home to the apparently more alluring locale of Missing Mile, North Carolina, home of a Goth band he likes called "Lost Souls?" The band is composed of two teenagers, Steve and Ghost, the latter a psychic, an uncanny empath. Hitchhiking his way to them, Nothing meets a van of weird, gothically dressed and eerily beautiful boys (Zillah, Molochai, and Twigg). They turn out to like the same thing he does: pretending to be vampires. But of course, they *are* vampires, real ones who kill their victims and drink their blood. And Nothing realizes he is more than willing to join their family. After a brief and chaotic stop in Missing Mile, they head onward to New Orleans.

With these two locales, Brite plays with two distinct but familiar sets of southern gothic convention. The name Missing Mile suggests a place forgotten by time and erased by history, and in seeking it out, Nothing is looking for the site of a magical queer parentage, a stylishly haunting alternative to suburbia: "The singer's voice [was] as strong and golden-green as some Appalachian summer mountain spring. . . . He pictured [Missing Mile] as a mysterious southern crossroads, a hamlet where the ordinary became exotic."[92] As a child of the Maryland suburbs, Nothing's vision emerges from the conventions in which the Lost Souls? tape traffics: the liner features "a picture of an old gravestone dappled with shadow and sunlight, surrounded by pine needles and twining kudzu vines."[93] But the image is a "grainy photocopy," suggesting its endless reproducibility.[94] Steve and Ghost, just as they create and sell the music of Lost Souls?, also frame their own lives through a marketable southern gothic aesthetic. Driving through the town and its adjacent rural expanse at night, Steve imagines the road as "a magic river, a river of shimmering asphalt banked by pined forest and thick, rioting expanses of kudzu. . . . They drove past a graveyard full of softly rotting monuments and flowers, an abandoned railyard[;] . . . a southern Pride car wash whose sign read, mysteriously, AS WE THIINK, SO WE ARE[;] . . . [and] one dilapidated nightclub outside which dark shapes always lurked, regardless of hour or temperature."[95] Magic, riot, rot, dilapidation, abandonment—what Steve and Ghost attune to on their drive are familiar terms of southern gothic. The car wash sign suggests the imaginative transformation that kudzu and darkness can enact: that of the natural into the supernatural, embodiment into "ghost"liness.

The inhabitants of Missing Mile are not unaware of the generic conventions of southern gothic. Steve's ex-girlfriend, Ann, is now dating a man who "had written his doctoral thesis on William Faulkner and had never really gotten over it," and Steve, when he's confronted by a couple of guys who catch him trying to rob a Coke machine, wonders if "they could make him *squeeeeal* like a pig," a la *Deliverance*.[96] References to cultural touchstones are more implicitly embedded in the narrative as well; Missing Mile seems haunted by O'Connor, by Caldwell. Nothing's first hitchhiking experience en route to Missing Mile is with an Evangelical albino who requests oral sex in lieu of fare, and Christian, an older vampire who seeks out the small town as a respite from New Orleans, finds, on his entrance, a town sign "swathed in kudzu, stained brown with blood long dry" and a mute child who stares at him with vacant eyes when he asks for directions.[97] But this is not *You Have Seen Their Faces*; when Christian "began to know their faces," it's those of "children in black, which he had not expected in a small southern town."[98] Bartending at The Sacred Yew, surprisingly "no redneck bar," he finds the same Gothic crowd of teens he was used to in New Orleans.[99]

And although the music of Lost Souls? is characterized by lyrics like, "walk the mountain roads with me and drink some clear water," Steve seems to drink only bourbon and Dixie beer.[100] The rural southern gothic of North Carolina, in other words, is fed on convention and branding as much as the cosmopolitan southern gothic of New Orleans. It proliferates in stories and images. On Halloween in Missing Mile, a "snaky night, riotous with the last October kudzu," Ghost "lean[s] back against his favorite gravestone[,] . . . a private in the Confederate army" and begins to tell Steve what he hears the man's ghost saying. Steve responds with, "Well, I can play that game too. Want me to tell you the story of the Hook again?"[101] These are excessively familiar stories for a spooky night. They are interrupted in their reveries by a kid from the Sacred Yew, with "Dracula makeup smudged on his nose," inviting them to a vampire film festival.[102] Gothic conventions (southern or otherwise) are visible here as conventions, but they are nonetheless a means of building community.

Missing Mile and New Orleans embody separate southern gothic traditions in the novel, but vampires of all kinds populate both spaces; they represent the desire for, and the presence of, an alternative community. When Ghost, in New Orleans, passes "a group of kids wearing black clothes, black lipstick, and eyeliners," he reflects that "vampires were their dream come true, their ideal to aspire to."[103] Ghost's musings suggest that the Dracula in the Sacred Yew is not so different from the Dracula on Bourbon Street—the difference is just that the kid on Bourbon Street has more clubs to choose from, and more likeminded friends to find there. But while community might be found through adherence to convention, convention also makes true membership in a community impossible to determine, as becomes clear from the anxieties about authenticity among the New Orleans vampires. It's the real vampire fans who "know enough to drink Chartreuse[;] . . . the distilled essence of the town burns in their bellies."[104] Their eyes turn bright green—a rather unnatural color that is, the novel frequently stresses, the color of Zillah's eyes.

But while anyone could resemble Zillah if they've had a wild enough night, *he* is the real distilled essence of the town, the real vampire, first "appear[ing] by some Mardi Gras magic."[105] The night of that celebration, he and his cronies prove their vampire nature to Christian at his bar by way of a doubloon "the same size and shape as those thrown from Mardi Gras parade floats"—a real silver one, not plastic.[106] And yet, separated by several generations from the original vampire race, they are themselves not quite the real deal, "wish[ing] they had fangs but ha[ving] to make do with teeth they filed sharp."[107] Zillah's sexual conquest that night, the human teenager Jessy, is not so different from him in her own wish for sharp fangs. She is a native of New Orleans, but her proximity to the vampire world comes from a "dog-eared and heavily underlined" copy of *Dracula* and the vials of "red dust" that she finds at voodoo shops.[108] The city's many global influences—French Chartreuse, Spanish coins, African voodoo—are on full display, but always in the context of tourism. Historical currency becomes difficult to distinguish from its many reproductions, and the tradition of voodoo is commodified for white teenagers who consider it a good pairing with Irish novels. The "essence of the town" is impossible to differentiate from its marketing.[109] Likewise, the "real" vampire can't separate himself from an idealized image. If his teeth aren't sharp, he files them. Like the disillusioned teenager, he adorns himself in black. He is ever having to compete with Dracula and his wannabes. As Jessy's father claims, the city "has become riddled with [vampires]."[110]

This southern gothic space must function simultaneously as familiar and exceptional to vampires and vampire-imitators alike. Nothing's reunion with his queer, vampiric chosen family is put not in terms of "finding" them in the South, but in the sense of inventing them; he fashions the South to be just the escape that he needs. Nothing paints the Maryland suburbs and the conventional families who live there as "boring and oppressive," home to clueless adults and disaffected kids, drained of vitality and imagination.[111] When he finds the note apparently pinned to him as a baby, leaving him at that suburban doorstep and identifying his original name as *Nothing* rather than Jason, the moniker becomes a blank slate, an open road of possibility. That road is one of invention, where he continually turns toward the story he needs, and refuses the one that represents the dullness of late-capitalist domesticity. On his travels, for instance, he is delighted to find "a truck-stop diner somewhere south of nowhere," but dismayed to find that the diner represents Everywhere USA: "The flashy jukebox . . . didn't have the decency to play green and mournful country music, but played the pop top twenty over and over[;] . . . the place reeked of hamburger grease and cardboard flavored coffee."[112]

He finds his ideal of southernness *with* vampirism, as a form of queer magic: "At last he was in the South, with its green cathedrals of kudzu[;] . . . he believed in [vampires] because they had to be there. . . . He had always known he could not live his whole life in the real world."[113] The cathedral of kudzu is as distant from "the real world" as the monster, and Nothing and his new vampire family inch further into that Gothic darkness by smoking opium and taking mysterious pills. To fully secure the bonds of his new magical life, Nothing sleeps with Zillah, the leader of the vampire pack, and participates in the killing of another hitchhiker, who turns out to be his old friend Lane. Vampiric murder does not come easy—it looks more like crazed cannibalism than elegant bloodsucking. But finally, as the van barrels southward, they throw the body of the suburban child, like the discarded "real" boy, Jason, onto the road, and travel onward toward New Orleans.

But although Nothing's search for home and family in New Orleans is about laying claim to queer transformation, the novel ultimately questions the extent to which community and radical antinormativity are compatible. Nothing seeks out a vampire family for the complete freedom it offers, but this family ventures so far beyond the constraints of normativity that he ultimately finds an atemporal anarchy, a nihilism that can't sustain the sense of continuity and commitment that "family" implies. For Zillah, Molochai, and Twigg, family means only sharing in a cycle of desire and gratification when doing so is convenient: in their most familial moment, they stand "naked and embracing, the three of them as much a family as anyone could be, anywhere," when Molochai expresses his hunger for "whipped cream and kidneys and chocolate truffles and baby's-blood ice cream."[114] However, little more connects the three than a physical and sexual hunger rewarded by hunting in packs. When Nothing finds out that Zillah is his birth father (in addition to being his lover) he is at first thrilled: "in a world of night, in a world of blood, what did such pallid rules matter?"[115] The description of the non-magical world's rules as "pallid," a word that so consistently cites to vampires, flips the script. It's the human world that is "bloodless," not quite alive, through its tedious adherence to "rules." But ultimately, Nothing's dream of a queerly constructed family is crushed by the very thing that made it an appealing fantasy in the first place—the prospect of hedonistic pleasure unlimited by the obligation of any rules or ethical system.

When the queerly constructed bond "become[s] flesh . . . *blood*," "family" represents just another body to be consumed for instant gratification.[116] As William Hughes notes, identity for Brite's vampires is "vested in what sensations can be given and what received"; as he argues, this "make[s] the family an erotic and recreational rather than an administrative and reproductive unit."[117] Identity based on sensation is so fluid as to be a highly unstable quantity—and "family" must in this context constantly reconfigure itself on the waves of desire. Although Hughes argues that "their polygamous commitment to each other" ensures the continuity of Nothing's new family, this continuity is short lived—because "commitment" is by nature incompatible with the vampire's beloved spontaneity.[118] Any form of commitment, after all, represents structures of obligation that jangle with the vampires' dream of life as an unending New Orleans bacchanalia.

Although Nothing is at first thrilled with his alternative family, he quickly finds that Zillah is as abusive as a "father" as he is as a lover. As Nothing pushes back, their union descends into violence. Nothing wants commitment, but Zillah is "a blank soul, a being with no morals and no passions except those that could be gratified at a moment's notice, a mad child allowed to rage out of control."[119] Rather than possessing either age and experience or the headstrong vitality of youth, Zillah is regularly described as a chaotic compendium of ages: he is apparently over 100 years old, but has the looks of a young teenager and "suck[s] like a baby before he could sleep."[120] Nothing has a similar experience of New Orleans: "time moves differently[,] . . . a sort of dream time[,] . . . that could stretch a single day or compress three hundred and eighty-three years."[121] Elizabeth Freeman argues that such "historical and temporal disjunction, experienced as illicit pleasure, define and enable queer sociability," but in Brite's novel, that sociability is precarious.[122] Both the vampire and New Orleans ultimately resist the possibility of sustained belonging through the very quality by which they first seem to offer it: endless mutability, the pleasures of instant transformation and wish fulfillment unchecked by the temporal and ethical rule, and boundaries of the "real" world.

Bourbon Street, finally, is the encapsulation of the radical but elusive pleasures of monstrous southern queer kinship. The vampires "tast[e] a memory of altars, of the Garden of Eden" on this street offering a buffet of "blood full of wine and beer and whiskey," where "sleazy lights" promise that "MEN WILL TURN INTO WOMEN BEFORE YOUR EYES!!"[123] Liquor, blood, and sex merge into a kind of sensory paradise where anything is possible, where transformation is both sensational and holy. But although Nothing is "dazzled by the carnival of Bourbon Street, drunk on Chartreuse," the magic of a carnival is that it remains just that—a carnival, in reactionary opposition to the structuring principles that would give him his longed-for family.[124] At the novel's end, Nothing is alone again, having killed Zillah in defense of the "brothers" he first fantasized about calling his—Steve and Ghost. He promises to watch over these first objects of his fantasy of queer family, but only from afar, in the vampire's conventional solitude. Nothing is left with the freedom of that solitude, even as he obligates himself to those he would—but cannot—call family.

Lands of Enchantment

Although *Lost Souls* and *The Gilda Stories* share a focus on the experiences of queer vampire families rather than their hunters, the similarities, for the most part, end there. *Gilda* is all about sustainable systems. As the first novel about a queer Black woman vampire,[125] Jewelle Gomez's *The Gilda Stories* has garnered a good deal of critical attention in the years since its publication. It has been interpreted through the framework of several traditions—among them Afrofuturism, the neoslave narrative, and the African American folk tradition—and work on *Gilda* has stressed its groundbreaking approach to intersectionality.[126] The novel has also had wide popular success, including, in 2016, a twenty-fifth anniversary edition. If you're looking for a story that reframes the vampire's unsettling border-crossing tendencies as anticapitalist, deeply relational, and sustaining, you need look no further than *Gilda*. As Anatol writes, "in embracing the previously abject space of the border" and imagining her protagonist as "a figure outside of the destructive tendencies of the West," Gomez "uses the vampire trope to continually stress the power and pleasure to be found in fluid relationships and roles rather than immobile, fixed dynamics."[127]

The novel begins with an enslaved young woman ("The Girl") fleeing a plantation in antebellum Mississippi. In Louisiana, she's discovered by a white woman in masculine clothes—Gilda—who gives her protection and a home at the brothel she runs just outside of New Orleans. The Girl admires the familial and romantic bond between Gilda and Bird, an indigenous woman who shares Gilda's strange power of communicating without language. Over time, the Girl learns that the two are vampires, and that Gilda, who has lived for many centuries, is ready to "finally see the end of the road."[128] In an exchange both sexual and maternal, Gilda begins the process of turning "The Girl," with her consent, believing that she will be a good companion for Bird. After the first Gilda is gone, the Girl takes her name, and after a time, she too becomes Bird's romantic partner. But she also explores the world independently, finding other family and romances along the way. The novel ranges broadly across time and space: from 1850 in Louisiana, to Yerba Buena in 1890, to Missouri in 1921, to Boston in 1955, to New York in 1971, to California in 1981, to New Hampshire in 2020, to a postnational "Land of Enchantment" in 2050. Not in one of these places and times is Gilda's journey to freedom complete, and Gilda is constantly aware of historical continuities and changes through her long life. Always, Gilda takes blood only to sustain herself and leaves in exchange a gift—a dream, a reassurance, a sense of strength. As Auerbach writes, the "true vampire," in *Gilda*, "is a guardian angel . . . in a contaminated society."[129]

The first scene sets the terms of the novel: the vampiric "beast" of exploitative white (masculine) power in the slaveholding South encounters the perceived monstrosity of the Black woman, who carries within her the dream of a better world. The Girl, running from enslavement, wakes in her hiding place to find a white man standing over her. Although the sounds of the Girl's body in the hay become, in dreams, "her mother [raking] the bristles through the Girl's thicket of dark hair," the sound of the man approaching "remained what it was: danger."[130] The scene shifts between dream and wakefulness; it is through her dreams that the reader learns of the Girl's family at the plantation, and their resistance to the white slaveholders, who "were not fully human."[131] According to the Girl's mother, this is a function of youth, humanity accruing only over time: "They ain't been here long 'enough. They just barely humans. Maybe not even. They suck up the world, don't taste it."[132] Her family's Fulani past, the "lost empires," is a "dream to the Girl, like the one she was having now."[133] The blurring of dreaming and waking life, for Gilda, suggests early on the possibility of alternative modes of relationality; she is attuned to what Gloria Anzaldúa calls the "other mode of consciousness," lost to Western "objectivity," which "facilitates images from the soul and the unconscious through dreams and the imagination" and keeps us from distancing ourselves from others.[134]

Her mother, in a dream, urges the Girl to awaken in time to see "the beast from this other land" and to avoid becoming his prey.[135] The Girl "see[s] into the past and future" as he approaches her, and the expansive temporality of her dreams allow her to gather strength in the moment.[136] As he prepares to "invade her[,] . . . stiff with conquest," she "enter[s] him with her heart which was now a wood-handled knife[;] . . . warmth spread from his center of power to his chest as the blood left his body."[137] The inversion of penetration, the drainage of the overseer's predatory power, is a vampiric scene. But as Christopher Lewis argues, even this moment of death is written through a lens of intimacy and some gentleness, as Gilda "move[s] quietly, as if he had really been her lover and she was afraid to wake him."[138] His death is a necessary and a significant one. From this opening scene, as Lewis argues, the novel "question[s] the desire to be recognized as human given that white humanity is practiced through greedy consumption and exploitative penetration."[139] The novel makes clear that we've built a society on miscalculated ideas of what makes us "human"; when Enlightenment humanism feeds itself on a conception of the non-white, non-male, non-Western, and sexually nonnormative subject as Other, that humanism is violent, beastly.[140] The more ethical alternative is to embrace what has been called monstrous and deviant.

In her life as a vampire, Gilda travels widely, but her time living with sex workers in a house outside of New Orleans marks a foundational home, the culmination of her birth into a vampiric family—and even as she travels and expands that family, the South remains oddly prominent. As in Brite's novel, the transformation of human to vampire is a queer affair, one with a fluidity of parental and sexual suggestion: "the Girl felt herself drawn into the flowing energy. . . . [Gilda] held the Girl's head to her breast and in a quick gesture opened the skin of her chest[;] . . . soon the flow was a tide."[141] But this monstrous queerness is, unlike in Brite's novel, a method of forming a sustainable family.[142] Bird, who completes Gilda's change, arrived in New Orleans after her family of origin "came south to burn away the disease from our spirits" brought by white settlers—a history she bears in the pockmarks on her skin.[143] In the 1970s, Gilda gives "birth" to a vampire "son," Julius, a man who has "come to New York City[,] . . . having nothing to keep him in the South."[144] Gilda's mentors, Anthony and Sorel, are a white gay couple who make New Orleans their home base although they travel widely.[145] In 2050, Gilda and all of these family members, hunted for their powerful vampire blood in the maelstrom of capitalism's collapse and climate apocalypse, travel southward. They are seeking an escape from a slavery that will drain their lifeblood literally rather than figuratively—and going south offers "less industrial lands where it was somewhat easier to remain undiscovered."[146]

Although the role of "the South" has not been much invoked in criticism of the novel, I want to emphasize especially Gomez's choice to retain the myth that the vampire must sleep with the soil of its homeland.[147] This is at first glance surprising, especially in a novel that rewrites most vampire conventions. Although vampires can "turn" one another, it is only ever a conscious decision that leads to a kind of birth, never framed as a moment of infection or disease. There are no silver crosses, no cloves of garlic. The vampire's super-speed is here, surely because it helps Gilda cross borders real and metaphorical with alacrity. But the myth of the soil asserts the vampire's link to coffins, death, and nativism, and as such the idea that soil contains magical powers conscripted by state or national borders seems expressly counter to the novel's politics. Mississippi soil might be "blood soil," but in this quality it is, in every meaning of the term, "much like the rest in the Delta sphere," as Gilda muses.[148] And yet one of her earliest discoveries in New Orleans is Gilda's "large feed bags filled with dirt," and through all her travels, she keeps her own Mississippi soil in the lining of her jacket.[149]

The migration of Mississippi soil dramatizes how the legacy of slavery extends across time and space. As critics have pointed out, the projects of the neoslave narrative and the Afrofuturist text join in the novel's emphasis on the pervasiveness of anti-blackness; Susana Morris, for example, emphasizes the connection between the novel's "apocalyptic past and future landscapes" and its representation of the "rabid inhumanity of white supremacist society."[150] *Gilda* demands an alternative future not just for one problem region (the South) but for an entire nation and the broader paradigm of Western culture—throwing all of our geographic imaginaries into question. Although the Mississippi soil holds the blood of her people, that (ongoing) history doesn't stop at state lines. As she travels southward in the novel's last episode, two centuries after escaping enslavement, she "avoid[s] Mississippi almost unconsciously as if bounty hunters might still be searching for the girl she had been."[151] She also carries Mississippi as the woman she has become, powerful but sought by bounty hunters in pursuit of valuable vampire blood. "Mississippi" becomes less a state than a symbol of the unfreedom Gilda carries as a Black woman, ever marked as an object for capitalist consumption.

Paradoxically, once Mississippi ceases to be geographically determined (the threat of enslavement is everywhere), the South becomes a place to claim. Just as soil can carry traumatic histories, it can also symbolize resistance and the claiming of alternative futures. As Horton-Stallings writes, "I rely upon my metaphorical use of dirt . . . to think through imaginative transnational, diasporic, and Indigenous sexuality, eroticism, embodiment, sensorium, and intimacy practices that have been rendered immoral, anonymous, or displaced."[152] The soil stresses an "intimate or spiritual relationship with land beyond ownership," a relationship of sexual and political resistance.[153] Carrying the soil of her land, Gilda imagines the South as a direction of possibility, rather than an existing geography of oppression: "Bird had made her way south early. . . . Inside she heard the voices[:] . . . *South to Peru*."[154] In the novel's final scene, she gazes toward her vampire comrades, "on a ridge to the south in the quickening sky[,] . . . silhouette[d] against a silver moonbow[,] . . . they turned southward to meet them. Gilda was no longer fleeing for her life."[155] The South's moonlight and magnolias are transmuted into moonbows on a southbound trail. This late post-apocalyptic age also looks like a very early one in the Earth's history, and Gilda moves south toward freedom instead of away from it.[156] In the novel's circular structure,[157] she fulfills the prediction the original Gilda gave: "You may feel you have nothing to go back to, but sooner or later we all want to go back to something."[158] As the crew travels southward, the newest vampire, Ermis, hums gospel hymns. Black southern history layers over an unimagined future. To go "back" is less a return than a rewriting.

Gilda heavily emphasizes the transformative possibilities of the written word. Writing one's own reality, and one's own future, is not an impossible dream (the very word, in the novel's first scene, loses its meaning as "unreal") but a vital possibility and a political imperative. From her first lessons with Bird, a teacher sensitive to the fact that what she finds in the written word does not reflect her own experiences, Gilda's upbringing into eternal life is not only in becoming a vampire, but in becoming a writer. Both are modes of transformation, "shamanistic," in Anzaldúa's words: "transform[ing] the storyteller and the listener into something else[,] . . . writer . . . as shape-shifter."[159] This is her way of building a world in which she can live, even as it constitutes a profession within and part of a (rapidly dying) capitalist society.

Gilda's work as a writer can be understood as a form of Muñoz's queer disidentification—changing a system from within. As Caroline Rody has pointed out, *The Gilda Stories* "shows a remarkable degree of self-consciousness about its own capitalization on market trends[;] . . . always astride the moment's current, Gilda cashes in on the late twentieth-century public craving for a mythified African American past. . . . She conceives the literary mission of linking ancestry to the future as a fitting consummation of this history."[160] Not only Gomez, but Gilda herself, as Jerry Rafiki Jenkins argues, "interrogates an assumption held by both the publishing establishment and the black literary community during the 1970s and 80s . . . that speculative fiction is a genre written for, by, and about white people."[161] As a bestselling author, Gilda writes romances as a way of remembering and reframing history, "cloaked in adventure and mysticism."[162] But while she's savvy about the market, Gilda takes a firm stance on the appropriate mode of subverting it. She's frustrated by Frank Yerby's *The Foxes of Harrow*: "a black man writing almost exclusively about white, southern society. . . . Who were the characters, really? Where could she fit him within her life, her experience of the past century? . . . She tossed the book back."[163] A fantasy of the white antebellum South, even if complex or ambivalent, is a fantasy of the white antebellum South. For Gilda, Yerby's sin is in confining the South in time and space rather than letting it run, bleeding out into a more expansive dream. Gilda's literary philosophy seems to mirror the terms in which Gomez articulates her own: as a project of "creat[ing] a *new mythology*."[164]

This vision of a new mythology strengthens as the US national imaginary dissolves. By 2020, in Gilda's world, the *New York Times* has folded, the populace not being much for reading anymore. When people cease to imagine themselves as part of a national imagined community, they do not see themselves as citizens of the world; instead, pollution and greed rage out of hand. The rich grow richer, while most people find themselves displaced. By 2050, there is no United States, and environmental conditions worldwide are dire. Although an organization called GrassRoots seems by its name to cling to the potential of local care and attachment, asking people to "turn around the way they lived," many scramble to emigrate "Off-World" into space.[165] Finally, the nation built on capitalism has hastened its own end; it is a "wasteland" where people are "dying of greed."[166] But within this bleak paradigm, southern space becomes one of open possibility, a place for Gilda, Bird, and their cohort of vampire refugees to stake their claim through land and through story. Gilda "has allowed Bird to transport most of her journals south with her," and Bird gently compels her: "We've not had time enough to know this world together[;] . . . we remain because this is our home. We both have lost land here. Should we leave it all to them?"[167]

The answer, of course, is no. When the nation that gave "the South" ideological meaning falls, this family, even in their precarity as marginalized and pursued "monsters" (racial and sexual others as well as vampires) are free to seek a more inclusive and ethical way of living on the southern land they claim.[168] They boldly pursue a dream that feels, in a post-apocalyptic landscape, almost certainly impossible. Rody's point that Gomez "sometimes cloaks her earnest politics in mawkish prose" is well taken.[169] Earnestness is vulnerability. And there is perhaps no creature like the vampire (creeping slowly to the exposed neck) to show us how risky vulnerability is. Even the vampire's unavoidable campiness suggests how distant, magical, and impossible *transformation* can feel from the day-to-day, on-the-ground realities of our lives. New novels are written every day, but not so much new mythologies, despite Gomez's professed aim. *Gilda* and *Lost Souls*, though they take up the queerness of the vampire in explicit terms, and boldly explore what such a creature does to our understanding of southern kinship, demand of the reader a steep buy-in. To ask that we accept the premise of a man who turns into a bat is in many ways an easier ask than the premise of a changeable social system.

Trans/formations

Bird's question in *Gilda*—"Should we leave it all to them?"—speaks to very real political fights for queer life in southern spaces of the United States. And more specifically, although neither Gomez nor Brite present their vampires as transgender, theorizations of the trans body resonate with the conception of the vampire as a figure of border-troubling queer monstrosity.[170] As Hil Malatino writes, trans becoming can be understood as a way of "valorize[ing] monstrosity, a means of affirming gendered embodiment as always already made, mutable, nonsovereign, intra-active, and in excess of the regulatory logics of the human."[171] Trans studies, too, are very much in dialogue with feminist posthumanism and its work of "perform[ing] a multiplicity of dislocations of sex, gender, sexuality, race, and ability," in Camille Nurka's words.[172] Understood as posthumanist meditations, these novels offer ways of thinking through trans embodiment in southern spaces—especially for people of color. Gomez's novel insists that the South remain open to queer Black lives that defiantly refuse those "regulatory logics of the human": Gilda and her cohort are fugitives at the borders of the possible, making the land they claim one of sanctuary and mutual care.[173] The monstrosity of their southernness, finally, seems to be the only true humanity. In *Lost Souls*, the magic of Bourbon Street, and of the southern gothic more broadly, is that it positions embodied and epistemological transformation as a true possibility. But the vampires of both novels also invoke complicated queer histories in real southern spaces like New Orleans.

The historical scene of antebellum decadence and horror as well as postbellum trade, New Orleans is a city where southernness and queerness long have met and still meet in "monstrosity," and as such it serves as a testing ground for the radical potential of that monstrosity. New Orleans's reputation as a haven for hedonism is surely connected to its fame as a "vampire city";[174] this kind of Gothic tourism, a way for the city to write itself and sell itself, blends the mythical with the erotic and the historical. But if tourism can be the basis of creative forms of community—polyamorous, freedom-loving vampires seeking same—it can also be deeply exploitative.[175] The city's centrality in the slave trade lies at the root of what is now its quite-marketable (and apparently toothless) Gothic aesthetic. As Rashauna Johnson writes, "chattel slavery allowed New Orleans to become a modern city," with all the sexual liberalism that "modern" connotes.[176] The city's reputation as a space for deviant sexualities, then, is partially rooted in legacies of abuse and unfreedom, even as such a reputation begets present-day scenes of radical liberation from the normative. Nor is "The Big Easy" an altogether accurate nickname; the "Dixie Bohemia" of the French Quarter and the city more widely has been home to queer writers and artists, but also to "reform" movements whose legacies are visible in contemporary policing and discriminatory city ordinances that especially hurt sex workers and people of color.[177]

But so, too, is New Orleans a southern city where transformation—the kind that Gilda hopes for at the end of the world—might look like a real possibility. Even in the post-apocalyptic landscape of Katrina, Andy Horowitz argues, "there was a radical potential to the way some New Orleanians theorized why they and their city mattered, because many came to see themselves as defending a vision of quality of life that could not be reduced to economic terms," a way of life that that "transformed the civic calendar" (and, we might say, a heteronormative temporality) into something much queerer: "a perennial ritual of social aid and pleasure."[178] The idea of such a ritual recalls Gilda's practice of taking blood; it's a moment of pleasure, rather than fear, that leaves those she feeds on with a fond dream, possibly even one powerful enough to improve their waking lives. Transformation is a powerful thing; and although not synonymous with progress, it is surely a necessary condition for hope—a hope that drives the many queer and trans communities and activists of New Orleans. As Johnson writes, "people of all backgrounds are working to transform bloody streets [in New Orleans] into places of justice and peace, in part through "stories remind[ing] us . . . that pretensions to unbounded power have been—and must be—checked by the determination of the defiant."[179] The queer "monstrosity" of New Orleans—as with other southern spaces—is best understood as a space of layered stories, its transformational potential underwritten by both hope and trauma.

Good Times at the End Times

In the first season of *True Blood*, our protagonist Sookie finds herself on two dates in quick succession: the first with Bill Compson, a Confederate soldier turned vampire, and the second with Sam, her human boss. When Sam finds out Sookie has been out with Bill, he's angry: "you've got no future with him," he yells. Sookie shoots back, "I've got nothing *but* a future with him."[180] This exchange sets the terms of the debate that we see played out across *Lost Souls* and *The Gilda Stories*, as well as within the field of queer theory. In his monstrosity, his untamed hunger, his closeness to Death, does the vampire/queer subject represent a pure (and purely nihilistic) opposition to reproductive futurity, even to futurity writ large? Or, in her alterity, her radical relationality, her long history, does she represent the dream of a nonnormative and vitally necessary futurity? If we return to Halberstam's identification of the vampire as a "meaning machine," the answer is, of course, both.

The vampires of *Lost Souls* align with Edelman's "sinthomosexual" nonsubject—cultural symbol of queer nonreproductivity, annihilating jouissance, inherently opposed to kinship structures and an illusory futurity promising happiness and wholeness.[181] The queer embraces the dissolution of subjecthood and refuses to be taken in by what Edelman calls the "puppet of humanism."[182] The vampires of *Lost Souls* certainly chime with this formulation of queerness—their wild life of drinking, drugs, sex, and killing for blood is all about self-shattering enjoyment.[183] When Nothing leaves behind his striving parents, the Maryland suburbs, and his name for the gothic South, he ostensibly moves away from the illusory futurity of a humanist progress narrative and toward a figuration of the death drive. But the problem is that Nothing is always searching for a family, always searching for a more magical (happy, whole) life—strivings after social organization and meaning that are precluded by queer negativity. Despite the void that is Nothing's name, the better figure for the embrace of the sinthomosexual is Zillah, whose name, fittingly, means "shadow": his relentless pursuit of jouissance makes him look rather like a two-dimensional narcissist. Notoriously, Muñoz labeled Edelman's particular brand of posthumanism "the white gay man's last stance"; we might apply this "last stand" argument to Zillah.[184] In its broad anti-identitarianism, the effect of this approach to queer monstrosity is a lack of empathy for the lives of others, resulting finally in the reinscription of a social hierarchy in which he conveniently resides at the top. In this, we might well link Zillah associatively to the statue that Ghost observes in Jackson Square, celebrating US imperialism within a southern aesthetic that invokes a different kind of "last stand": "Andrew Jackson rear[ing] up on his horse, sour-faced and pigeon-spotted, challenging the giant magnolias that surrounded the square."[185]

The critique that seeks to annihilate "the subject" ironically reinstates the universality of a white male subject and banishes understandings of those who, finding their futures already threatened, might not be so quick to reject the hope of futurity. As Sharon Holland has argued, the call for a subjectless feminism not only loses the complexity of theorizing lived experiences of race and gender, but can constitute a rejection of earlier theorists like Lorde, whose epigraph, from the prologue to her *Collected Poems*, introduces *The Gilda Stories*: "sometimes at noon I dream / there is nothing to fear. . . ."[186] Muñoz's assertion in *Cruising Utopia* that "queer feminist and queer of color critiques are the powerful counterweight to the antirelational" captures the spirit of Gomez's imagining of vampiric life.[187] Queer monstrosity as a collectivity embraces multiple marginalized subject positions to insistently occupy "the 'should be' of utopia, its indeterminacy and its deployment of hope . . . against capitalism's ever expanding and exhausting force field."[188] Gilda's awareness of how different subjects can be differently marginalized and othered, her experience of deep time, her distrust of capitalist as well as nationalist ideologies, her insistence on staking a claim to utopia even on a land that's dying—all of these are very much in line with Muñoz's vision.[189] For Gilda, to be a vampire is to insist upon a past and a future as much as a present.

Whether frozen in a youthful present or embodying centuries of weighty history, the vampire has a queer relationship to time—that is, one in some way "out of joint," in Freeman's words.[190] The way "the South" functions in popular culture (as in *True Blood*) posits southern temporality as queer, too: not linear or stable in shape and rate, driving us ever toward progress, but subject to stagnation, curves, odd accelerations and slowdowns. This monstrous space is fitting for vampires: Gilda and Zillah both, their distinct models of queerness dwelling uncomfortably adjacent to one another. When Sookie defends her future with Bill, she does so from the dark swampiness of Bon Temps—"Good Times"—and it is, really, what constitutes "good time" (and, relatedly, good place) that comes into question. No future or nothing but a future: these options hang together in the humid air. I have argued that the borders of "the South" begin to shift and dissolve at the vampire's touch—just as the vampire becomes visible as an ever-replicating and changeable story. Through that changing story, the monstrosity of queerness gives us multiple ways of understanding southern space within national, postnational, and global imaginaries; and southern monstrosity consolidates a temporally and ideologically deviant space from which to stage distinct narratives arising out of conflicting models of queer relationality.

Counter to Auerbach's prediction in 1998, vampirism is not "need[ing] a long restorative sleep."[191] On the contrary, vampires are enduringly popular for their ability to help us imagine transformation—to inspire, as Nurka puts it, "radical challenges to 'the human' as configured through the binaries of human/animal, human/nonhuman, sex/gender, hetero/homo.... epistemological upheavals [that] can effect a powerful theoretical becoming."[192] Anne Rice's *Interview with the Vampire* has recently enjoyed a revamp in which the relationship between Louis and Lestat is made explicitly queer. The Frenchman first takes his "little drink" of Louis—in this adaptation a Black man in early-twentieth-century New Orleans—during a lurid sex scene. The city itself is opulent, decadent, but its pleasures are initially limited for Louis; as he tells it, "In New Orleans you could be a lot of things, but a gay, Black man wasn't one of them."[193] He finds that he can be, however, a gay Black vampire. He tells his story from a great distance (in Dubai, 2022) to an older journalist who has of late been preoccupied with other kinds of monsters: COVID, Putin, and his own decline to Parkinson's disease. The show's first episode teases, through this cynical journalist, the idea that we are creeping toward midnight on humanity's "doomsday clock." Louis's story is one he needs badly: by no means utopian, it nevertheless offers a scene of wonder, transformation, and monstrous becoming, a beginning (however bloody) rather than an end. The viewer, too, might find hope in this story—and, in the New Orleans set, the sexy fangs, the palimpsests of performances past—a queer southernness that spills out over its limits, and gestures perhaps unsettlingly to the ways we spill out over the imagined borders of our own lives.

Coda
Dragging Southernness

• •

In September of 2022, my partner and I attended Pride in Murfreesboro, Tennessee—small as prides go, in a park designed to take visitors back to the Civil War era: Cannonsburgh Village, dedicated to "represent[ing] 100 years of early Tennessee life from the 1830s to the 1930s."[1] Rainbow flags paired curiously with log cabins. Queer couples held hands and admired one of the park's main attractions, the "World's Largest Cedar Bucket." Although the park was bordered by angry citizens with signs warning of God's wrath, the event was scrappy and welcoming, with booths for inclusive churches, family-friendly attorneys, and theatre collectives. We collected the usual mix of vibrant local art and corporatized rainbow swag. There were karaoke booths, food trucks—and, closing our small-town pride with spirit and style, a drag show that evening. A little over a month later, word came down that the city would not renew the license for Pride the next year, due to *"the exposure of children to a harmful prurient interest . . . inconsistent with the community standards of Murfreesboro"* in a public space.[2] In language and sentiment, the fate of pride in Murfreesboro presaged the wider drag ban to be proposed in Tennessee in early 2023.[3] My home state once again made news for all the wrong reasons. Most obviously, the bill situated queerness as antithetical to an obscure standard of community decency, and claimed to protect children, paragons of the future, against "prurient interest" (a "protective" impulse, as many have already argued, that would be better directed toward the NRA). In the flood of reactions against the proposed ban, it didn't take long before a high-school yearbook photograph surfaced: Tennessee's governor, Bill Lee, wearing a skirt and heels. Although it baffles the mind that the emergence of such a photo would come as a surprise to Governor Lee, his shocked indignance at being compared to the drag performers he indicted was remarkable: "What a ridiculous, ridiculous question that is[,] . . . conflating something like that to sexualized entertainment in front of children, which is a very serious question."[4]

This response—the apparent amazement that anyone would compare *his* cross-dressing to that of drag artists—would seem to betray a fundamental belief that the effect of a performance is stable and predictable based on the intent behind it. How could anyone mistake the harmless fun of a straight white man for the "sexualized entertainment" of deviants? But of course, performance is never stable in its effects. It risks escaping the limits of our intentions, taking on myriad meanings, possibilities, and fantasies for those who see it.

The anger of Lee's response points to the threat that drag poses to white southern masculinity. I've spent the pages of this book tracing the many ways that southernness and queerness align; but when it comes to patriarchy, they often seem to repel one another with the force of two magnets. The plantation myth that serves as an urtext for white southern masculinity and femininity is built on an exalted paternalism; and on a smaller scale, of course, patriarchy describes the source and the expression of the white man's privilege that dominates much of the South politically—the kind that abhors "identity politics." Queerness, on the other hand, is fundamentally opposed to patriarchy in theory and in practice: in its form, its temporality, and its history, patriarchy is the ultimate form of normativity. It's the structure of oppression that feminists and queer activists have spent a lifetime fighting.

A drag performance in a space claimed as southern, or by someone claiming a southern identity, has the potential to bring these loyalties—these politics—into conflict. That conflict is especially sharp when the southernness at stake (those "community standards") has its roots in the delicate constellation of gender, race, and class arising out of Old South fantasy. The southern belle and cavalier gentleman have been well-circulated in American culture, particularly in the twentieth century, as genteel and romantic figures. Magnolias, hoop skirt, white suit. But that gentility, of course, is at once created and threatened by a parallel iconography of Blackness: the predatory, powerful sexuality of the Black man and the perpetual sexual receptivity of the Black woman. The plantation romance was long a site of erotic interest for its national readership, and still, the figures of the belle and the cavalier are not legible without the shadow of racialized sexual violence.[5]

The southern lady always needs protection from the white gentleman, whether from the ravenous Black man, or from the aggression of the North. Her (white) femininity, the gentleman's (white) masculinity, and the South itself, are coextensive effects of this oft-told (and eroticized) story. As Mr. Compson tells Quentin in *Absalom, Absalom!*, "years ago we in the South made our women into ladies. Then the War came along and made the ladies into ghosts" (7). Although he posits the South as a landscape of creation, and the War as the event of its destruction, he might also have said that making women into ladies made a region into the South; or that stories of "the War" multiplied those ladies, and by replication they became ghosts—traces, simulacra. As McPherson writes, in the wake of the war, the "hyperfeminized figure of the southern woman" became a "discursive figure for the region," to be written and rewritten ad infinitum.[6]

Crucially, southern femininity, which does the work of reinforcing sexual, racial, and regional difference, is inextricable from "a notion of masquerade or performance"; think Scarlett O'Hara, using her wiles to accomplish exactly what she wants.[7] Paradoxically, "real" southern femininity is both naturally white and pure, *and* expertly "put on." This performative aspect of southern femininity has by no means died away; it's still visible in cultural traditions like pageantry and debutante balls, in which a "passing" southern femininity relies on highly specific dress codes and expertly made-up faces. It's visible in the enduringly popular discourse about what it means to be a "modern" southern woman: a 2011 *Garden & Gun* feature on "Redefining the Southern Woman," for example, features an image of a (white) woman in a white blouse, a magnolia in her hair.[8] The article begins with a claim to authenticity through distinctiveness ("Southern women are different. That is a fact.") and goes on to defend that authenticity as an effect of "rules[,] . . . expectations[,] . . . the basic template, which is, fundamentally[,] . . . Southern women make the effort." That means a good portion of the day given over to time in front of the makeup mirror; it means "never leaving the house with wet hair. Not even in the case of fire." The "fact" of Southern femininity is a function of history, the article argues—but it's expressed through a lot of very intentional daily work.

The icon of southern hyperfeminization might well be Dolly Parton, with her perfect hair (who could ever imagine seeing Dolly's hair wet?), high voice, exaggerated figure, and long nails. Dolly is, notoriously, an icon to both southern and queer audiences for precisely this reason—possibly more so than for her music, brilliant though it is. Famously, she quipped that if she hadn't been born a girl, she "would've had to be a drag queen";[9] on a talk show, she once told a story of entering and losing a Dolly drag contest.[10] This is surely a strong argument for the performative quality of southern femininity—but more than that, Dolly, with her self-deprecating stories and her instantly recognizable laugh, links performativity to play and humor—key aspects of the queerness of drag.[11]

At least in the terms of queer theory, masquerade is a form of play—and of storytelling. To masquerade is to imagine oneself as another, occupying a different life than one's own. Play can be quite queer: in Halberstam's words, "being taken seriously means missing out on the chance to be frivolous[;] . . . terms like *serious* and *rigorous* . . . do not allow for visionary insights or flights of fancy."[12] For drag queens, the imaginative play involved in conceptualizing a character and performing hyperfemininity is connected to Muñoz's disidentification: seeking to change a system from within it.[13] To inhabit femininity as a social construction, rather than a natural state, is subversive, liberatory. As Butler writes, "woman itself is a term in process, a becoming, a constructing that cannot rightfully be said to originate or to end. As an ongoing discursive practice, it is open to intervention and resignification." Drag, in highlighting the constructedness of gender, is a political act.[14]

Southern gender conventions, and white southern femininity especially, are particularly "drag"able because they are already highly imitative: performative, well-circulated, and accordingly ripe for parody that deconstructs the idea of a natural gender. But as Lauryl Tucker writes, the effects of parody are "unpredictable and unproductive"; parody is "reliable neither as a formal way to re-dress late capitalism in ever-spiffier suits, nor as an inherent form of redress."[15] The capacity of the white southern lady to tip over easily into drag (which by extension drags white southern masculinity) by no means makes her an inherently radical figure. The belle's hyperfeminization, even if it suggests gender as performative, does not necessarily subvert gender roles—nor complicate sharp demarcations along lines of class and race.[16]

I'm thinking of Capote's *Other Voices, Other Rooms*, in which Joel, the displaced child at the center of the novel, glimpses a "queer lady" in the window.[17] Unbeknownst to Joel, the woman is his Uncle Randolph, in evening gown and wig, donning the costume he wore to a masquerade ball to which he can never return. That masquerade, for Randolph, was a joyful performance of gender parody; but now he repeats the performance in isolation. He moves through dissipated days in a dilapidated plantation house, living on the dregs of family wealth, caring for Joel's disabled father, bickering with his neurotic sister, and relying on the service of their Black servant, Missouri. Their lives are farcical shadows of Old South fantasy; he and his sister have already queered southern masculinity and femininity before he ever puts on a dress, although to no particularly progressive effect. In drag (alone), he is more vividly a ghost of the southern gothic than an embodiment of queer possibility—Joel, seeing the ghostly face in the window, comes to the conclusion that the house is haunted. And of course, the house *is* haunted: by the traumas of racialized and gendered violence, by the specter of wealth possessed and lost, and by the loneliness of thwarted connections and forbidden desires. The room in which Randolph puts on white southern femininity is a densely pressurized space of southern and queer deviance. But whether the sight of the face in the window ultimately expands or constricts Joel's world is up for debate. And as for the ghost—that room is not a space of empowerment for Randolph, nor even a space he can truly escape.

If masquerade is another term linking southernness and queerness, where do such performances take shape in a way that proves generative rather than claustrophobic? One answer, once again, might lie in the capacity of many Souths to exist beside one another, and thus to speak to one another, to open doors, to layer performances of regional and queer attachment. There's the Atlanta of debutante balls, and there's the Atlanta of RuPaul; the Memphis of the elite country clubs of Peter Taylor's fiction, and the Memphis of "Atomic Rose," a drag bar featuring performances by Bella DuBalle[18]; there's the Ole Miss of Faulkner's ghost, strolling through the Grove in his white suit and corncob pipe, and the Ole Miss of the little stage in that same park, the site of drag shows past and, I hope, future. It's worth saying again: I want to avoid an unmerited optimism in any inherent queer potential of "Old South" gender conventions. Bill Lee, a few years after he posed in drag for his high school yearbook, was pictured dressed as a Confederate soldier, standing next to a woman dressed as a southern belle, at an "Old South" party at Auburn University.[19] To compare this masquerade to drag would no doubt also seem "ridiculous" to him—as it does to me, since it in no way "drags" the values of Dixie. And yet to place these two images of Lee side by side has the potential to complicate, for an observer, the value of both. The photos compose a micro-archive that hums with unstable interactions: between South and nation, past and present, disguise and demasking, masculinity and femininity, queer possibility and violent heteronormativity.

Those interactions matter. Telling stories of southernness and queerness is a way of exploring the many shifting forms of kinship between them, and in doing so, of widening our visions, our expectations, and our dialogues about what both terms can mean. In this book, I've sought to trace some of those forms of connection. And yet we don't live in an abstract, theoretical world, but in a concrete, political one. Even when queerness and southernness share conceptual frameworks, the on-the-ground experience of queer and southern identities can often feel irreconcilable. "The South" is undeniably a red political bloc, curtailing LGBTQ rights and leaning in hard to an enforcement of heteronormativity and white privilege. Not only self-expression, but lives, are under threat in states like Tennessee. A drag ban, at its insidious core, is not only a restriction on so-called "sexualized entertainment," but a restriction on any form of antinormative gender expression, and especially trans identities—all the more so for people of color, who doubly threaten the sanctity of southern gender conventions and, by extension, "community standards." It must be said that in such a place, stories of queer southernness can feel like paltry refuge.

Shortly before Tennessee's drag bans were set to take effect in April of 2023, the artist Lizzo performed in Knoxville. She brought a group of drag queens on stage with her for the finale, speaking explicitly to their act of resistance: "I was told by people on the internet, 'Don't go to Tennessee' . . . but why would I not come to the people who need to hear this message the most? The people who need to feel this release the most?"[20] This might strike a familiar note, gesturing to a story that still needs debunking: that the South is a backwards place, and we need missionaries to shine a light because we won't find it ourselves down here. And yet these were local drag performers, and Lizzo wasn't wrong: her audience *did* need to feel the release she offered, to see a different kind of southern community onstage, and to cultivate forms of allyship that both embrace and transcend regional identifications.

There's been a great deal of important work in making queerness outside of dominant coastal urban cities more visible: *Queer as Folk*, *We're Here*, and the reboot of *Queer Eye*, for example, make a point of telling stories—true and fictional—of queer life in southern spaces.[21] But it's a different experience entirely to attend a concert and find queerness there in abundance, radiating from Lizzo and those Tennessee drag queens and from the audience who cheered them on: performative, real, playful, political. Lizzo's song "Everybody's Gay," from her 2022 album *Special*, keys into that feeling of community—one emerging from a paradoxical relationship between authenticity and masquerade:

> Tonight I wanna be nobody else (nobody else)
> This costume feels so real, almost scared myself[22]

The "real" here is not incompatible with the costume, and being "nobody else" is a choice, a desire, that doesn't conscribe the speaker to a singular "me." The "freaky ball" she describes, in which everyone is "play[ing] dress up," queerly collapses the debutante ball and the monster ball: there's a not-so-coy Mona Lisa alongside "sisters drinking bitches brew." When she sings that "we can take our mask off," it's an *us*—a community—that finds freedom in the removal of a singular mask, and that same community that finds pleasure in the donning of many scarily real costumes. This image resonates with C. Riley Snorton's theorization of transness as "attentive to the possibilities of valorizing—without necessarily redeeming—different ways of knowing and being" and "invested in reviving and inventing strategies for inhabiting unlivable worlds."[23]

Those unlivable worlds are everywhere—even, at times, the very sites where we're promised livability. Lizzo's support of the LGBTQ community at her show in Knoxville was widely celebrated, but in the autumn of that same year, allegations arose that she had created a hostile work environment, characterized by body shaming and sexual harassment. I followed Lizzo's denial of these accusations, the Twitter (X?) storm, the debates among disappointed and defensive fans, the articles that denounced her as "progressivecore"—politically progressive, that is, only as an aesthetic, a style, to be put on and taken off at will.[24] This term suggests another type of masquerade: the successful performer who garners fame and wealth by championing inclusion onstage, but does the opposite behind the scenes. It gestures to the terrible, always-present possibility that what appears to be queer antinormativity, a bold and vital deviance, is anything but. As of this writing, I don't know how the Lizzo story ends, but I point to it as an example of how the violence of late capitalism creeps into the precarious utopianism of our monster balls.

Still, we can search out ways to inhabit our unlivable world. Still, we can search for moments—at a concert, at other localized scenes of joyful community—that hold the potential not only to reconcile southernness and queerness, but to actively join them. In these moments, however small or fleeting, we practice forms of kinship that serve as homing devices: home to ourselves, to the stories we read and live through, to hope.

Notes

Introduction

1. Nicolaou, "Watch *Tiger King's* Joe Exotic."
2. p*op dealer, "If Tiger King has taught me anything"; Chris Gonzalez, "Tiger King is delivering": soft era Cris, "Y'all Tiger King on Netflix."
3. Yurcaba, "DeSantis Signs 'Don't Say Gay' Expansion."
4. See Martyn Bone's introduction to *Creating and Consuming the American South*: "contemporary responses to the suburbanization, modernization, or homogenization of Dixie are fairly consistent with those narratives of decline and endurance, invasion and resistance, that have shaped discussions of southern identity for decades" (2).
5. See Smith, "For They Know Not What They Do," and Romine, *The Real South*.
6. See particularly the work of Jon Smith, Scott Romine, Tara McPherson, Jennifer Rae Greeson, and Leigh Anne Duck. Duck's phrasing here can be found in "Southern Nonidentity" (329.)
7. See Greeson, *Our South*, introduction.
8. Greeson, *Our South*, 3.
9. See Lassiter, et al, *The Myth of Southern Exceptionalism*: "In rejecting the framework of southern exceptionalism, we are not arguing that there are no variations among regions. . . . but by the second half of the twentieth century, if not well before, focusing on the South's aberrant qualities compared to the rest of the US obscures much more than it reveals about the fundamental questions of modern American history" (12).
10. Duck, *The Nation's Region*, 18.
11. See Romine, *The Real South*; Bone, Ward, and Link, *Creating and Consuming the American South*; and Hinrichsen, *Possessing the Past*.
12. McPherson, *Reconstructing Dixie*, 17.
13. See also Cox, *Dreaming of Dixie*.
14. Brasell, *Possible South*, 8.
15. For these theorizations in relation to the South's discursivity, see, respectively, Brasell, *The Possible South* (citing Edward Said's *Orientalism*); McPherson, *Reconstructing Dixie* (citing Benedict Anderson's *Imagined Communities*); and Romine, *The Real South* (citing Slavoj Žižek's *The Plague of Fantasies*).
16. Greeson, *Our South*, 10.
17. See Saturday Night Live, "Colonel Angus Comes Home."
18. Bibler, "Queer/Quare," 202.
19. Harker, *The Lesbian South*, 100.
20. "The ACLU is tracking."

21. For more on rurality and queerness, see Johnson, *Just Queer Folks*, and Herring, *Another Country: Queer Anti-Urbanism*. As Rosenthal (*Living Queer History*) points out, a 2019 study identified the South as home to more LGBTQ people than any other region (7).

22. Rosenthal, *Living Queer History*, 3.

23. For a survey of some of these "hip" Souths and their histories, see Bingham and Freeman, *The Bohemian South*. See also Howard, *Carryin' on in the Lesbian and Gay South*.

24. See Halberstam, *In a Queer Time and Place*. See also Herring, "Southern Backwardness."

25. See Halberstam, *The Queer Art of Failure*, Love, *Feeling Backward*, and Ahmed, *The Promise of Happiness*, respectively.

26. Nyong'o, "Do You Want Queer Theory," 103. Although I'm simplifying the relational/anti-relational divide here, Nyong'o argues persuasively that there are "grounds for moving queer politics beyond the 'binary stalemate' of having to choose between resisting the hegemonic fantasy of the homosexual or acceding to it" (107).

27. Ruti, *The Ethics of Opting Out*.

28. Bradway and Freeman, *Queer Kinship*, 3.

29. Ruti, *The Ethics of Opting Out*, 37.

30. Johnson, "'Quare' studies," 5.

31. Manalansan, "Messing Up Sex," 1288.

32. Cohen, "Punks, Bulldaggers, and Welfare Queens," 142.

33. See also Davis, *Southscapes*: as Davis argues, the South remains a "spatial object and ideological landscape" with "persistent conceptual power" in making "matters of race . . . both opaque and transparent" (2).

34. See Spillers, "Mama's Baby, Papa's Maybe."

35. Hale, *Making Whiteness*, 3. See also Lassiter and Crespino, *The Myth of Southern Exceptionalism*.

36. See Joshi and Desai, *Asian Americans in Dixie*.

37. Holland, *Erotic Life*, 11. See also Somerville, *Queering the Color Line*: "the challenge is to recognize the instability of multiple categories of difference simultaneously rather than to assume the fixity of one to establish the complexity of another" (5).

38. See also Smith, "Toward a Post-Postpolitical Southern Studies": "Like 'late' capitalism, the 'postmodern condition' . . . is hardly something one can imagine oneself out of," and New Southern Studies does well to turn to realities of regional experience (83).

39. Johnson, *Sweet Tea*, 6–7.

40. See Johnson's oral histories of Black queer life in the South, *Sweet Tea* and the more recent *Black. Queer. Southern. Women*. Other examples of works in this category include John Howard's *Men Like That*, Johnson's *Just Queer Folks*, Allen's *Real Queer America* (2019), and Rosenthal's *Living Queer History* (2021).

41. In addition to Richards and Bibler, see also Pugh's *Precious Perversions* and *Queer Chivalry* and Gordon's *Gay Faulkner*. Pugh's work argues for the inclusion of more gay comic voices into the southern canon and interrogates the literary repre-

sentation of Southern forms of masculinity; Gordon's work gives the southern literary patriarch a place in gay history.

42. Bibler, *Cotton's Queer Relations*, 2.
43. Richards, *Lovers and Beloveds*, 2.
44. Quoted in Carr, *Understanding Carson McCullers* (9).
45. Brasell, "The Degeneration of Nationalism," 53.
46. As Harker writes, 'The South has long been associated with deviant sexuality . . . This creates an unexpected bridge between the South and queer theory, for which deviance is a site of resistance against the normative. Most southern lesbian feminist writers in this study embraced the southern grotesque as a way to explore a wide range of hitherto unspeakable sexual practices" (*The Lesbian South,* 16).
47. For a history of this shift, see Fetner, *How the Religious Right Shaped Lesbian and Gay Activism*.
48. See Bone, Ward, and Link, *Creating and Consuming the American South*.
49. See Ashby, *With Amusement for All*.
50. And earlier: I'm thinking here of the documentary work of James Agee and Erskine Caldwell, their highlighting of the peculiar region's vexed relation with "the modern."
51. See Thompson, *American Culture in the 1980s*.
52. McPherson, *Reconstructing Dixie*, 18.
53. See for example Nagourney, "The Sun Belt, Eclipsed," and Guillory, "From Nixon to Trump."
54. Jameson, *The Political Unconscious*, x.
55. Waugh, *Metafiction*, 2.
56. See Waugh, *Metafiction*, and Hutcheon, *Narcissistic Narrative*.
57. Hutcheon, *Narcissistic Narrative*, 8.
58. For these theorists, as in my work, the vocabulary of narratology arises from structuralist and Russian formalist origins, as well as the reader response theories of critics such as Wolfgang Iser and Stanley Fish.
59. See Hutcheon's 2013 preface to her 1980 monograph, *Narcissistic Narrative*.
60. Chadd, *Postsouthern*, 23.
61. See Kreyling, *The South That Wasn't There*.
62. Chadd, *Postregional Fictions*, 29.
63. Hutcheon, *Narcissistic Narrative*, 13.
64. Horton-Stallings, *Dirty South Manifesto*, 5–9.
65. Phelan ("Narrative Ethics") identifies two wings of the "ethical turn" in narrative theory since the 1980s: poststructuralist narrative ethics, after Levinas, brings our attention to the immutable alterity of the Other, whereas humanist ethics emphasizes the importance of connection across difference.
66. Booth, "Why Ethical Criticism," 354.
67. For a more in-depth analysis of this argument, see Bradway, "Queer Narrative Theory."
68. Bradway, "Queer Narrative Theory," 712.
69. Edelman, *Bad Education*, 19; Fawaz, *Queer Forms*, 6.
70. Wiegman, "Eve's Triangles," 57.
71. hooks, "Theory as Liberatory Practice," 59–60.

Chapter 1

1. Romine, "God and the Moon Pie," 50.
2. Davis and Powell, *Writing in the Kitchen*, 13; Stokes and Atkins-Sayre, *Consuming Identity*, 6.
3. See, for example, the work of the Southern Foodways Alliance at the University of Mississippi.
4. See Ferris, *The Edible South*, and Twitty, *The Cooking Gene*.
5. Ferris, *The Edible South*, 189. See also Stanonis, "Just Like Mammy Used to Make." As Stanonis writes, "Southern food," rather than describing a set of dishes, has long been that which suggests a way of "preserving the region's mores" against the impact of modernity, as well as "fortify[ing] [a] commitment to Jim Crow" (216).
6. See Berlant, *The Female Complaint*: Aunt Jemima's "condensation of racial nostalgia, white national memory, and progressive history was a symptomatic, if not important, vehicle for post–Civil War national consolidation" (122).
7. Stanonis, "Just Like Mammy Used to Make," 226. So, too, we see that echo in the KFC Colonel.
8. Ferris, *The Edible South*, 323.
9. Duffin-Ward, *Suddenly Southern*, 67.
10. For more on the natural foods movement that emerged in southern states in the 1970s, see Ferris, *The Edible South*: "Many first-time members of southern food co-ops became more deeply entrenched in the counterculture, as well as in the continuing civil rights movement, in part because of food" (308–09).
11. Tompkins, *Racial Indigestion*, 5.
12. Tompkins, *Racial Indigestion*, 5.
13. See Berlant, *Cruel Optimism*: "Eating . . . is best seen as activity releasing the subject into self-suspension" (116).
14. See Probyn, *Carnal Appetites*: "The ways that sex and eating intersect" reflects that "eating refracts who we are[,] . . . as alimentary assemblages, eating recalls with force the elemental nature of class gender, sexuality, nation" (33).
15. Scott, *Extravagant Abjection*, 17.
16. Tompkins, *Racial Indigestion*, 3.
17. For a brief history of this trend, see Deans, "A History of Eating Disorders."
18. Engelhardt, "Beating the Biscuits," 159.
19. Hatherley, "Pleasures of 'Unfit' Femininities," 67.
20. McPherson, *Reconstructing Dixie*, 18.
21. See Brooks, *Reading for the Plot*: framed narratives "speak of the investments of desire on the parts of both addresser and addressee, author and reader, a place of rhetorical exchange or transaction. The two most predominant motivations for storytelling, as Brooks sees it, are seduction and aggression, both "inextricably linked to the erotic" (236).
22. All reviews here, including Harper Lee's, are taken from the novel's inside cover.
23. Ebert, "Fried Green Tomatoes."
24. Flagg, *Fried Green Tomatoes*, 37.
25. "The Vocabularist."

26. See Duck, *The Nation's Region*: "Increasingly, after the Civil War, the dominant national time was understood to be that of capitalist modernity . . . regional cultures . . . were understood to be shaped by tradition (5).

27. Flagg, *Fried Green Tomatoes*, 8.

28. Flagg, *Fried Green Tomatoes*, 101.

29. Flagg, *Fried Green Tomatoes*, 95.

30. That is to say that Whistle Stop participates in the economy of late capitalism even as it mourns its arrival. See Romine: In "the late South" of our contemporary moment, "nostalgia—utopianism with a backward glance—function[s] as both a discrete industry and a diffuse cultural practice in a South whose past is almost uniformly undesirable" (*The Real South*, 24).

31. Flagg, *Fried Green Tomatoes*, 9, 212.

32. Flagg, *Fried Green Tomatoes*, 5

33. Flagg, *Fried Green Tomatoes*, 4.

34. Flagg, *Fried Green Tomatoes*, 6.

35. Flagg, *Fried Green Tomatoes*, 73–74.

36. Flagg, *Fried Green Tomatoes*, 244.

37. Flagg, *Fried Green Tomatoes*, 244.

38. Wallace-Sanders, *Mammy*, 3. See also McPherson: "The wishful figuration of Mammy as keeper of white femininity echoes life in the early-twentieth-century South while erasing the networks of power that controlled black women' bodies and mobility in that era" (*Reconstructing Dixie*, 55).

39. Flagg, *Fried Green Tomatoes*, 241, 67.

40. Flagg, *Fried Green Tomatoes*, 84.

41. See Anderson, *Imagined Communities*: the newspaper allows us to conceive of ourselves as part of a national whole because seemingly disparate events are placed in the news layout on the same page, under the same date, suggesting invisible threads connecting citizens (33). The news strip, on the other hand, undermines that project, emphasizing the isolation of the singular region—Birmingham, for example.

42. See Felski, *The Limits of Critique*: the critic has long functioned as detective, reading suspiciously searching out clues and determining how everything relates to everything else in a text that reveals itself to her scrutiny—a reading style that contributes to the critic's image as "archaeologist who 'digs deep'" or "ironist who 'stands back'" (7).

43. Flagg, *Fried Green Tomatoes*, 5.

44. Flagg, *Fried Green Tomatoes*, 157.

45. Flagg, *Fried Green Tomatoes*, 62

46. Flagg, *Fried Green Tomatoes*, 44

47. See Butler, *Gender Trouble*: "Drag is an example that is meant to establish that 'reality' is not as fixed as we generally assume it to be. The purpose . . . is to expose the tenuousness of gender 'reality' in order to counter the violence performed by gender norms" (xxv).

48. Flagg, *Fried Green Tomatoes*, 60.

49. Flagg, *Fried Green Tomatoes*, 63.

50. Flagg, *Fried Green Tomatoes*, 9.
51. Flagg, *Fried Green Tomatoes*, 10.
52. Flagg, *Fried Green Tomatoes*, 10.
53. Flagg, *Fried Green Tomatoes*, 18.
54. Flagg, *Fried Green Tomatoes*, 9.
55. Flagg, *Fried Green Tomatoes*, 75.
56. Flagg, *Fried Green Tomatoes*, 44.
57. Flagg, *Fried Green Tomatoes*, 43.
58. See Tompkins, *Racial Indigestion*, and bell hooks, "Eating the other."
59. Flagg, *Fried Green Tomatoes*, 45.
60. Flagg, *Fried Green Tomatoes*, 44.
61. Flagg, *Fried Green Tomatoes*, 46.
62. Although I read the text as connecting white queerness to blackness in this way, structuring them as similar, it should be emphasized that white queerness and blackness are not comparable identity positions, nor do they have comparable histories as objects of consumption (for more on this, see Tompkins). I use the term "abjection" after Scott's theorization in *Extravagant Abjection*, referring both to a history of "traumatizing violent domination," from Fanon's theorization, and to Kristeva's "all-too-typically deracinated" psychoanalytical framework, adopted in much queer theory for the role of the abject in shattering the illusion of stable, bound subjecthood (5, 14).
63. Flagg, *Fried Green Tomatoes*, 5.
64. Flagg, *Fried Green Tomatoes*, 66.
65. Flagg, *Fried Green Tomatoes*, 69; Dunne, "Bakhtin Eats Some Fried Green Tomatoes," 30.
66. Flagg, *Fried Green Tomatoes*, 112.
67. Barbecue taps into a host of "southern" feelings. See Stokes, *Consuming Identity*, on the importance of "authenticity" in conversations around barbecue, and see also Opie, *Hog and Hominy*, and Ferris, *The Edible South*, on the racial oppression in the history of this cultural tradition.
68. Flagg, *Fried Green Tomatoes*, 359. For Artis, eating Frank is "something that would give him power when he was feeling weak . . . He would never have to feel the anger, the hurt, the humiliation of the others, ever again" (352).
69. Nunes, *Cannibal Democracy*.
70. Flagg, *Fried Green Tomatoes*, 300.
71. Flagg, *Fried Green Tomatoes*, 300.
72. Flagg, *Fried Green Tomatoes*, 296.
73. Nunes, *Cannibal Democracy*, 6.
74. Flagg, *Fried Green Tomatoes*, 298.
75. I'm using blackness-as-fever-dream here in the sense that Toni Morrison, in *Playing in the Dark*, understands the "Africanist presence" in United States literature, against which the white subject is constructed.
76. Flagg, *Fried Green Tomatoes*, 299.
77. Flagg, *Fried Green Tomatoes*, 78.

78. Flagg, *Fried Green Tomatoes*, 79.

79. Flagg, *Fried Green Tomatoes*, 80.

80. See Williams-Forson, *Building Houses Out of Chicken Legs*, for an analysis of the stereotype of fried chicken as a "Black" food. In this moment of identity formation and perhaps feminist consciousness—Idgie and Ruth go after their *own* pleasure, their *own*, female-directed erotic interests—Sipsey's work is central, although she does not get to consume her own meal.

81. Flagg, *Fried Green Tomatoes*, 314.

82. Flagg, *Fried Green Tomatoes*, 318.

83. See Evans, "Not Your Auntie," on the complicated history behind the term "auntie"—and its adjacency to the "mammy" image.

84. Nunes, *Cannibal Democracy*, 12.

85. Flagg, *Fried Green Tomatoes*, 200–202.

86. Flagg, *Fried Green Tomatoes*, 252.

87. Flagg, *Fried Green Tomatoes*, 336.

88. Credit goes to Jennifer Rae Greeson for finding this pun.

89. We can think of this temporal layering through the lens of what Freeman terms "queer time": queer time "elongates and twists chronology . . . generates its own discontinuous history" in the "lost moments of official history," of national narratives (*Time Binds*, xi).

90. Flagg, *Fried Green Tomatoes*, 361.

91. Flagg, *Fried Green Tomatoes*, 346.

92. Flagg, *Fried Green Tomatoes*, 367.

93. Flagg, *Fried Green Tomatoes*, 370.

94. For more on the tension between Mary Kay and second-wave feminism, see Kreydatus, "Enriching Women's Lives."

95. Flagg, *Fried Green Tomatoes*, 362.

96. For more on the late-capitalist commodification of southernness, see Romine, *The Real South*.

97. Flagg, *Fried Green Tomatoes*, 373.

98. Flagg, *Fried Green Tomatoes*, 376.

99. Flagg, *Fried Green Tomatoes*, 375.

100. See Parsons, "I Just Can't Wait to Get to Heaven": "Instead of emphasizing Ninny's memories of Klan violence, the devastating effects of poverty and hunger, and the decimation of the region's agricultural industry and primary source of livelihood, the novel uses the repetitive motif of southern cooking to tie the story firmly to the region, a motif that also enhances the text's nostalgic quality" (193).

101. Ebert, "Fried Green Tomatoes."

102. Ebert, "Fried Green Tomatoes."

103. Holmlund, "Cruisin' for a Bruisin'," 32.

104. Berglund, "The Secret's in the Sauce," 127.

105. Vickers, "*Fried Green Tomatoes*."

106. Egerton, "As God Is My Witness," 17.

107. Egerton, "As God Is My Witness," 18.

108. Smith, "Cultural Studies' Misfit," 376–77.

109. All cited reviews are printed in the edition of the cookbook referenced in the bibliography.

110. See Sontag, "Notes on Camp." "Not camp" is a slippery designation. Sontag's abstruse notes on what camp *is* make for a kind of Fight Club rule: "to talk about Camp is therefore to betray it" (1). And yet if we must talk about it, the essence of camp is "its love of the unnatural: of artifice and exaggeration" (1). *Not* camp, then, would mean *not* unnatural, *not* artificial, *not* exaggerated. The insistence on "genuine" here—especially coming from *Vogue*, a magazine devoted to the art(ifice) of style—seems to protest too much.

111. For more on the Ledbetter suit, see Smith, "Cultural Studies' Misfit."

112. Mickler, *White Trash Cooking*, 13, 94, 74.

113. To segregate soul food from "white trash food" according to "spice" and "variety" is a bizarre choice with clear ideological implications. In focusing, in this chapter, on the intersection between food and ideas of white southernness, space does not allow an exploration of the complex history of soul food, but see Opie's *Hog and Hominy* and Twitty's *The Cooking Gene*.

114. Smith, "Cultural Studies' Misfit," 370–71.

115. Smith, "Cultural Studies' Misfit," 374.

116. See also Taylor, "Untimely Subjects": white trash functions to "'trash' both Old South virtues and New South progress" in the popular imagination—accordingly, the burgeoning "cottage industry of 'white trash' cooking, etiquette and culture" constructs, through camp, a pose of racial innocence for the post-civil rights era (70, 73).

117. Hart, "Constellations," 17.

118. See Wray, *Not Quite White*: the class called white trash was "institutionalized as a banal social fact, resulting in the indignities of segregation and . . . harm of involuntary sterilization" (67). Southern states were prominent in the national imagination as the locale of this "degenerate" class: Carrie Buck, through Buck v. Bell, came to be "representative of an entire social group, the degenerate poor whites of the South" (92).

119. See Anderson, "Ernest Matthew Mickler, 48, Dies."

120. Sublette and Martin, "Let Them Eat Cake," 32.

121. Harker, *The Lesbian South*, 56.

122. Allison, interview by Kelly Anderson.

123. In Allison's introduction to the 2002 introduction of *Trash*, she meditates on the complexity of reclaiming the word trash, "tak[ing] it on deliberately, as I had 'dyke'." But the longer term *white trash*, she writes, cites too acutely to "the other side of the hatefulness in the words," producing instant discomfort in Black listeners. That discomfort "took me right back to being a girl and hearing the uncles I so admired spew racist bile and callous homophobic insults" (xv). Although I explore here how Allison reclaims "trash," this passage is significant for her declaration that "some phrases cannot be reclaimed" (xv).

124. Allison, *Trash*, 9.

125. Allison, *Trash*, 11.

126. Allison, *Trash*, 9, 13.
127. Allison, *Trash*, 12.
128. Allison, *Trash*, 11.
129. Allison, *Trash*, 87.
130. Allison, *Trash*, 87.
131. Allison, *Trash*, 85.
132. O'Connor, *The Complete Stories*, 121.
133. O'Connor, *The Complete Stories*, 122.
134. O'Connor, *The Complete Stories*, 121.
135. Allison, *Trash*, 76. See also Ellis, "Preface," *The Sexual Life of Savages*, who prefaces Malinowski's work with an interest in differentiating—and reveling in similarities between—the "savage" and the "civilized" man. To devour stories of the "savage," in other words, is to create an image of ourselves.
136. Allison, *Trash*, 77.
137. Allison, *Trash*, 131.
138. Allison, *Trash*, 136.
139. See Allison, interview by Kelly Anderson, for Allison's discussion of ideological battlegrounds within second-wave feminism.
140. Allison, *Trash*, 133
141. Allison, *Trash*, 129.
142. Allison, *Trash*, 146.
143. Allison, *Trash*, 169.
144. Lindenmeyer, "Lesbian Appetites," 477.
145. Allison, *Trash*, 165.
146. Allison, *Trash*, 172.
147. See Romine, "God and the Moon Pie," on the Moon Pie specifically as "guarantor of something called 'southern culture'" (51).
148. Allison, *Trash*, 162.
149. Jarvis, "Gendered Appetites," 764.
150. Jarvis, "Gendered Appetites," 769.
151. Allison, *Trash*, 163.
152. Cantrell, "Down Home and Out," 122.
153. Lindenmeyer, "Lesbian Appetites," 481.
154. Quoted in Harker, *The Lesbian South*, 53.
155. See Harker, *The Lesbian South*.
156. Twitty, *The Cooking Gene*, xii.

Chapter 2

1. Quoted in Crank, *Understanding Randall Kenan*, 10.
2. For more on the swampy South's role in understandings of the American wilderness and our ability to conquer and civilize it, see Smith, "Hot Bodies and 'Barbaric Tropics'."
3. Allewaert, *Ariel's Ecology*, 33. See also Wilson, *Shadow and Shelter*.
4. "Team Avatar vs. The Swampbenders."

5. Ahmed, *Queer Phenomenology*, 66.
6. Ahmed, *Queer Phenomenology*, 67–8.
7. Keeling, *Queer Times*, 17–18.
8. Keeling, *Queer Times*, 16, 36.
9. Keeling, *Queer Times*, 15, 18, 19, 32. See also Glissant, with whom Keeling is in dialogue. For Glissant, the swamp is a place that "resists" by taking us beyond the "separation" of the Plantation—here a figure for isolation—and instead draws us into an unmappable, disorienting, and ultimately sustaining *we* (*Poetics of Relation*, 206).
10. McKittrick, *Demonic Grounds*, 6, 17. See also Gopinath, *Unruly Visions*: queerness is "the conduit through which to experience the shadow histories of the past . . . shift[ing] our field of vision so that alternative possibilities, landscapes, and geographies come into view" beyond the "abiding legacy of . . . imperial, racial, and settler colonial projects" (16, 7, 9).
11. See Allewaert, *Ariel's Ecology*, and Wilson, *Shadow and Shelter*.
12. See McKittrick, *Demonic Grounds*: Black geographies form alternatives to the oppressive structures of "transparent space," which "assumes that geography—specifically, physical and material geographies—is readily knowable," an assumption that occludes the ways in which imperialist practices of domination have worked to keep "unruly deviant bodies 'in place'" (9).
13. Camp, *Closer to Freedom*, 7. Camp applies Edward Said's term, "rival geographies," to the contested terrains of the slaveholding South.
14. Alleawart, *Ariel's Ecology*, 38.
15. See Kuhn, "Garden Variety": "The existence of Maroon communities within North Carolina's Dismal Swamp has been well documented, although . . . the historical record has largely ignored their presence" (498).
16. Alleawart, *Ariel's Ecology*, 9.
17. Sayers, *A Desolate Place*, 5.
18. Thananopavarn, "Digging Up the Past," 204.
19. Johnson, *Just Queer Folk*, 18. See also Weston, "Get Thee to a Big City," and Halberstam, *In a Queer Time and Place*.
20. Griffin, *"Who Set You Flowin'?,"* 3, 5.
21. Horton-Stallings, *Dirty South Manifesto*, 1.
22. Bibler, *Cotton's Queer Relations*, 1, 2.
23. See Spillers, "Mama's Baby, Papa's Maybe": The enslaved body is weighted by "externally imposed meanings and uses[,] . . . the source of an irresistible, destructive sensuality" (67).
24. Kenan, *Black Folk Could Fly*, 264.
25. Kenan, *Black Folk Could Fly*, 36.
26. Kenan, interview by Charles Rowell, "An Interview with Randall Kenan," 139.
27. Harris, *The Power of the Porch*, 114.
28. Harris, *The Power of the Porch*, 194. See also Gates, *The Signifying Monkey*.
29. See also Guinn, *After Southern Modernism*: "Kenan struggles to clear a place for himself in the region's literature. Through his masterful Signifyin(g) on the recurrent tropes of African American fiction, he revitalizes the impulse of those, like Hurston and Wright, intent on expanding the discourse of southern culture" (140).

30. Kenan, *Visitation*, 13

31. Kenan, *Visitation*, 216. See also Herring's theorization of "queer urbanism," the ways in which the metropole is framed "as the epicenter of contemporary [queer] life" (*Another Country* 4–5).

32. Kenan, *Visitation*, 210.

33. Kenan, *Visitation*, 210.

34. Kenan, *Visitation*, 211.

35. Kenan, *Visitation*, 213. See also McMahand, "Strange Bedfellows," which argues that this actors' residence is a cue to Keenan's "intense rhetorical interplay" with the literature of the Southern Renaissance in the novel (44). My argument is in line with his conclusion that Kenan's work "radically reorients southern subjectivity" (51).

36. Kenan, *Visitation*, 222–23.

37. Kenan, *Visitation*, 223.

38. Kenan, *Visitation*, 225.

39. Kenan, *Visitation*, 232.

40. Walker, "Queering Black Nationalism," 70. Walker argues that this white face minstrelsy is Kenan's "critique of the ways in which black gay men's racial identities are negated because, as black nationalist rhetoric reminds us, authentic black men are not bisexual or gay" (70).

41. This possibility is suggested elsewhere in the novel as an option for Reverend Jimmy Greene, Horace's uncle. Jimmy remembers his mentor telling him, in a coded conversation about the kind of "curiosity" Jimmy has, to "go North, young man" (*Visitation*, 34).

42. Kenan, *Visitation*, 11.

43. Kenan, *Visitation*, 251. See also McRuer, "Queer Locations, Queer Transformations." McRuer critiques "the need to transport characters like Kenan's Horace Cross off to 'the big city'" as "symptomatic of a regional elision in queer theory generally . . . despite the hardships Horace endured, this rural setting is not simply the site of 'backwardness' or 'repression'. . . . Tims Creek, North Carolina, is a site of struggle and possible transformation" (185, 190).

44. Kenan, *Let the Dead*, 56.

45. Kenan, *Let the Dead*, 49, 56.

46. Kenan, *Let the Dead*, 54.

47. Kenan, *Let the Dead*, 69.

48. Kenan, *Let the Dead*, 59.

49. Kenan, *Let the Dead*, 59.

50. Kenan, *Let the Dead*, 50.

51. Kenan, *Let the Dead*, 72.

52. Kenan, *The Carolina Table*.

53. Kenan, *If I Had Two Wings*, 116.

54. Kenan, *If I Had Two Wings*, 114.

55. Kenan, *If I Had Two Wings*, 114.

56. Kenan, *If I Had Two Wings*, 140.

57. Kenan, *If I Had Two Wings*, 140.

58. Kenan, *If I Had Two Wings*, 114.

59. Hartman, *Lose Your Mother*, 169. As Hartman writes, to imagine the free territory is "the dream of an elsewhere, with all its promises and dangers" (234).

60. "Cane" here plays on Toomer's *Cane*, which, like Kenan's work, offers a multivocal and generically hybrid counter to a white southern pastoral. The name also invokes the Biblical Cain, progenitor of a "marked" race.

61. As an ethnographer in his own hometown, Greene occupies the complicated position that E. Patrick Johnson identifies, in *Black. Queer. Southern. Women*, of being both outsider and insider, (queerly) disoriented by this liminal positionality. Johnson quotes Della Pollock's account of this experience, which very much evokes the swamp: The ethnographer is "propelled into landscapes of knowing and not knowing I would not otherwise have dared enter" (12).

62. On multivocality, see Bakhtin, *Problems of Dostoevsky's Poetics*: "constructed not as the whole of a single consciousness, absorbing other consciousnesses as objects into itself, but as a whole formed by the interaction of several consciousnesses, none of which entirely becomes an object for the other" (18).

63. Kenan, *Let the Dead*, 284.

64. Kenan, *Let the Dead*, 305.

65. Kenan, *Let the Dead*, 334.

66. Quoted in Thananopavarn, "Digging Up the Past," 206.

67. Kenan, *Let the Dead*, 279. Not only are these themes frequently cited in discussions of Kenan's work, but the white and Black "Cross" families, with their intertwined histories, are derived from Kenan's own experience. See Betts, "Randall Garrett Kenan: Myth and Reality in Tims Creek."

68. Kenan, *Let the Dead*, 280.

69. This passage also echoes the authenticating and editorial function of white abolitionists' framing of slave narratives: see Lydia Maria Child, with Harriet Jacobs's *Incidents in the Life of a Slave Girl* (1861), and William Lloyd Garrison, with Frederick Douglass's *Narrative of the Life of Frederick Douglass* (1849), for example.

70. Cannon, "Disturbing the African American Community," 107.

71. Tucker, "Gay Identity," 323.

72. Thananopavarn, "Digging Up the Past," 207.

73. See Cannon, "Disturbing the African American Community," 109, and Norman, *Dead Women Talking*, 123, respectively.

74. Kenan, *Let the Dead*, 279.

75. Kenan, *Let the Dead*, 319.

76. Kenan, *Let the Dead*, 276.

77. Kenan, *Let the Dead*, 287.

78. Kenan, *Let the Dead*, 322.

79. Thananopavarn, "Digging Up the Past," 212.

80. Thananopavarn, "Digging Up the Past," 212.

81. Kenan, *Let the Dead*, 323. Phineas's self-satisfaction at not being the predator that the girl believes he is recalls Agee's gaze onto a Black couple in *Let Us Now Praise*

Famous Men: "I decided to go after them and speak to them. . . . Following them, I watched aspects of them which are less easily seen. . . . At the sound of the twist of my shoe in the gravel, the young woman . . . sprang forward into the first motion of a running not human but that of a suddenly terrified wild animal . . ." (37–38).

82. Kenan, *Let the Dead*, 324.

83. Rieger, *Clear-Cutting Eden*, 4. Here, Rieger is specifically discussing Thomas Nelson Page and Joel Chandler Harris, although he warns that "a concise definition of pastoral is not possible" (2).

84. See Catriona Mortimer-Sandiland and Bruce Erickson, *Queer Ecologies*: "Darwin's wake generally coincided with the rise of sexological thought," leading to "notions of natural sexuality from which nonreproductive sexualities [were] considered as deviant" (7). See also Somerville, *Queering the Color Line*.

85. Mortimer-Sandilands and Erickson, *Queer Ecologies*, 12. See also Outka, *Race and Nature*.

86. Mortimer-Sandilands and Erickson, *Queer Ecologies*, 12.

87. Kenan, *If I Had Two Wings*, 38.

88. Kenan, *If I Had Two Wings*, 36.

89. Kenan, *If I Had Two Wings*, 38.

90. Kenan, *If I Had Two Wings*, 38.

91. Kenan, *If I Had Two Wings*, 48.

92. Kenan, *If I Had Two Wings*, 45.

93. Kenan, *If I Had Two Wings*, 47.

94. See Jones, *Race Mixing*: Dean, swinging on rope swing, totally dejected and abject, is a "contemporary image of strange fruit hanging from a southern tree" that "conjures up, even as it reverses in a way, old images of black men lynched after rumored offenses to white women" (160).

95. The prominence of the folk tale in this story evokes Hurston's fiction as well as her ethnographic work. See Sorenson, "Modernity on a Global Stage": In Hurston's work, the folk tale, rather than emerging "organically from a collective voice" of the past or offering universal moral lessons, "results from a series of negotiations with and across difference" (5).

96. Kenan, *Let the Dead*, 164.

97. Kenan, *Let the Dead*, 164–65.

98. Kenan, *Let the Dead*, 176.

99. Kenan, *Let the Dead*, 168.

100. Kenan, *Let the Dead*, 176–77.

101. Kenan, *Let the Dead*, 178–79.

102. Kenan, *Let the Dead*, 175.

103. Crawley, "Circum-Religious Performance," 203.

104. Kenan, *Let the Dead*, 40. See Holland's discussion of *Visitation* in *Raising the Dead*, in which she argues that Kenan critiques the role of the Black church in perpetuating a "heterosexual paradigm" that erases Black queer visibility (107). See also Crawley, "Circum-Religious Performance."

105. Kenan, *If I Had Two Wings*, 254.

106. Littler, "The Implications of 'Chosenness,'" 39.
107. Holland, *Raising the Dead*, 118.
108. Kenan, *Visitation*, 14.
109. Kenan, *Visitation*, 23.
110. Kenan, *Visitation*, 23.
111. Berlant, *Queen of America*, 3.
112. See Morrison, "Home": "so much of what seems to lie about in discourses on race concerns legitimacy, authenticity, community, belonging. In no small way, these discourses are about home . . ." (5)
113. hooks, "Homeplace," 42.
114. hooks, "Homeplace," 42.
115. See Holland, *Erotic Life of Racism*.
116. See Allen, "Black/Queer/Diaspora," for his discussion of "liberatory models from the past" that "project our imaginations forward, to possible futures" (214).
117. McBride, "Straight Black Studies," 70.
118. Johnson, "'Quare' Studies," 148.
119. Kenan, *Let the Dead*, 305.
120. Kenan, *If I Had Two Wings*, 105.
121. Kenan, *If I Had Two Wings*, 103, 108.
122. Kenan, *If I Had Two Wings*, 102.
123. Kenan, *If I Had Two Wings*, 106.
124. Kenan, *If I Had Two Wings*, 105.
125. Kenan, *If I Had Two Wings*, 109.
126. Kenan, *If I Had Two Wings*, 109.
127. See Stockton, *The Queer Child*, on the queer possibilities of "growing sideways" rather than up: "Growth is a matter of extension, vigor, and volume as well as verticality" (11).
128. Kenan, *Let the Dead*, 175.
129. Kenan, *Let the Dead*, 176.
130. Kenan, *Let the Dead*, 183.
131. Kenan, *Let the Dead*, 177.
132. Kenan, *If I Had Two Wings*, 133.
133. Kenan, *If I Had Two Wings*, 120.
134. Kenan, *If I Had Two Wings*, 119.
135. Kenan, *If I Had Two Wings*, 133.
136. Kenan, *If I Had Two Wings*, 37.
137. Kenan, *If I Had Two Wings*, 34.
138. Kenan, *If I Had Two Wings*, 46.
139. Kenan, *If I Had Two Wings*, 47.
140. Kenan, *If I Had Two Wings*, 40.
141. Kenan, *If I Had Two Wings*, 40.
142. Kenan, *If I Had Two Wings*, 39–40.
143. Kenan, *If I Had Two Wings*, 43. In the atmospheric musicality of this scene, Cicero's praise of breakfast takes on the tune of "Amazing Grace," a song about being lost and then found, led "home.."

144. Kenan, *If I Had Two Wings*, 45.
145. Kenan, *If I Had Two Wings*, 46.
146. Browne, *Dark Matters*, 9.
147. Browne, *Dark Matters*, 52, 57.
148. Browne, *Dark Matters*, 21.
149. Browne, *Dark Matters*, 21.
150. Kenan, *If I Had Two Wings*, 175.

151. See Ellis, *Antebellum Posthuman*: "By the 1850s, the center of gravity in the debate over US slavery had noticeably shifted from the question of whether it is morally acceptable to enslave a human being toward the question of whether Black bodies should be considered human in the first place . . . an empirical question 'upon which science alone has the right to pronounce'" (3).

152. Kenan, *If I Had Two Wings*, 175–76.

153. Browne, *Dark Matters*, 58. Here, Browne is in dialogue with bell hooks's theorization of "black looks" Maurice Wallace's formulation of the "eyeballing disposition."

154. Kenan, *If I Had Two Wings*, 187.
155. Kenan, *If I Had Two Wings*, 180.
156. Kenan, *If I Had Two Wings*, 177.
157. Kenan, *If I Had Two Wings*, 181, 185.
158. Kenan, *If I Had Two Wings*, 190.
159. Kenan, *If I Had Two Wings*, 179.
160. Kenan, *If I Had Two Wings*, 187.
161. Kenan, *If I Had Two Wings*, 189.
162. Kenan, *If I Had Two Wings*, 188.
163. Kenan, *If I Had Two Wings*, 197.
164. Kenan, *If I Had Two Wings*, 101.
165. Kenan, *If I Had Two Wings*, 101.
166. Kenan, *If I Had Two Wings*, 101.
167. Kenan, *If I Had Two Wings*, 101.

168. For more on the racially fetishizing gaze of the camera, specifically as it relates to representations of Black masculinity, see Wallace, *Constructing the Black Masculine*.

169. Kenan, *If I Had Two Wings*, 102. Their encounter here signifies the Diana/Actaeon myth, in which Actaeon, a hunter, comes across Diana bathing in a pool. Enraged, she transforms him into a stag, and he's then hunted down by his own dogs.

170. Kenan, *If I Had Two Wings*, 105.
171. Kenan, *If I Had Two Wings*, 108.

172. Kenan, *If I Had Two Wings*, 109. The radical alterity of the swamp, its landscape only fully visible to some, bears similarities to Du Bois's *Quest of the Silver Fleece*: "'And what's beyond the swamp?' . . . 'Dreams!'" (4).

173. See Wallace, *Constructing the Black Masculine*, for a critical analysis of the Black male body as having a "doubly spectral and spectacle perceptibility in the public eye" (6).

174. Kenan, *Visitation*, 13. See also Somerville, *Queering the Color Line*, on the overlap of racial and sexual "passing" narratives in the twentieth century.
175. Kenan, *Visitation*, 87.
176. See Browne, *Dark Matters*.
177. Kenan, *Visitation*, 13.
178. Kenan, *Visitation*, 28.
179. Kenan, *Visitation*, 143.
180. Kenan, *Visitation*, 27.
181. Kenan, *Visitation*, 100.
182. Kenan, *Visitation*, 151, 154.
183. Kenan, *Visitation*, 154.
184. See Foucault, *Discipline and Punish*: The "soul" is produced by "methods of punishment, supervision and restraint" (29); and Horace's paranoia recalls Panopticism: "a state of conscious and permanent visibility that assures the automatic functioning of power" (201).
185. Kenan, *Visitation*, 163.
186. Kenan, *If I Had Two Wings*, 108.
187. Kenan, *Visitation*, 166.
188. Kenan, *Visitation*, 166.
189. Kenan, *Visitation*, 155.
190. See Ahmed, *Queer Phenomenology*: "To be orientated is . . . to be turned toward certain objects, these that help us to find our way. . . . They gather on the ground, and they create a ground upon which we can . . . gather," 1.
191. Kenan, *Visitation*, 254.
192. Holland, *Raising the Dead*, 123.
193. Kenan, *Visitation*, 254, 245.
194. See Levine, *Forms*, and Fawaz, *Queer Forms*. I use "form" here loosely, in the spirit that Levine adopts it: "all shapes and configurations, all ordering principles, all patterns of repetition and difference. . . . It is the work of forms to make order" (3). And yet, as Fawaz points out, the structuring or ordering work that form imposes does not have to equate to a political restrictiveness: "far from normalizing or delimiting gender and sexual variety, queer forms g[i]ve specificity to, and diversif[y] the range of, possible genders and sexualities that can be conceived (10).
195. Kenan, *Let the Dead*, 166–67.
196. Kenan, *Let the Dead*, 168.
197. Kenan, *Let the Dead*, 183, 191.
198. Kenan, *Let the Dead*, 179.
199. Kenan, *Let the Dead*, 175.
200. Johnson, *Sweet Tea*, 5.
201. Johnson, *Sweet Tea*, 547.
202. Johnson, *Sweet Tea*, 11.
203. Kenan, *Black Folk Could Fly*, 253.
204. Kenan, *Let the Dead*, 305.
205. Kenan, *Let the Dead*, 305.
206. Kenan, *Let the Dead*, 275–76.

Chapter 3

1. I have used "melancholy," rather than "melancholia," throughout this chapter, but it's worth noting that the distinction has been approached in different ways by various theorists. See Anne Anlin Cheng, *The Melancholy of Race*.
2. See Lybrand, "Man Who Carried Confederate Flag."
3. See Kreyling, *The South That Wasn't There*: "the twin subjects of the South and memory are dusty commonplaces in the history of southern literary studies" (x).
4. Gwin, "Introduction," 2.
5. See Duck, *The Nation's Region*.
6. Tate, "The New Provincialism," 272.
7. Faulkner, *Absalom, Absalom!*, 7.
8. See also Woodward, *The Burden of Southern History* (1960) and Simpson, "The Closure of History in a Postsouthern America" (1980).
9. Smith, *Finding Purple America*, 29.
10. Eng and Kazanjian, "Introduction: Mourning Remains," 3.
11. See Kim, *Postcolonial Grief*; Cheng, *The Melancholy of Race*; Winter, *Hope Draped in Black*; Rifkin, *The Erotics of Sovereignty*; and Crimp, *Melancholia and Moralism*.
12. Žižek, "Melancholy and the Act," 658.
13. Quoted in Žižek, "Melancholy and the Act," 661.
14. See Crimp, *Melancholia and Moralism*.
15. See Muñoz, *Cruising Utopia*.
16. Love, *Feeling Backward*, 4.
17. Love, *Feeling Backward*, 2.
18. Butler, "Afterword: After Loss, What Then?", 470.
19. See also Ahmed, *The Promise of Happiness*, on the role of alienation in "revolutionary consciousness": "You become estranged from the world as it has been given: the world of good habits and manners, which promises your comfort in return for obedience and good will. As a structure of feeling, alienation is an intense burning presence" (168).
20. Muñoz, *Cruising Utopia*, 29.
21. Muñoz, *Cruising Utopia*, 24–5.
22. Ahmed, *What's the Use?*, 196–97.
23. See also Freeman, *Time Binds*.
24. See also Gilroy, *Postcolonial Melancholy*.
25. Munro, "Neo-Confederates Take Their Stand," 147.
26. For more on southernness and authenticity, see Romine, *The Real South*.
27. Bone, *The Postsouthern Sense of Place*, 5. As Bone points out, "it is highly debatable whether such images of a traditional agrarian South standing firmly rooted against the abstracting, displacing tendencies of capitalist land speculation had any historical basis. Southern slave owners were *human* capitalists: their investment was concentrated chiefly in slaves rather than land" (8).
28. Smith, *Finding Purple America*, 18.
29. Smith, *Finding Purple America*, 38.

30. Taylor, *Reconstructing the Native South*, 3.
31. Taylor, *Reconstructing the Native South*, 3.
32. Benjamin, "Theses on the Philosophy of History," 257–58.
33. Yaeger, "Ghosts and Shattered Bodies," 88, 90.
34. See Muñoz, *Cruising Utopia*: "employing key words and thematics such as 'ghosts,' 'memory,' 'longing,' and 'utopia'" serves to "decipher the networks of commonality and the structures of feeling that link queers across different identity markers . . . as well as bodies separated along generational lines" (47).
35. Stockton, *The Queer Child*, 4. For queer formulations of childhood, see also Halberstam, *The Queer Art of Failure*, and Freeman, *Time Binds*.
36. Saunders, *Lincoln in the Bardo*, 208.
37. Saunders, *Lincoln in the Bardo*, 296.
38. Saunders, *Lincoln in the Bardo*, 6.
39. Saunders, *Lincoln in the Bardo*, 5.
40. Saunders, *Lincoln in the Bardo*, 25.
41. Saunders, *Lincoln in the Bardo*, 5.
42. Saunders, *Lincoln in the Bardo*, 27–8.
43. Saunders, *Lincoln in the Bardo*, 39.
44. Here, I'm thinking particularly of Edgar Lee Masterson's *Spoon River Anthology* and Sherwood Anderson's *Winesburg, Ohio*. See Booth, "*S-Town*, Small Town Literature, and the Uses of Queerness": works like these can be said to represent the small town as a microcosm of anxieties about America more broadly at a moment of transition, with grotesque queerness coming to represent the "horror beneath the town, and therefore beneath America itself" (276).
45. Specific southern regional place-names appear here and there: Fort Sumter, Fredericksburg, Cedar Creek Bridge.
46. Saunders, *Lincoln in the Bardo*, 222.
47. Saunders, *Lincoln in the Bardo*, 90.
48. Saunders, *Lincoln in the Bardo*, 90.
49. Saunders, *Lincoln in the Bardo*, 97.
50. Saunders, *Lincoln in the Bardo*, 96, 104.
51. Saunders, *Lincoln in the Bardo*, 96.
52. Saunders, *Lincoln in the Bardo*, 103.
53. Saunders, *Lincoln in the Bardo*, 105–06.
54. Edelman, *No Future*, 13.
55. See Duck, *The Nation's Region*: during Reconstruction, "understandings of southern cultural difference served to suppress public concern about the presence of racial segregation in an ostensibly liberal democracy" (26).
56. Saunders, *Lincoln in the Bardo*, 308.
57. Saunders, *Lincoln in the Bardo*, 309.
58. Saunders, *Lincoln in the Bardo*, 308.
59. See Shenk, *Lincoln's Melancholy*.
60. Saunders, *Lincoln in the Bardo*, 277–78.
61. There have been many speculations about Lincoln's sexuality: see Tripp, *The Intimate World of Abraham Lincoln*. His presence in Saunders's bardo, it's worth not-

ing, compounds the queerness of Vollman's and Bevins's relationship, mysteriously allowing them the "intensely pleasurable" new experience of "intermingl[ing] with one another" (172).

62. Saunders, *Lincoln in the Bardo*, 311.
63. Saunders, *Lincoln in the Bardo*, 331.
64. See Outka, "Whitman and Race" on Whitman's boundary-blurring poetry and "the unsettlement of fixed epistemologies" (301); Hartman, *Scenes of Subjection*, on empathy and embodiment; and Haggarty on the Gothic's "long history of obsessive queer desire" that often asserts itself through "the language of penetration" (24), a "shattering of male subjectivity leading to the 'dissolution of the self'" (44).
65. Parrish, *From the Civil War to the Apocalypse*, 4.
66. Parrish, *From the Civil War to the Apocalypse*, 1.
67. Truong, *Bitter in the Mouth*, 4.
68. Truong, *Bitter in the Mouth*, 53.
69. Truong, *Bitter in the Mouth*, 4.
70. Truong, *Bitter in the Mouth*, 4–5.
71. Truong, *Bitter in the Mouth*, 4–5.
72. Truong, *Bitter in the Mouth*, 156–57.
73. Hinrichsen, *Possessing the Past*, 192.
74. Truong, *Bitter in the Mouth*, 6.
75. Truong, *Bitter in the Mouth*, 21.
76. Truong, *Bitter in the Mouth*, 102.
77. Truong, *Bitter in the Mouth*, 115.
78. Truong, *Bitter in the Mouth*, 158.
79. Thomas, "Queer Formalism," 58; Cruz, "Monique Truong's Literary South," 720.
80. See also Janette, who offers that the novel "palimpsestically constructs its protagonist and narrator with layered secrets" (155), and Dykema, who argues that Truong's approach to race and synesthesia "reveal the archive's complicity in flattening difference under the politico-economic regimes of liberal and neoliberal multiculturalism" (108).
81. Truong, *Bitter in the Mouth*, 169. See also Simal-González, "Judging the Book by its Cover": transracial adoption can "act as a litmus test for Asian Americanness and introduce the ultimate Asian American phantom" (10).
82. Eng, *The Feeling of Kinship*, 3.
83. Truong, *Bitter in the Mouth*, 171.
84. Jerng, *Claiming Others*, xiii. As Jerng writes, transracial adoption forges the kinship bonds that serve as "crucial sites through which persons are both nationalized and naturalized" (xvii).
85. Truong, *Bitter in the Mouth*, 55.
86. Truong, *Bitter in the Mouth*, 108.
87. Lowe, *Immigrant Acts*, 18.
88. Truong, *Bitter in the Mouth*, 171.
89. Truong, *Bitter in the Mouth*, 172.
90. Nguyen, *America's Vietnam*, 2.

91. We might compare this to Bobbie Ann Mason's *In Country* (1985), in which the setting of small-town Kentucky in 1984 is unmistakably textured by the Vietnam War.

92. Truong, *Bitter in the Mouth*, 216.

93. Owen, *The Vietnam War in the Southern Imagination*, 25.

94. See Owen, *The Vietnam War in the Southern Imagination*: with the main training for Vietnam located in Louisiana, the South "assume[d] a crucial, albeit passing, formative role in the background of many soldiers who left 'the World'" of the US for an "unreal" foreign land (46). Owen cites James Dickey's novel *Deliverance*, in its plotline of an ill-fated trip into the wilderness, as a tale "in essence, [of] Vietnam fought in the South" (21).

95. Truong, *Bitter in the Mouth*, 169.

96. Truong, *Bitter in the Mouth*, 223.

97. Truong, *Bitter in the Mouth*, 117.

98. Truong, *Bitter in the Mouth*, 110.

99. Truong, *Bitter in the Mouth*, 173.

100. Cheng, *The Melancholy of Race*, 10.

101. Cheng, *The Melancholy of Race*, 13.

102. Truong, *Bitter in the Mouth*, 162

103. Truong, *Bitter in the Mouth*, 117.

104. Cheng, *The Melancholy of Race*, 8.

105. Heather Love and Ann Cvetkovich, for example, emphasize the kinship that forms around archives of feeling—lost, non-normative, and ephemeral histories, as well as personal memories unrecognized by public memorials.

106. Truong, *Bitter in the Mouth*, 53.

107. For an overview of critical reception to Truong's novel, see Kaus, "Reimagining the South."

108. Lee, *To Kill a Mockingbird*, 4.

109. Truong, *Bitter in the Mouth*, 133.

110. Truong, *Bitter in the Mouth*, 1.

111. Truong, *Bitter in the Mouth*, 171.

112. Bow, "Racial Interstitiality," 55.

113. Bow, "Racial Interstitiality," 56.

114. Joshi and Desai, *Asian Americans in Dixie*, 1.

115. Truong, *Bitter in the Mouth*, 213.

116. Truong, *Bitter in the Mouth*, 7.

117. Truong, *Bitter in the Mouth*, 12.

118. Truong, *Bitter in the Mouth*, 13.

119. Truong, *Bitter in the Mouth*, 13.

120. Throughout the novel, Linda's desires are layered and compounded, from her triangulated relationships with her best friend Kelly and her middle school boyfriend Wade, to her affection for the taste of her fiance's name, which seems, at times, to overpower her affection for the man himself (Leo*parsnip*).

121. These southern children, even the white and privileged, are starkly distinct from the nation-oriented Child of the Future that Saunders's Willie Lincoln embod-

ies because they emerge from the story of a past that is always incomplete and interrupted. Their future is ever haunted by that past. Accordingly, they grow sideways and refuse to be civilized and fully "straightened" out: Twain's Huck, Wolfe's Eugene Gant, Faulkner's Caddie Compson, and McCullers's Frankie, to name just a few. In this way, literary southern children tend to queer a national progress narrative, offering a melancholy backward glance instead of (or in addition to, as is perhaps the case with Scout) a forward-looking optimism.

122. Harper Lee and Dill, in turn, inevitably conjure up Truman Capote, icon of southern queerness. The "Baby" in front of Harper's name suggests the way that both queerness and southernness revise or subvert narratives of progress and maturation. See Bibler, "Queer/Quare."

123. Truong, *Bitter in the Mouth*, 154.

124. Truong, *Bitter in the Mouth*, 44.

125. Truong, *Bitter in the Mouth*, 117–19. As is evidenced by Bobby's different treatment of Linda's friend Kelly and her adoptive mother DeAnne, his assault is likely racially motivated.

126. Truong, *Bitter in the Mouth*, 3.

127. Truong, *Bitter in the Mouth*, 232.

128. Truong, *Bitter in the Mouth*, 185.

129. Love, *Feeling Backward*, 7.

130. Love, *Feeling Backward*, 4.

131. Truong, *Bitter in the Mouth*, 8.

132. Truong, *Bitter in the Mouth*, 174.

133. Cruz, "Monique Truong's Literary South," 717, 719.

134. Truong, *Bitter in the Mouth*, 206.

135. Because Linda uses he/him/his pronouns in her narrative, I do here as well.

136. Cruz, "Monique Truong's Literary South," 731.

137. It is important to note that this approach, however much it seeks to rewrite narrow definitions of southernness, is itself problematic. By claiming South America as his own extended southern play space, Harper is engaging in a kind of neo-imperialism. Much like *Gone with the Wind* capitalizes on a fantasy of the plantation South, the "drunken reds" of "that other South" both hide and suggest the costs of the "exotic" resort space.

138. Truong, *Bitter in the Mouth*, 258.

139. Truong, *Bitter in the Mouth*, 200.

140. Cruz, "Monique Truong's Literary South," 732.

141. Truong, *Bitter in the Mouth*, 122.

142. Truong, *Bitter in the Mouth*, 75.

143. Truong, *Bitter in the Mouth*, 15.

144. Truong, *Bitter in the Mouth*, 161.

145. Truong, *Bitter in the Mouth*, 164.

146. Truong, *Bitter in the Mouth*, 165.

147. Manoff, "Theories of the Archive," 11.

148. Manalansan, "Messing up Sex," 94

149. Truong, *Bitter in the Mouth*, 53.

150. See Kaus, "Reimagining the Southern Gothic": It's through *North Carolina Parade* that Linda is able to "reimagine the stories of marginalized figures . . . envision forces for progressive social change that cut[s] across races, genders, and times" and ultimately "highlight the stakes involved in historiographical methods" (85, 92).

151. Janette, "Alternative Historical Tetherings," 194.

152. Truong, *Bitter in the Mouth*, 140.

153. Truong, *Bitter in the Mouth*, 243.

154. Truong, *Bitter in the Mouth*, 141.

155. Truong, *Bitter in the Mouth*, 53.

156. Janette, "Alternative Historical Tetherings," 206.

157. Truong, *Bitter in the Mouth*, 203.

158. Truong, *Bitter in the Mouth*, 202.

159. Truong, *Bitter in the Mouth*, 262.

160. Truong, *Bitter in the Mouth*, 260.

161. Truong, *Bitter in the Mouth*, 260.

162. Truong, *Bitter in the Mouth*, 260.

163. Truong, *Bitter in the Mouth*, 260.

164. See Flood, "The Vietnamese refugees in Thailand."

165. Truong, *Bitter in the Mouth*, 143.

166. Truong, *Bitter in the Mouth*, 143.

167. Truong, *Bitter in the Mouth*, 143.

168. See Lassiter and Crespino, *The Myth of Southern Exceptionalism*.

169. Truong, *Bitter in the Mouth*, 183.

170. Truong, *Bitter in the Mouth*, 184.

171. Truong, *Bitter in the Mouth*, 117.

172. Truong, *Bitter in the Mouth*, 41, 122.

173. Truong, *Bitter in the Mouth*, 165. As Heather Love has written, the fate of Eurydice is "a central myth of queer existence," which "describes the paralyzing effects of loss" as well as "the consequences of the refusal to forget such losses" (5).

174. Truong, *Bitter in the Mouth*, 268.

175. Truong, *Bitter in the Mouth*, 268.

176. Truong, *Bitter in the Mouth*, 268.

177. Truong, *Bitter in the Mouth*, 269.

178. Truong, *Bitter in the Mouth*, 281.

179. Truong, *Bitter in the Mouth*, 280.

180. Truong, *Bitter in the Mouth*, 212.

181. Truong, *Bitter in the Mouth*, 268.

182. Truong, *Bitter in the Mouth*, 279.

183. Truong, *Bitter in the Mouth*, 279.

184. Truong, *Bitter in the Mouth*, 265.

185. Truong, *Bitter in the Mouth*, 282.

186. Simal-González, "Judging the Book by Its Cover," 27.

187. Truong, *Bitter in the Mouth*, 271.

188. See Gates, *Stony the Road*, for a discussion of the optimism of the early Obama years and the vitriol of the Trump era, and his comparison of this seismic shift to that of the post-Civil War years through the failures of Reconstruction.

189. Baudrillard, "Disneyworld Company."

190. See Stanonis, "Introduction": "As the racial regime represented by the Confederacy fell into disrepute during the civil rights movement, icons of the Confederacy grew less dignified, thereby becoming subversive symbols that function simultaneously as means of ridiculing the past and of celebrating that discredited past" (10).

191. Saunders, *CivilWarLand*, 14.
192. Romine, *The Real South*, 24, 9.
193. Saunders, *CivilWarLand*, 10.
194. Saunders, *CivilWarLand*, 3.
195. Saunders, *CivilWarLand*, 11.
196. Saunders, *CivilWarLand*, 8, 17.
197. Saunders, *CivilWarLand*, 5.
198. Saunders, *CivilWarLand*, 6.
199. Saunders, *CivilWarLand*, 6.
200. Saunders, *CivilWarLand*, 6.
201. Saunders, *CivilWarLand*, 6.
202. Saunders, *CivilWarLand*, 14.
203. Saunders, *CivilWarLand*, 12.
204. Saunders, *CivilWarLand*, 24.
205. Saunders, *CivilWarLand*, 26.
206. Saunders, *CivilWarLand*, 25.
207. Saunders, *CivilWarLand*, 26.
208. Saunders, *CivilWarLand*, 9.
209. Saunders, *CivilWarLand*, 14.
210. Saunders, *CivilWarLand*, 26.
211. Muñoz, *Cruising Utopia*, 47.
212. See Smith, *Finding Purple America*.
213. Smith, *Finding Purple America*, 49.
214. Žižek, "Melancholy and the Act," 658.

Chapter 4

1. See McPherson's *Reconstructing Dixie* on the hyperfeminized figure of the Southern woman as discursive symbol for the region, and how the land itself is figured as feminine as well.

2. Examples include Adam Messer's *Blood Thrasher* series (Savannah), Susannah Sandlin's *Penton Legacy* series (Alabama), Charlaine Harris's *Southern Vampire Mysteries* (Louisiana), Brandon Massey's *Dark Corner* (Mississippi), K. Murray Johnson's *Image of Emeralds and Chocolate* (Louisiana), and, in addition to Hendrix, the novels I discuss in this chapter: George R. R. Martin's *Fevre Dream* (Louisiana),

Poppy Z. Brite's *Lost Souls* (Louisiana and North Carolina), and Jewelle Gomez's *The Gilda Stories* (Louisiana and Mississippi).

3. I use male pronouns here for ease of continuity in describing the vampire generally.

4. Stephanie Meyers's *Twilight* as well as Octavia Butler's *Fledgling*, for example, both take place in the great dark forests of the Pacific Northwest.

5. Butler, "Afterword. Animating Autobiography," 41; Cohen, "Monster Culture," 4.

6. Anderson, Hagood, and Turner, *Undead Souths*, 5.

7. See Watson, "So Easy a Child Can Do It."

8. This association is so robust that David Chariandy's novel *Soucouyant*, about a man's fraught relationship with his mother and the trauma she endured as a Caribbean immigrant to Canada, was described by a *Toronto Star* review as "Southern in its historical preoccupation with racism" (Nurse, "Gothic on the Bluffs").

9. Halberstam, *Skin Shows*, 17. See also Palmer, *The Queer Uncanny*: "the ability of the Gothic to transgress, in both the 'itinerant' and 'unorthodox' senses of the term, is particularly apparent in its encounter with queer"—in his boundary-destroying tendencies, the vampire queers the South from within (11).

10. Dahl, "(The promise of) Monstrous Kinship?", 196. See also DasGupta, "Cartographies of Friendship, Desire, and Home."

11. Halberstam, *Skin Shows*, 99.

12. Anatol, *Things That Fly in the Night*, 90. See Anatol's discussion of the Afro-Caribbean figure of the soucouyant. For the pre-Stoker vampire in the Gothic tradition, it's worth noting Carmen Maria Machado's markedly queer 2019 edition of Joseph Sheridan Le Fanu's *Carmilla*.

13. Anatol, *Things That Fly in the Night*, 116.

14. These Southern origins often upset the vampire's male gendering. See Anatol, *Things that Fly in the Night*: Zora Neale Hurston adopts the soucouyant figure to complicate stereotypes of femininity in her novel *Joseph's Gourd Vine* (162).

15. Sedgwick, *Between Men*, 91.

16. Hughes and Smith, *Queering the Gothic*, 4, 1.

17. Brasell, "Mass Production of Degeneracy," 81.

18. Watson, "So Easy Even a Child Can Do It," 2.

19. Quoted in Watson, "So Easy Even a Child Can Do It," 1.

20. "S. A. Cosby on *Razorblade Tears*," 9:42.

21. "S. A. Cosby on *Razorblade Tears*," 12:50–13:05.

22. Brasell, "Mass Production of Degeneracy," 71.

23. Goddu, "Vampire Gothic," 136.

24. Kent, "'The Bloody Transaction,'" 739.

25. See Hagood, "Gone to Ground."

26. Kent, "'The Bloody Transaction,'" 740.

27. See Patterson, *Slavery and Social Death*.

28. Dracula's aristocratic vibe is particularly strong in Lugosi's tuxedoed 1931 adaptation. But see also Arata, "The Occidental Tourist": Dracula is a powerful racial Other to imperial Britain, provoking horror in part because he so effectively "deracinates his victims[;] . . . they receive a new racial identity" (630).

29. See Horton-Stallings, *Dirty South Manifesto*: "southern public spheres [have been] largely erected out of the sexual economy of slavery and sustained by settler colonialism" (5); see also Greeson, "Expropriating *The Great South*": "to represent the Southern states under Reconstruction as a colonized region of the United States . . . was, fundamentally, to assert a new stature of equality for the United States among the imperial nations of the world" (120).

30. See Benefiel, "Blood Relations."

31. Mythologies of the Old South and its fall rely on both genderings; see Bibler, *Cotton's Queer Relations* and McPherson, *Reconstructing Dixie*.

32. On Dracula-as-capital, see Halberstam, *Skin Shows*: "The money that had been buried comes back to life, becomes capital and embarks on the conquest of the world: this and none other is the story of Dracula the vampire" (91).

33. See Patterson, *Slavery and Social Death*: the enslaved undergo social death and are reborn as capital on the southern plantation. See also Holland, *Raising the Dead*: the South so regularly appears as the nation's "space of death" for the Black body that the region itself is itself frequently figured as undead (5).

34. Halberstam, *Skin Shows*, 21.

35. Halberstam, *Skin Shows*, 92.

36. Halberstam, *Skin Shows*, 2.

37. *Alucard*, as the film painstakingly tells us several times, is *Dracula* backward—this is a monster apparently too lazy for a more robust anagram.

38. See Clukey, "Monstrous Plantations": "the monsters of plantation horror register anxieties about how Americans can maintain imperial control abroad without losing self-control and their white identities. If romance idealizes the white man's burden to take up the civilizing mission, then horror suggests that the white man's own claims to civilization are tentative at best" (134).

39. Hagood, "Gone to Ground," 254.

40. Hagood, "Gone to Ground," 254.

41. Hagood, "Gone to Ground," 254. See also McPherson, "Revamping the South," for its discussion of the series' "indulg[ence] in a bit of southern mythmaking" and real-life-Louisiana's importance to contemporary Hollywood (341).

42. Auerbach, *Our Vampires, Ourselves*, 1.

43. Wald, *Contagious*, 2. *Dracula*'s fin-de-siècle fears about increased mobility across physical and ideological borders are the same that Wald studies in her analysis of early outbreak narratives. In more recent literature, as Auerbach explores, the vampire becomes a way to process anxieties about HIV/AIDS.

44. Wald, *Contagious*, 9.

45. Wald, *Contagious*, 53.

46. Hendrix, *The Southern Book Club's Guide*, 8.

47. Hendrix, *The Southern Book Club's Guide*, 361.

48. Hendrix, *The Southern Book Club's Guide*, 349.

49. Hendrix, *The Southern Book Club's Guide*, 378.

50. Hendrix, *The Southern Book Club's Guide*, 278.

51. Hendrix, *The Southern Book Club's Guide*, 343.

52. Hendrix, *The Southern Book Club's Guide*, 348.

53. I'm invoking queerness here in the broad sense of sexual antinormativity. This scene sees Patricia not only desiring the monster and enjoying (even as a mom!) a nonreproductive sexual act, but it also flirts with sadomasochism and exhibitionism.

54. Hendrix, *The Southern Book Club's Guide*, 365.

55. Hendrix, *The Southern Book Club's Guide*, 351.

56. Hendrix, *The Southern Book Club's Guide*, 382.

57. For more on AIDS and the outbreak narrative, see Wald, *Contagious*. For the effect of the AIDS epidemic on vampire narratives of the 80s and 90s, see Auerbach, *Our Vampires, Ourselves*.

58. Hendrix, *The Southern Book Club's Guide*, 395.

59. See "Grady Hendrix." These reviews are from Kirkus Reviews and Paul Tremblay, respectively, on the author's website.

60. See Harrison, *American Culture in the 1990s*: "Between . . . two positions outlined[,] . . . the gesture of defiance with its appeal to a world without borders, and the sense of being entirely contained within a system that incorporates all dissent—lie much of the cultural politics of the 1990s" (201).

61. Schwartz and Savage, *Gossip Girl*, s1ep1; Ball, *True Blood*, s1ep3.

62. *True Blood*'s oddly outdated aesthetics have gone, from what I can find, mostly unremarked, showing our readiness to accept the South as a region of anachronism.

63. New Orleans is the vampire's home base to some extent in three of the four texts I read in this chapter. Beyond its heavily marketed Gothic aesthetics, this can be understood through the city's history in the slave trade (see Marler, *The Merchants' Capital*); its centrality to a "southern" literary history (See Johnson, *New Orleans: A Literary History*); its twentieth-century and contemporary relationship to the Global South and discourses of creolization (See Gruesz, "The Mercurial Space of 'Central' America"); and its status as a countercultural haven (See Bingham and Freeman, *The Bohemian South*).

64. Martin, *Fevre Dream*, 8.

65. Martin, *Fevre Dream*, 8.

66. Martin, *Fevre Dream*, 2.

67. Martin, *Fevre Dream*, 3.

68. Martin, *Fevre Dream*, 3.

69. Martin, *Fevre Dream*, 396.

70. Martin, *Fevre Dream*, 366.

71. Vampirism, here (especially as it centers on white men) resembles the social role into which gay men are placed, and which they should adopt, as Bersani argues in "Is the Rectum a Grave?": "Male homosexuality advertises the risk of the sexual itself as the risk of self-dismissal, of *losing sight* of the self, and in so doing it proposes and dangerously represents *jouissance* as a mode of ascesis" (30).

72. Martin, *Fevre Dream*, 247.

73. Martin, *Fevre Dream*, 123.

74. Martin, *Fevre Dream*, 213.

75. Martin, *Fevre Dream*, 213.

76. See Marler, *The Merchants' Capital*: "the city's cosmopolitan character caused New Orleans to be widely disparaged as corrupt and dissolute by most southerners" (5).

77. Martin, *Fevre Dream*, 158.

78. Martin, *Fevre Dream*, 237, 291. See also Gruesz, "The Mercurial Space of 'Central' America": in the first half of the nineteenth century and even more so in the second, to separate itself from the "degenerate" South of the national imagination, "New Orleans itself registered and made canny use of this vision of the city as a transit point between the 'Latin' and 'Saxon' worlds in order to further economic development agendas" (143); but the understanding of the city as "a transit point" also elicits the fears of moral and physical contagion that Wald discusses (149).

79. Martin, *Fevre Dream*, 139.

80. Martin, *Fevre Dream*, 148, 391.

81. Martin, *Fevre Dream*, 148.

82. Martin, *Fevre Dream*, 291.

83. See Marler, *The Merchants' Capital*: "As a result of numerous interrelated changes to the structures of regional, national, and global commerce, the fortunes of the quondam 'Queen City of the South' plummeted during and after the Civil War. Neither before nor since has a first-rank American city fallen from economic grace so swiftly and decisively" (8).

84. Martin, *Fevre Dream*, 431.

85. Martin, *Fevre Dream*, 460.

86. Martin, *Fevre Dream*, 460.

87. Martin, *Fevre Dream*, 460.

88. A year apart, both novels were nominated for a Lambda Literary Award; *The Gilda Stories* received the award.

89. See Grady, "Vampire Culture": he argues that Anne Rice's vampires are primarily humanists, "immortal custodians of Western culture" (226).

90. Hughes, "The taste of blood," 142.

91. Block, "Review of *Lost Souls*."

92. Brite, *Lost Souls*, 74.

93. Brite, *Lost Souls*, 116. Brite's novel is filled with kudzu. See "Invasive Queer Kudzu": like the vampire, this plant is parasitic, hyper-mobile, and queer in its "monstrous . . . tenacity" (and, of course, it is all over the southern United States).

94. Brite, *Lost Souls*, 116.

95. Brite, *Lost Souls*, 17, 40.

96. Brite, *Lost Souls*, 106, 249.

97. Brite, *Lost Souls*, 125.

98. Brite, *Lost Souls*, 119.

99. Brite, *Lost Souls*, 119.

100. Brite, *Lost Souls*, 167.

101. Brite, *Lost Souls*, 235.

102. Brite, *Lost Souls*, 239.

103. Brite, *Lost Souls*, 303.

104. Brite, *Lost Souls*, 3.

105. Brite, *Lost Souls*, 90.

106. Brite, *Lost Souls*, 7.

107. Brite, *Lost Souls*, 5.

108. Brite, *Lost Souls*, 78.

109. Brite, *Lost Souls*, 3. See Hagood, "The Gothic Tradition in New Orleans": "This touristic streak of New Orleans Gothicism is more complex than it might at first appear, for, at the same time that it fulfills an important role in the marketing of the city, it also expresses an aspect of New Orleans's sense of itself as evidenced in both its Gothic literary tradition and architecture" (278). See also Johnson, *Slavery's Metropolis*: "the commodification of slave culture [in New Orleans] is as ubiquitous as slaves are invisible" (17).

110. Brite, *Lost Souls*, 281.

111. Brite, *Lost Souls*, 115.

112. Brite, *Lost Souls*, 115.

113. Brite, *Lost Souls*, 150, 156.

114. Brite, *Lost Souls*, 83.

115. Brite, *Lost Souls*, 228.

116. Brite, *Lost Souls*, 229.

117. Hughes, "The taste of blood," 149.

118. Hughes, "The taste of blood," 156. See also Greenberg, "Sins of the Blood": Greenberg positions the vampire gang of *Lost Souls* as "an alternative family" that represents "escape from the tyranny of hegemonic order" (177).

119. Brite, *Lost Souls*, 186.

120. Brite, *Lost Souls*, 141.

121. Brite, *Lost Souls*, 227.

122. Freeman, *Time Binds*, 122.

123. Brite, *Lost Souls*, 6.

124. Brite, *Lost Souls*, 279. See also Palmer, *The Queer Uncanny*, on the carnivalesque as a mode of celebrating "queer vitality and jouissance" (15).

125. On *Gilda* and subsequent Black vampire novels, see Jenkins, *The Paradox of Blackness in African American Vampire Fiction*.

126. See Lewis, "Queering Personhood," and Kent, "The Bloody Transaction," for a discussion of *The Gilda Stories* as a neo-slave or fugitive slave narrative; see Morris, "More Than Human," for a discussion of *Gilda* as an Afrofuturist text. See also Fulton Minor, *Speaking Power*, who discusses the novel in terms of "African American oral traditions of call and response and the ring shout in structure in content," which serve to "actualize Black feminist orality" (116).

127. Anatol, *Things That Fly in the Night*, 174, 175, 180. In the context of her own project of understanding the vampiric figure through other than a white and Western lens, Anatol also points out that "while not explicitly a soucouyant narrative . . . [*Gilda*] is a productive extension of the trope simply because of its focus on a Black female vampire" (174). In looking to the recuperative possibilities of the border, Gomez's novel is a reflection of the third-wave intersectionalist feminist politics that she invokes with an epigraph by Audre Lorde. See also Anzaldúa, *Borderlands*: "The

prohibited and forbidden are its inhabitants[,] . . . the perverse, the queer, the troubled, the mongrel, the mulatto, the half-breed, the half dead" (25).

128. Gomez, *The Gilda Stories*, 34.

129. Auerbach, *Our Vampires, Ourselves*, 186, 184. See also Patterson, "Haunting Back": "Unlike her white female counterparts in works such as Stoker's *Dracula*[,] . . . the Girl is neither corrupted nor destroyed when she shares her blood with a vampire[;] . . . on the contrary, as she develops a fuller understanding of the Western world and of the place that it has allotted her [as a Black woman], she acquires the psychological and physical stamina to effectively begin to challenge that placement" (39).

130. Gomez, *The Gilda Stories*, 9.

131. Gomez, *The Gilda Stories*, 10.

132. Gomez, *The Gilda Stories*, 11.

133. Gomez, *The Gilda Stories*, 11.

134. See Anzaldúa, *Borderlands*: "In trying to become 'objective,' Western culture made 'objects' of things and people when it distanced itself from them, thereby losing 'touch' with them. This dichotomy is the root of all violence" (59).

135. Gomez, *The Gilda Stories*, 11.

136. Gomez, *The Gilda Stories*, 11.

137. Gomez, *The Gilda Stories*, 11.

138. Gomez, *The Gilda Stories*, 12.

139. Lewis, "Queering Personhood in the Neo-Slave Narrative," 449.

140. For a fuller articulation of this dialectic, see Ferguson, *Aberrations in Black*, and Wynter, "Unsettling the Coloniality of Being."

141. Gomez, *The Gilda Stories*, 46.

142. By placing these vampiric exchanges of both sexual and maternal/paternal intimacy in New Orleans, both *Gilda* and *Souls* enter into and change the terms of dialogues around incest and the South. See Harkins, "Surviving the Family Romance?"

143. Gomez, *The Gilda Stories*, 22.

144. Gomez, *The Gilda Stories*, 172. When Gilda changes Julius, it begins with "a kiss both passionate and chaste, leaving Julius feeling like a child in her arms, yet still a man," and ends with a kind of post-coital exhaustion after he has sucked at the blood she gives him from her breast (192).

145. In this, Gomez cites back to Rice, and to the vampire myths she seeks to rewrite. Anthony's and Sorel's flaneur-like existence suggests a familiar link between cosmopolitanism, mobility, and freedom. See Johnson, *Slavery's Metropolis*: this is an association that must be "decoupled . . . in Atlantic world studies" (8), and one that *Gilda* more broadly challenges. Mobility might be a necessary component of freedom, but it is not, itself, freedom.

146. Gomez, *The Gilda Stories*, 240.

147. This myth seems to originate with Stoker.

148. Gomez, *The Gilda Stories*, 37.

149. Gomez, *The Gilda Stories*, 39.

150. Gomez, *The Gilda Stories*, 39–40. See also Lewis, "Queering Personhood."
151. Gomez, *The Gilda Stories*, 243.
152. Horton-Stallings, *Dirty South Manifesto*, 43.
153. Horton-Stallings, *Dirty South Manifesto*, 39.
154. Gomez, *The Gilda Stories*, 240, 249.
155. Gomez, *The Gilda Stories*, 252.
156. See Anzaldúa, *Borderlands*: The Aztec figure Coatlicue, a woman with a serpent head, also invokes non-Western "vampiric" figures, in this case the woman with a mouth "guarded by rows of dangerous teeth, a sort of *vagina dentata*[,] . . . the most sacred place on earth, a place of refuge, the creative womb from which all things were born and to which all things returned" (56).
157. See Fulton Minor, *Speaking Power*, for her discussion of the novel's "cyclical format that draws on multiple literary and oral traditions" (118); in this, the novel evokes a kinship with Toomer's *Cane*.
158. Gomez, *The Gilda Stories*, 43.
159. Anzaldúa, *Borderlands*, 88.
160. Rody, *The Daughter's Return*, 84.
161. Jenkins, "Race, Freedom, and the Black Vampire," 313.
162. Gomez, *The Gilda Stories*, 220.
163. Gomez, *The Gilda Stories*, 198.
164. Gomez, "Recasting the Mythology," 87. See also Anzaldúa, *Borderlands*: "I write the myths in me, the myths I am, the myths I want to become" (93).
165. Gomez, *The Gilda Stories*, 233, 240.
166. Gomez, *The Gilda Stories*, 241.
167. Gomez, *The Gilda Stories*, 242, 250.
168. See Spillers, "Mama's Baby, Papa's Maybe," on "claim[ing] monstrosity" in its potential for a radical empowerment. See also Jenkins, "Race, Freedom, and the Black Vampire": "While the multicultural conservative conceptualizes assimilation as the path to freedom, Gomez's conception of the vampiric family rejects assimilation altogether," rejecting, too, the "deeply held cultural fiction that the body is a legible text" (319).
169. Rody, *The Daughter's Return*, 78.
170. See Malatino, *Queer Embodiment*: Foucault's definition of monstrosity as "mixity" grounds her discussion of the ways in which intersex and trans bodies were historically considered "monstrous" before they were pathologized (4).
171. Malatino, *Queer Embodiment*, 13.
172. Nurka, "Animal Techne," 210. See also Ellison, Green, Richardson, and Snorton, "We Got Issues": "transness is always and already theorized and theorizable from literature on 'racialized gender'" (165).
173. See Chávez, "From Sanctuary," on the importance of aligning queer politics with "a commitment to what I can only think of as 'fugitivity.' A long tradition of theorizing the concept of fugitivity among radical and feminist black intellectuals traces this line of thinking directly to Frederick Douglass and fugitive slaves" (67).
174. For more on New Orleans's reputation as a "vampire city," see Piatti-Farnell, "The Blood Never Stops Flowing."

175. See Hagood, "The Gothic Tradition in New Orleans."
176. Johnson, *Slavery's Metropolis*, 17–18.
177. See Grant, "The New Orleans Police Raid," and Long, "Queers, Fairies, and Ne'er-Do-Wells."
178. Horowitz, *Katrina*, 186.
179. Johnson, *Slavery's Metropolis*, xv.
180. Ball, *True Blood*, s1ep4.
181. See Edelman, *No Future*.
182. Quoted in Caserio et al., "Antisocial Thesis," 821.
183. We find this idea crystallized in the elder vampire Christian's encounter with a young boy at a Gothic gay club in New Orleans: the boy offers himself up to the vampire's predation, and Christian finds the mingling tastes of his semen and blood, in the boy's moment of "little death" and actual death, "almost too exquisite to bear" (*Lost Souls* 67).
184. Quoted in Caserio et al., "Antisocial Thesis," 825.
185. Brite, *Lost Souls*, 261.
186. See Holland, *The Erotic Life of Racism*.
187. Muñoz, *Cruising Utopia*, 17.
188. Muñoz, *Cruising Utopia*, 99. See Ruti, *The Ethics of Opting Out*, for an analysis of the Edelman/Muñoz and Edelman/Berlant debates.
189. See Berlant and Edelman, *Sex, or the Unbearable*: as Berlant writes, "I am interested in optimism as a mode of attachment to life. I am committed to the political project of imagining how to detach from lives that don't work. . . . I aim, along with many antinormative activists, to expand the field of affective potentialities, latent and explicit fantasies, and infrastructures for how to live beyond survival, toward flourishing not later but in the ongoing now" (5).
190. Freeman, *Time Binds*, 19.
191. Auerbach, *Our Vampires, Ourselves*, 192.
192. Nurka, "Animal Techne," 210.
193. Jones, *Interview with the Vampire*, s1ep1.

Coda

1. "Cannonsburgh Village."
2. Giffin, "City Restricts BoroPride."
3. Cochrane, "Judge Finds Tennessee Law."
4. Lavietes, "Tennessee Governor Appears to Have Dressed in Drag."
5. See Bibler, *Cotton's Queer Relations*.
6. McPherson, *Reconstructing Dixie*, 19.
7. McPherson, *Reconstructing Dixie*, 21.
8. Glock, "Redefining the Southern Belle."
9. Dolly Parton, "It's a good thing."
10. Chang and Thompson, "Dolly Parton on Gay Rumors."
11. See Horowitz, "The Trouble with 'Queerness'.".
12. Halberstam, *The Queer Art of Failure*, 6.

13. See Muñoz, *Cruising Utopia*.
14. Butler, *Gender Trouble*, 43.
15. Tucker, *Unexpected Pleasures*, 8, 11.
16. See McPherson, *Reconstructing Dixie*.
17. Capote, *Other Voices, Other Rooms*, 67.
18. "Atomic Rose."
19. Allison, "Tennessee Gov. Bill Lee Says He Regrets Participating."
20. Associated Press, "Grammy-Winning Singer Lizzo."
21. The reality shows *We're Here* and *Queer Eye*, between them, include episodes set in South Carolina, Alabama, Mississippi, Georgia, and Louisiana, while the most recent season of the drama *Queer as Folk* is set in New Orleans.
22. Jefferson and Thomas, "Everybody's Gay."
23. Snorton, *Black on Both Sides*, 7.
24. Barzilai, "Lizzo Was Never as Progressive as We Wanted Her to Be."

Bibliography

Agee, James and Walker Evans. *Let Us Now Praise Famous Men*. 1941. New York: Houghton Mifflin Harcourt, 2000.
Ahmed, Sara. *The Promise of Happiness*. Durham: Duke University Press, 2010.
———. *Queer Phenomenology*. Durham: Duke University Press, 2006.
———. *What's the Use? On the Uses of Use*. Durham: Duke University Press, 2019.
Allen, Jafari. "Black/Queer/Diaspora at the Current Conjuncture." *GLQ* 18, no. 2 (2012): 211–48.
Allen, Samantha. *Real Queer America: LGBT Stories from Red States*. Boston: Little, Brown & Company, 2019.
Allewaert, Monique. *Ariel's Ecology: Plantations, Personhood, and Colonialism in the American Tropics*. Minneapolis: University Press of Minnesota, 2013.
Allison, Dorothy. "Dorothy Allison." By Kelly Anderson. *Voices of Feminism Oral History Project* (November 2007): https://www.smith.edu/libraries/libs/ssc/vof/transcripts/Allison.pdf.
———. *Trash: Stories*. 1988. New York City: Plume, 2002.
Allison, Natalie. "Tennessee Gov. Bill Lee Says He Regrets Participating in 'Old South' Parties at Auburn University." *The Tennessean*, 20 February 2019, https://www.tennessean.com/story/news/politics/2019/02/20/tn-gov-bill-lee-kappa-alpha-old-south-party-auburn/2904953002/.
Anatol, Giselle Liza. *The Things That Fly in the Night: Female Vampires in Literature of the Circum-Caribbean and African Diaspora*. New Brunswick: Rutgers University Press, 2015.
Anderson, Benedict. *Imagined Communities: Reflections on the Origin and Spread of Nationalism*. London: Verso, 1983.
Anderson, Eric Gary, Taylor Hagood, and Daniel Cross Turner, eds. *Undead Souths: The Gothic and Beyond in Southern Literature and Culture*. Baton Rouge: Louisiana State University Press, 2015.
Anderson, Susan Heller. "Ernest Matthew Mickler, 48, Dies; Author of Best-Selling Cookbook." *The New York Times*, 18 November 1988, https://www.nytimes.com/1988/11/18/obituaries/ernest-matthew-mickler-48-dies-author-of-best-selling-cookbook.html.
Anzaldúa, Gloria. *Borderlands/La Frontera: The New Mestiza*. 1987. San Francisco: Aunt Lute, 25th anniversary edition, 2012.
Arata, Stephen. "The Occidental Tourist: *Dracula* and the Anxiety of Reverse Colonization." *Victorian Studies* 33, no. 4 (1990): 621–45.
Ashby, LeRoy. *With Amusement for All: A History of American Popular Culture Since 1830*. Lexington: University Press of Kentucky, 2012.

Associated Press. "Grammy-Winning Singer Lizzo Protests Tennessee Law Restricting Drag Shows." *The Guardian*, 23 April 2023, https://www.theguardian.com/music/2023/apr/23/singer-lizzo-protests-tennessee-anti-drag-law-on-stage.

"Atomic Rose," Atomic Rose, accessed 31 July 2023, https://www.atomicrosememphis.com/about.

Auerbach, Nina. *Our Vampires, Ourselves*. Chicago: University of Chicago Press, 1995.

Bakhtin, Mikhail. *Problems of Dostoevsky's Poetics*. Translated by Caryl Emerson. Minneapolis: University of Minnesota Press, 1984.

Ball, Alan, director. *True Blood*. 2008–2014; New York City: HBO.

Barzilai, Ben. "Lizzo Was Never as Progressive as We Wanted Her to Be." *The Daily Beast*, 6 August 2023, https://www.thedailybeast.com/lizzo-was-never-as-progressive-as-we-wanted-her-to-be.

Baudrillard, Jean. "Disneyworld Company." 1996. Translated by Francois Debrix. *CTHEORY*, 24 August 2015, https://journals.uvic.ca/index.php/ctheory/article/view/14846.

Benefiel, Candace. "Blood Relations: The Gothic Perversion of the Nuclear Family in Anne Rice's *Interview with the Vampire*." *The Journal of Popular Culture* 38, no. 2 (2004): 261–73.

Benjamin, Walter. "Theses on the Philosophy of History." In *Illuminations*, edited by Hannah Arendt, translated by Harry Zohn, 253–65. New York: Harcourt, 1968.

Berglund, Jeff. "'The Secret's in the Sauce': Dismembering Normativity in *Fried Green Tomatoes*." *Camera Obscura* 14, no. 3 (1999): 124–59.

Berlant, Lauren. *Cruel Optimism*. Durham: Duke University Press, 2011.

———. *The Female Complaint*. Durham: Duke University Press, 2008.

———. *The Queen of America Goes to Washington City*. Durham: Duke University Press, 1997.

Berlant, Lauren and Lee Edelman. *Sex, or the Unbearable*. Durham: Duke University Press, 2013.

Bersani, Leo. "Is the Rectum a Grave?" In *Is the Rectum a Grave? And Other Essays*, 3–30. Chicago: University of Chicago Press, 2009.

Betts, Doris. "Randall Garrett Kenan: Myth and Reality in Tims Creek." In *Southern Writers at Century's End*, edited by Jeffrey Folks and James A. Perkins, 9–20. Lexington: University Press of Kentucky, 1997.

Bibler, Michael. *Cotton's Queer Relations: Same-Sex Intimacy and the Literature of the Southern Plantation, 1936–1968*. Charlottesville: University of Virginia Press, 2009.

———. "Queer/Quare." In *Keywords for Southern Studies*, edited by Jennifer Rae Greeson and Scott Romine, 200–215. Athens: University of Georgia Press, 2016.

Bingham, Shawn Chandler and Lindsey A. Freeman, eds. *The Bohemian South: Creating Countercultures, from Poe to Punk*. Berkeley: University of North Carolina Press, 2017.

Block, Marylaine. "Review of *Lost Souls*, by Poppy Z. Brite." *Library Journal Review*, October 1992.

Bone, Martyn. *The Postsouthern Sense of Place in Contemporary Fiction*. Baton Rouge: Louisiana State University Press, 2005.

Bone, Martyn, Brian Ward, and William A. Link, eds. *Creating and Consuming the American South*. Gainesville: University Press of Florida, 2015.

Booth, Nathanael. "*S-Town*, Small Town Literature, and the Uses of Queerness." *Mississippi Quarterly* 72, no. 2 (2019): 273–96.

Booth, Wayne. "Why Ethical Criticism Can Never Be Simple." *Style* 32, no. 2 (1998): 351–64.

Bow, Leslie. "Racial Interstitiality and the Anxieties of the 'Partly Colored': Representations of Asians under Jim Crow." In *Asian Americans in Dixie: Race and Migration in the South*, edited by Khyati Y. Joshi and Jigna Desai, 54–76. Champaign: University of Illinois Press, 2013.

Bradway, Tyler. "Queer Narrative Theory and the Relationality of Form." *PMLA* 136, no. 5 (2021): 711–27.

Bradway, Tyler and Elizabeth Freeman, eds. *Queer Kinship: Race, Sex, Belonging, Form*. Durham: Duke University Press, 2022.

Brasell, Bruce R. "Mass Production of Degeneracy: Queer Genre-Ship and Southern Gothic Film." In *Queering the South Onscreen*, edited by Tison Pugh, 67–87. Athens: University of Georgia Press, 2020.

———. "'The Degeneration of Nationalism': Colonialism, Perversion, and the American South." *The Mississippi Quarterly* 56, no. 1 (Winter 2002–03): 33–54.

———. *The Possible South: Documentary Film and Limitations of Biraciality*. Oxford: University Press of Mississippi, 2015.

Brite, Poppy Z. *Lost Souls*. New York City: Penguin, 1992.

Brooks, Peter. *Reading for the Plot: Design and Intention in Narrative*. New York City: Knopf, 1984.

Browne, Simone. *Dark Matters: On the Surveillance of Blackness*. Durham: Duke University Press, 2015.

Butler, Judith. "Afterword: After Loss, What Then?" In *Loss: The Politics of Mourning*, edited by David Eng and David Kazanjian, 467–73. Berkeley: University of California Press, 2002.

———. "Afterword. Animating Autobiography: Barbara Johnson and Mary Shelley's Monster." In *A Life with Mary Shelley*, edited by Barbara Johnson, 37–50. Redwood City: Stanford University Press, 2014.

———. *Gender Trouble: Feminism and the Subversion of Identity*. 1990. Milton Park: Routledge, 2006.

Camp, Stephanie. *Closer to Freedom: Enslaved Women and Everyday Resistance in the Plantation South*. Chapel Hill: University of North Carolina Press, 2005.

Cannon, Uzzie. "Disturbing the African American Community: Defamiliarization in Randall Kenan's *Let the Dead Bury Their Dead*." *Southern Literary Journal* 42, no. 1 (2009): 102–21.

"Cannonsburgh Village." Murfreesboro Parks and Recreation, accessed 31 July 2023, dhttps://www.murfreesborotn.gov/164/Cannonsburgh-Village.

Cantrell, Jaime. "Down Home and Out: Southern Lesbian Writers and the Sex Life of Food." In *The Bohemian South: Creating Countercultures, from Poe to Punk*, edited by Shawn Chandler Bingham and Lindsey A. Freeman, 107–27. Berkeley: University of North Carolina Press, 2017.

Caplan, Pat, ed. *Food, Health, and Identity*. Milton Park: Routledge, 1997.

Capote, Truman. *Other Voices, Other Rooms*. 1948. New York: Vintage International, 1994.

Carr, Virginia Spencer. *Understanding Carson McCullers*. Columbia: University of South Carolina Press, 2005.

Carruth, Allison. *Global Appetites: American Power and the Literature of Food*. Cambridge: Cambridge University Press, 2013.

Caserio, Robert, Lee Edelman, Jack Halberstam, José Esteban Muñoz, and Tim Dean. "The Antisocial Thesis in Queer Theory." *PMLA* 121, no. 3 (2006): 819–28.

Chadd, Claire. *Postregional Fictions: Barry Hannah and the Challenges of Southern Studies*. Baton Rouge: Louisiana State University Press, 2021

Chang, Juju and Victoria Thompson. "Dolly Parton on Gay Rumors, Losing a Drag Queen Look-Alike Contest and New Memoir." *ABC News*, 26 November 2012, https://abcnews.go.com/Entertainment/dolly-parton-gay-rumors-losing-drag-queen-alike/story?id=17812138.

Chávez, Karma R. "From Sanctuary to a Queer Politics of Fugitivity." *QED: A Journal in GLBTQ Worldmaking* 4, no. 2 (2017): 63–70.

Cheng, Anne Anlin. *The Melancholy of Race: Psychoanalysis, Assimilation, and Hidden Grief*. Oxford: Oxford University Press, 2000.

Chris Gonzalez (@livesinpages). "Tiger King is delivering the batshit, chaotic queer content I need right now." Twitter, 23 March 2020, 9:26 pm, https://twitter.com/livesinpages/status/1242276585492881415/.

Clukey, Amy. "Monstrous Plantations: *White Zombie* and the Horrors of Whiteness." In *Undead Souths: The Gothic and Beyond in Southern Literature and Culture*, edited by Eric Gary Anderson, Taylor Hagood, and Daniel Cross Turner, 124–35. Baton Rouge: Louisiana State University Press, 2015.

Cochrane, Emily. "Judge Finds Tennessee Law Aimed at Restricting Drag Shows Unconstitutional." *The New York Times*, 3 June 2023, https://www.nytimes.com/2023/06/03/us/politics/tennessee-drag-ruling.html.

Cohen, Cathy. "Punks, Bulldaggers, and Welfare Queens: The Radical Potential of Queer Politics?," *GLQ* 3, no. 4 (1997): 437–65.

Cohen, Jeffrey Jerome. "Monster Culture (Seven Theses)." In *Monster Theory: Reading Culture*, edited by Jeffrey Jerome Cohen, 3–25. Minneapolis: University of Minnesota Press, 1996.

Cox, Karen. *Dreaming of Dixie: How the South Was Created in American Popular Culture*. Chapel Hill: University of North Carolina Press, 2011.

Crank, James. *Understanding Randall Kenan*. Columbia: University Press of South Carolina, 2019.

Crawley, Ashon. "Circum-Religious Performance: Queer[ed] Black Bodies and the Black Church." *Theology and Sexuality* 14, no. 2 (2008): 201–22.

Crimp, Douglas. *Melancholia and Moralism: Essays on AIDS and Queer Politics*. Cambridge: MIT Press, 2002.

Cruz, Denise. "Monique Truong's Literary South and the Regional Forms of Asian America." *American Literary History* 26, no. 4 (2014): 716–41.

Cvetkovich, Ann. *An Archive of Feelings: Trauma, Sexuality, and Lesbian Public Culture*. Durham: Duke University Press, 2003.

Dahl, Ulrika. "(The promise of) Monstrous Kinship? Queer Reproduction and the Somatechnics of Sexual and Racial Difference." *Somatechnics* 8, no. 2 (2018): 195–211.

DasGupta, Debunaj. "Cartographies of Friendship, Desire, and Home; Notes on Surviving Neoliberal Security Regimes." *Disability Studies Quarterly* 34, no. 4 (2014).

Davis, David and Tara Powell, eds. *Writing in the Kitchen: Essays on Southern Literature and Foodways*. Oxford: University Press of Mississippi, 2014.

Davis, Thadious. *Southscapes: Geographies of Race, Region, and Literature*. Chapel Hill: University of North Carolina Press, 2011.

Deans, Emily. "A History of Eating Disorders." *Psychology Today*, 11 December 2011, https://www.psychologytoday.com/us/blog/evolutionary-psychiatry/201112/history-eating-disorders.

de Lauretis, Teresa. "Queer Texts, Bad Habits, and the Issue of a Future." *GLQ* 17, no. 2–3 (2011): 243–63.

Dolly Parton (@DollyParton). "It's a good thing I was born a girl, otherwise I'd be a drag queen." Twitter, 12 July 2010, 10:26 am, https://twitter.com/DollyParton/status/18362065644?lang=en.

Du Bois, W. E. B. *The Quest for the Silver Fleece*. 1911. New York City: Penguin Random House, 2012.

Duck, Leigh Anne. *The Nation's Region: Southern Modernism, Segregation, and US Nationalism*. Athens: University of Georgia Press, 2009.

———. "Southern Nonidentity." *Safundi: The Journal of South African and American Studies* 9, no. 3 (July 2008): 319–30.

Duffin-Ward, Maureen. *Suddenly Southern: A Yankee's Guide to Living in Dixie*. New York City: Atria, 2004.

Dunne, Michael. "Bakhtin Eats Some Fried Green Tomatoes: Dialogic Elements in Fannie Flagg's Famous Novel." *Studies in Popular Culture* 28, no. 1 (2005): 25–36.

Dykema, Amanda. "Embodied Knowledge: Synesthesia and the Archive in Monique Truong's *Bitter in the Mouth*." *MELUS* 39, no. 1 (2014): 106–29.

Ebert, Roger. "Fried Green Tomatoes." RogerEbert.com, 10 January 1992, https://www.rogerebert.com/reviews/fried-green-tomatoes-1992.

Edelman, Lee. *Bad Education: Why Queer Theory Teaches Us Nothing*. Durham: Duke University Press, 2023.

———. *No Future*. Durham: Duke University Press, 2004.

Egerton, John. "As God Is My Witness, I'll Never Go Hungry Again." *Southern Quarterly* 44, no. 2 (2007): 16–18.

Eng, David. *The Feeling of Kinship: Queer Liberalism and the Racialization of Intimacy*. Durham: Duke University Press, 2010.

Eng, David and David Kazanjian. "Introduction: Mourning Remains." In *Loss: The Politics of Mourning,* edited by David Eng and David Kazanjian, 1–26. Berkeley: University of California Press, 2002.

Engelhardt, Elizabeth. "Beating the Biscuits in Appalachia: Race, Class, and Gender Politics of Women Baking Bread." In *Cooking Lessons: the Politics of Gender and Food,* edited by Sherrie A. Inness, 151–68. Lanham: Rowman & Littlefield, 2001.

Ellis, Cristin. *Antebellum Posthuman: Race and Materiality in the Mid-Nineteenth Century.* New York City: Fordham University Press, 2018.

Ellis, Havelock. "Preface." In *The Sexual Life of Savages in North-Western Melanesia,* by Bronislaw Malinowski, vii–xii. London: Routledge, 1929.

Ellison, Treva, Kai M. Green, Matt Richardson, and C. Riley Snorton. "We Got Issues: Toward a Black Trans*/Studies." *TSQ* 4, no. 2 (2017): 162–69.

Evans, Stacie. "Not Your Auntie." *The Rumpus,* 1 November 2017, https://therumpus.net/2017/11/not-your-auntie/.

Everett, Percival. "The Appropriation of Cultures." *Callaloo* 19, no. 1 (1996): 24–30.

Faulkner, William. *Absalom, Absalom!* 1936. New York City: Vintage International, 1991.

Fawaz, Ramzi. *Queer Forms.* New York City: New York University Press, 2023.

Felski, Rita. *The Limits of Critique.* Chicago: University of Chicago Press, 2015.

Fetner, Tina. *How the Religious Right Shaped Lesbian and Gay Activism.* Minneapolis: University of Minnesota Press, 2008.

Ferguson, Roderick A. *Aberrations in Black: Toward a Queer of Color Critique.* Minneapolis: University of Minnesota Press, 2003.

Ferris, Marcie Cohen. *The Edible South: The Power of Food and the Making of an American Region.* Chapel Hill: University of North Carolina Press, 2016.

Flagg, Fannie. *Fried Green Tomatoes.* 1987. New York City: Ballantine, 2016.

Flood, E. Thadeus. "The Vietnamese Refugees in Thailand: Minority Manipulation in Counterinsurgency," *Critical Asian Studies* 9, no. 3 (1977): 31–47.

Ford, Sarah Gilbreath. *Tracing Southern Storytelling in Black and White.* Tuscaloosa: University of Alabama Press, 2014.

Foucault, Michel. *Discipline & Punish: The Birth of the Prison.* 1975. Translated by Alan Sheridan. New York: Vintage, 1995.

Freeman, Elizabeth. *Time Binds: Queer Temporalities, Queer Histories.* Durham: Duke University Press, 2010.

"Fried Green Tomatoes." *Variety,* 31 December 1990, https://variety.com/1990/film/reviews/fried-green-tomatoes-1200428905.

Fulton Minor, DoVeanna S. *Speaking Power: Black Feminist Orality in Women's Narratives of Slavery.* Albany: SUNY Press, 2006.

Gates, Henry Louis, Jr. *The Signifying Monkey: A Theory of African-American Literary Criticism.* Oxford: Oxford University Press, 1988.

———. *Stony the Road: Reconstruction, White Supremacy, and the Rise of Jim Crow.* New York City: Penguin, 2019.

Giffin, Matthew. "City Restricts BoroPride Org from Hosting Future Events on Public Property." *Middle Tennessee State University Sidelines,* 2 November 2022, https://mtsusidelines.com/2022/11/02/city-bans-boropride-org-from-hosting-future-events-on-public-property/.

Gilroy, Paul. *Postcolonial Melancholia*. New York City: Columbia University Press, 2006.

Glissant, Édouard. *Poetics of Relation*. 1990. Translated by Betsy Wing. Ann Arbor: University of Michigan Press, 1997.

Glock, Allison. "Redefining the Southern Belle." *Garden & Gun*, August/September 2011, https://gardenandgun.com/feature/redefining-southern-belle/.

Goddu, Teresa. "Vampire Gothic." *American Literary History* 11, no. 1 (1999): 125–41.

Gomez, Jewelle. *The Gilda Stories*. 1991. 25th anniversary edition. San Francisco: City Lights, 2016.

———. "Recasting the Mythology: Writing Vampire Fiction." In *Blood Read: The Vampire as Metaphor in Contemporary Culture*, edited by Joan Gordon and Victoria Hollinger, 85–92. Philadelphia: University of Pennsylvania Press, 1997.

Goode, Eric and Rebecca Chaiklin, creators. *Tiger King*. 2020–2021; Los Gatos, CA: Netflix.

Gopinath, Gayatri. *Unruly Visions: The Aesthetic Practices of Queer Diaspora*. Durham: Duke University Press, 2018.

Gordon, Philip. *Gay Faulkner: Uncovering a Homosexual Presence in Yoknapatawpha and Beyond*. Oxford: University Press of Mississippi, 2019.

Grady, Frank. "Vampire Culture." In *Monster Theory: Reading Culture*, edited by Jeffrey Jerome Cohen, 225–41. Minneapolis: University of Minnesota Press, 1996.

"Grady Hendrix." Gradyhendrix.com, accessed 10 December 2023, http://www.gradyhendrix.com/#/southernbookclub/.

Grant, Melissa Gira. "The New Orleans Police Raid That Launched a Dancer Resistance." In *We Too: Essays on Sex Work and Survival*, edited by Natalie West and Tina Horn, 94–103. New York City: The Feminist Press, 2021.

Greenberg, Louis. "Sins of the Blood: Rewriting the Family in Two Postmodern Vampire Novels." *JLS/TLW* 26, no. 1 (2010): 163–78.

Greeson, Jennifer Rae. "Expropriating *The Great South* and Exporting 'Local Color': Global and Hemispheric Imaginaries of the First Reconstruction." In *Hemispheric American Studies*, edited by Caroline F. Levander and Robert S. Levine, 116–39. New Brunswick: Rutgers University Press, 2008.

———. *Our South: Geographic Fantasy and the Rise of National Literature*. Cambridge: Harvard University Press, 2010.

Griffin, Farah Jasmine. *"Who Set You Flowin'?": The African American Migration Narrative*. Oxford: Oxford University Press, 1995.

Gruesz, Kirsten Silva. "The Mercurial Space of 'Central' America: New Orleans, Honduras, and the Writing of the Banana Republic." In *Hemispheric American Studies*, edited by Caroline F. Levander and Robert S. Levine, 140–65. New Brunswick: Rutgers University Press, 2008.

Guillory, Ferrel. "From Nixon to Trump." Southern Cultures, accessed 1 November 2023, https://www.southerncultures.org/article/southern-strategy-from-nixon-to-trump/.

Guinn, Matthew. *After Southern Modernism: Fiction of the Contemporary South.* Oxford: University Press of Mississippi, 2000.

Gwin, Minrose. "Introduction: Reading History, Memory, and Forgetting." *Southern Literary Journal*, 40, no. 2 (2008): 1–10.

Haggarty, George. *Queer Gothic.* Champaign: University Press of Illinois, 2006.

Hagood, Taylor. "Gone to Ground." In *Undead Souths: The Gothic and Beyond in Southern Literature and Culture*, edited by Eric Gary Anderson, Taylor Hagood, and Daniel Cross Turner, 248–60. Baton Rouge: Louisiana State University Press, 2015.

———. "The Gothic Tradition in New Orleans." In *New Orleans: A Literary History*, edited by T. R. Johnson, 278–91. Cambridge: Cambridge University Press, 2019.

Halberstam, Jack. *The Queer Art of Failure.* Durham: Duke University Press, 2011.

———. *In A Queer Time and Place: Transgender Bodies, Subcultural Lives.* New York City: NYU Press, 2005.

———. *Skin Shows: Gothic Horror and the Technology of Monsters.* Durham: Duke University Press, 1995.

Hale, Grace. *Making Whiteness: The Culture of Segregation in the South, 1890–1940.* New York: Vintage, 1998.

Harker, Jaime. *The Lesbian South: Southern Feminists, the Women in Print Movement, and the Queer Literary Canon.* Chapel Hill: University of North Carolina Press, 2018.

Harkins, Gillian. "Surviving the Family Romance? Southern Realism and the Labor of Incest." *The Southern Literary Journal* 40, no. 1 (2007): 114–39.

Harris, Trudier. *The Power of the Porch: The Storyteller's Craft in Zora Neale Hurston, Gloria Naylor, and Randall Kenan.* Athens: University Press of Georgia, 1996.

Harrison, Colin. *American Culture in the 1990s.* Edinburgh: Edinburgh University Press, 2010.

Hart, William David. "Constellations: Capitalism, Anti-Blackness, Afro-Pessimism, and Black Optimism." *American Journal of Theology & Philosophy* 39, no. 1 (2018): 5–33.

Hartman, Saidiya. *Lose Your Mother: A Journey Along the Atlantic Slave Route.* New York: Farrar, Strauss and Giroux, 2008.

———. *Scenes of Subjection.* Oxford: Oxford University Press, 1997.

Hatherley, Frances. "Pleasures of 'Unfit' Femininities." In *Fat Sex: New Directions in Theory and Activism*, edited by Helen Hester and Caroline Walters, 67–84. Milton Park: Routledge, 2016.

Hendrix, Grady. *The Southern Book Club's Guide to Slaying Vampires.* Philadelphia: Quirk Books, 2020.

Herring, Scott. *Another Country: Queer Anti-Urbanism.* New York City: New York University Press, 2010.

———. "Southern Backwardness: Metronormativity and Regional Visual Culture." *American Studies* 48, no. 2 (2007): 37–48.

Hinrichsen, Lisa. *Possessing the Past: Trauma, Imagination, and Memory in Post-Plantation Southern Literature.* Baton Rouge: Louisiana State University Press, 2015.

Holland, Sharon. *The Erotic Life of Racism*. Durham: Duke University Press, 2012.

———. *Raising the Dead: Readings of Death and (Black) Subjectivity*. Durham: Duke University Press, 2000.

Holmlund, Chris. "Cruisin' for a Bruisin': Hollywood's Deadly (Lesbian) Dolls." *Cinema Journal* 34, no. 1 (1994): 31–51.

hooks, bell. "Eating the Other: Desire and Resistance." In *Black Looks: Race and Representation*, 21–39. Boston: South End Press, 1992.

———. "Homeplace (A Site of Resistance.)" In *yearning: race, gender, and cultural politics*, 41–49. Boston: South End Press, 1990.

———. "Theory as Liberatory Practice." In *Teaching to Transgress: Education as the Practice of Freedom*, 59–75. Milton Park: Routledge, 1994.

Horowitz, Katie R. "The Trouble with 'Queerness': Drag and the Making of Two Cultures." *Signs* 38, no. 2 (2013): 303–326.

Horton-Stallings, LaMonda. *A Dirty South Manifesto*. Berkeley: University of California Press, 2019.

Horowitz, Andy. *Katrina: A History, 1915–2015*. Cambridge: Harvard University Press, 2020.

Howard, John, ed. *Carryin' on in the Lesbian and Gay South*. New York City: New York University Press, 1997.

———. *Men Like That: A Southern Queer History*. Chicago: University of Chicago Press, 2001.

Hughes, William. "'The Taste of Blood Meant the End of Aloneness': Vampires and Gay Men in Poppy Z. Brite's Lost Souls." In *Queering the Gothic*, edited by Andrew Smith and William Hughes, 189–201. Manchester: Manchester University Press, 2009.

Hughes, William and Andrew Smith, eds. *Queering the Gothic*. Manchester: Manchester University Press, 2009.

Hutcheon, Linda. *Narcissistic Narrative: The Metafictional Paradox*. 1981. Waterloo: Wilfrid Laurier University Press, 2013.

"Invasive: Amassing Southern LGBTQ Stories." Invasive Queer Kudzu, accessed 1 February 2022, https://cargocollective.com/invasivequeerkudzu.

Isenberg, Nancy. *White Trash: The 400-Year Untold History of Class in America*. New York City: Penguin, 2017.

Jameson, Fredric. *The Political Unconscious: Narrative as a Socially Symbolic Act*. Ithaca: Cornell University Press, 1982.

Janette, Michele. "Alternative Historical Tetherings: Wilbur Wright, George Moses Horton, and Virginia Dare in Monique Truong's *Bitter in the Mouth*." *Journal of Asian American Studies* 19, no. 2 (2016): 193–212.

Jarvis, Christina. "Gendered Appetites: Feminisms, Dorothy Allison, and the Body." *Women's Studies* 29 (2000): 763–92.

Jefferson, Melissa and Theron Thomas, writers. "Everybody's Gay." *Special*. Nice Life and Atlantic Records, 2022.

Jenkins, Jerry Rafiki. "Race, Freedom, and the Black Vampire in Jewelle Gomez's *The Gilda Stories*." *African American Review* 46, no. 2–3 (2013): 313–28.

Jenkins, Rafiki. *The Paradox of Blackness in African American Vampire Fiction.* Columbus: Ohio State University Press, 2019.

Jerng, Mark. *Claiming Others: Transracial Adoption and National Belonging.* Minneapolis: University of Minnesota Press, 2010.

Johnson, Colin. *Just Queer Folk: Gender and Sexuality in Rural America.* Philadelphia: Temple University Press, 2013.

Johnson, E. Patrick. *Black. Queer. Southern. Women. An Oral History.* Chapel Hill: University of North Carolina Press, 2018.

———. "'Quare' Studies, or (Almost) Everything I Know about Queer Studies I Learned from My Grandmother." *Text and Performance Quarterly* 21, no. 1 (2001): 1–25.

———. *Sweet Tea: Black Gay Men of the South.* Chapel Hill: University of North Carolina Press, 2011.

Johnson, Rashauna. *Slavery's Metropolis: Unfree Labor in New Orleans.* Cambridge: Cambridge University Press, 2016.

Johnson, T. R., ed. *New Orleans: A Literary History.* Cambridge: Cambridge University Press, 2019.

Jones, Rolin, creator. *Interview with the Vampire.* 2022; New York: AMC.

Jones, Suzanne. *Race Mixing: Southern Fiction Since the Sixties.* Baltimore: Johns Hopkins University Press, 2004.

Joshi, Khyati and Jigna Desai, eds. *Asian Americans in Dixie: Race and Migration in the South.* Champaign: University of Illinois Press, 2013.

Kaus, Alaina. "Reimagining the Southern Gothic: The Two Souths in Monique Truong's *Bitter in the Mouth*." *MELUS* 2, no. 3 (2017): 84–101.

Keeling, Kara. *Queer Times, Black Futures.* New York City: New York University Press, 2019.

Kempley, Rita. "Fried Green Tomatoes." *The Washington Post*, 10 January 1992, https://www.washingtonpost.com/wp-srv/style/longterm/movies/videos/friedgreentomatoespg13kempley_a0a28a.htm.

Kenan, Randall. *Black Folk Could Fly: Selected Writings.* New York City: Norton, 2022.

———. *If I Had Two Wings.* New York City: Norton, 2020.

———. "An Interview with Randall Kenan." By Charles H. Rowell. *Callaloo* 21, no. 1 (1998): 133–48.

———. *Let the Dead Bury Their Dead.* San Diego: Harcourt, 1992.

———. *A Visitation of Spirits.* New York City: Vintage, 1989.

———, ed. *The Carolina Table: North Carolina Writers on Food.* Hillsborough: Eno Publishers, 2016.

Kent, Sarah. "'The Bloody Transaction': Black Vampires and the Afterlives of Slavery in *Blacula* and *The Gilda Stories*." *The Journal of Popular Culture* 53, no. 3 (2020): 739–59.

Kim, Jinah. *Postcolonial Grief: The Afterlives of the Pacific Wars in the Americas.* Durham: Duke University Press, 2019.

King, Dennis. "Fried Green Tomatoes." *Tulsa World*, 31 January 1992, https://tulsaworld.com/archives/fried-green-tomatoes/article_7899e5fc-cbe9-5e26-baed-60433b6b7209.html.

Kreydatus, Beth. "'Enriching Women's Lives': The Mary Kay Approach to Beauty, Business, and Feminism." *Business and Economic History On-Line* 3 (2005): 1–32.

Kreyling, Michael. "Fee, Fie, Faux Faulkner: Parody and Postmodernism In Southern Literature." *Southern Review* 29, no. 1 (Winter 1993): 1–15.

———. *The South That Wasn't There: Postsouthern Memory and History*. Baton Rouge: Louisiana State University Press, 2010.

Kuhn, Mary. "Garden Variety: Botany and Multiplicity in Harriet Beecher Stowe's Abolitionism." *American Literature* 87, no. 3 (2015): 489–516.

Lassiter, Matthew and Joseph Crespino, eds. *The Myth of Southern Exceptionalism*. Oxford: Oxford University Press, 2009.

Lavietes, Matt. "Tennessee Governor Appears to Have Dressed in Drag, an Art Form He Wants to Restrict." NBC, 27 February 2023, https://www.nbcnews.com/nbc-out/out-politics-and-policy/tennessee-governor-appears-dressed-drag-art-form-wants-restrict-rcna72569.

Lee, Harper. *To Kill a Mockingbird*. 1960. New York City: Harper Perennial, 2002.

Levine, Caroline. *Forms: Whole, Rhythm, Hierarchy, Network*. Princeton: Princeton University Press, 2015.

Lewis, Christopher. "Queering Personhood in the Neo-Slave Narrative: Jewelle Gomez's *The Gilda Stories*." *African American Review* 47, no. 4 (2014): 447–59.

Lindenmeyer, Antje. "'Lesbian Appetites': Food, Sexuality and Community in Feminist Autobiography." *Sexualities* 9, no. 4 (2006): 469–85.

Littler, Lucy. "The Implications of 'Chosenness': Unsettling the Exodus Narrative as a Model for Black Liberation in Randall Kenan's *A Visitation of Spirits*." *Southern Literary Journal* 44, no. 1 (Fall 2011): 37–55.

Long, Alecia P. "Queers, Fairies, and Ne'er-Do-Wells." In *Remaking New Orleans: Beyond Exceptionalism and Authenticity*, edited by Thomas Jessen Adams and Matt Sakakeeny, 179–198. Durham: Duke University Press, 2019.

Love, Heather. *Feeling Backward: Loss and the Politics of Queer History*. Cambridge: Harvard University Press, 2003.

Lowe, Lisa. *Immigrant Acts: On Asian American Cultural Politics*. Durham: Duke University Press, 1996.

Lybrand, Holmes. "Man Who Carried Confederate Flag in US Capitol and Son Found Guilty of Felonies." *CNN*, 15 June 2022, https://www.cnn.com/2022/06/15/politics/kevin-hunter-seefried-confederate-flag-capitol-riot/index.html.

Malatino, Hil. *Queer Embodiment: Monstrosity, Medical Violence, and Intersex Experience*. Lincoln: University of Nebraska Press, 2019.

Manalansan, Martin. "Messing up Sex: The Promises and Possibilities of Queer of Color Critique." *Sexualities* 21, no. 8 (2018): 1287–90.

Manoff, Marlene. "Theories of the Archive from Across the Disciplines." *Portal: Libraries and the Academy* 4, no. 1 (2004): 9–25.

Marler, Scott. *The Merchant's Capital: New Orleans and the Political Economy of the Nineteenth-Century South*. Cambridge: Cambridge University Press, 2013.

Martin, George R. R. *Fevre Dream*. New York City: Poseidon, 1982.

Mason, Bobbie Ann. *In Country*. New York City: Harper, 1985.

McBride, Dwight. "Straight Black Studies: On African American Studies, James Baldwin, and Black Queer Studies." In *Black Queer Studies: A Critical Anthology*, edited by E. Patrick Johnson and Mae G. Henderson, 68–89. Durham: Duke University Press, 2005.

McKittrick, Katherine *Demonic Grounds: Black Women and the Cartographies of Struggle*. Minneapolis: University Press of Minnesota, 2006.

McMahand, Donnie. "Strange Bedfellows: Randall Kenan Talks Back to the Southern Renaissance." *The Southern Literary Journal* 47, no. 2 (2015): 36–54.

McPherson, Tara. *Reconstructing Dixie: Race, Gender, and Nostalgia in the Imagined South*. Durham: Duke University Press, 2003.

——. "Revamping the South: Thoughts on Labor, Relationality, and Southern Representation." *American Cinema and the Southern Imaginary*, edited by Deborah Barker and Kathryn McKee, 336–51. Athens: University of Georgia Press, 2011.

McRuer, Robert. "Queer Locations, Queer Transformations: Randall Kenan's *A Visitation of Spirits*." In *South to a New Place: Region, Literature, Culture*, edited by Suzanne W. Jones, 184–195. Baton Rouge: Louisiana State University Press, 2002.

Mickler, Ernest Matthew. *White Trash Cooking*. 1986. Berkeley: Ten Speed Press, 2011.

Morris, Susana M. "More Than Human: Black Feminisms and the Future in Jewelle Gomez's *The Guilda Stories*." *The Black Scholar* 46, no. 2 (2016): 33–45.

Morrison, Toni. "Home." In *The House That Race Built*, edited by Wahneema Lubiano, 3–12. New York City: Vintage, 1997.

——. *Playing in the Dark: Whiteness and the Literary Imagination*. Cambridge: Harvard University Press, 1992.

Mortimer-Sandilands, Catriona and Bruce Erickson. *Queer Ecologies: Sex, Nature, Politics, Desire*. Bloomington: Indiana University Press, 2010.

Muñoz, José Esteban. *Cruising Utopia: The Then and There of Queer Futurity*. New York City: New York University Press, 2009.

Munro, Niall. "Neo-Confederates Take Their Stand: Southern Agrarians and the Civil War." *European Journal of American Culture* 39, no. 2 (2020): 141–62.

Nagourney, Adam. "The Sun Belt, Eclipsed." *The New York Times*, 25 August 2012, https://www.nytimes.com/2012/08/26/sunday-review/the-sun-belt-eclipsed.html.

Nguyen, Marguerite. *America's Vietnam: The Longue Durée of US Literature and Empire*. Philadelphia: Temple University Press, 2018.

Nicolaou, Elena. "Watch *Tiger King's* Joe Exotic Marry His Husbands in This Wedding Video." Oprah Daily, 27 March 2020, https://www.oprahdaily.com/entertainment/tv-movies/a31955806/tiger-king-joe-exotic-wedding-video/.

Norman, Brian. *Dead Women Talking: Figures of Injustice in American Literature*. Baltimore: Johns Hopkins University Press, 2012.

Nunes, Zita. *Cannibal Democracy: Race and Representation in the Literature of the Americas*. Minneapolis: Minnesota University Press, 2008.

Nurka, Camille. "Animal Techne: Transing Posthumanism." *TSQ* 2, no. 2 (2015): 209–26.

Nurse, Donna. "Gothic on the Bluffs." *The Toronto Star*, 28 October 2007, https://www.thestar.com/entertainment/2007/10/28/gothic_on_the_bluffs.html.

Nyong'o, Tavia. "Do You Want Queer Theory (or Do You Want the Truth)? Intersections of Punk and Queer in the 1970s." *Radical History Review* 100 (Winter 2008): 103–19.

O'Connor, Flannery. *The Complete Stories*. 1946. New York: Farrar, Strauss and Giroux, 1981.

Opie, Frederick Douglass. *Hog and Hominy: Soul Food from Africa to America*. New York City: Columbia University Press, 2010.

Outka, Paul. *Race and Nature from Transcendentalism to the Harlem Renaissance*. London: Palgrave, 2008.

———. "Whitman and Race ('He's Queer, He's Unclear, Get Used to It')." *Journal of American Studies* 36, no. 2 (2002): 292–318.

Owen, Gilman. *The Vietnam War in the Southern Imagination*. Oxford: University Press of Mississippi, 1992.

Palmer, Paulina. *The Queer Uncanny: New Perspectives on the Gothic*. Cardiff: University of Wales Press, 2012.

Parrish, Timothy. *From the Civil War to the Apocalypse: Postmodern History and American Fiction*. Amherst: University of Massachusetts Press, 2008.

Parsons, Abigail. "I Just Can't Wait to Get to Heaven." In *Sex and Sexuality in Modern Southern Culture*, edited by Trent Brown, 185–206. Baton Rouge: Louisiana State University Press, 2017.

Patterson, Kathy Davis. "'Haunting Back': Vampire Subjectivity in *The Gilda Stories*." *Femspec* 6, no. 1 (2005): 35–57.

Patterson, Orlando. *Slavery and Social Death: A Comparative Study*. Cambridge: Harvard University Press, 1982.

Phelan, James. "Narrative Ethics." The Living Handbook of Narratology, 21 November 2013, https://www-archiv.fdm.uni-hamburg.de/lhn/node/108.html.

Piatti-Farnell, Lorna. "'The Blood Never Stops Flowing and the Party Never Ends': The Originals and the Afterlife of New Orleans as a Vampire City." *M/C Journal* 20, no. 5 (2017): 1–9.

p*op dealer (@malerbud). "If Tiger King has taught me anything, it's that the Southern United States is the most batshit insane place on earth. It's not real. It can't be real". Twitter, 24 March 2020, 11:47 pm, https://twitter.com/malerbud/status/1242674545997332480.

Probyn, Elspeth. *Carnal Appetites: FoodSexIdentities*. Milton Park: Routledge, 2000.

Pugh, Tison. *Precious Perversions: Humor, Homosexuality, and the Southern Literary Canon*. Baton Rouge: Louisiana State University Press, 2016.

———. *Queer Chivalry: Medievalism and the Myth of White Masculinity in Southern Literature*. Baton Rouge: Louisiana State University Press, 2013.

Rice, Anne. *Interview with the Vampire*. New York City: Knopf, 1976.

Richards, Gary. *Lovers and Beloveds: Sexual Otherness in Southern Fiction, 1936–1961*. Baton Rouge: Louisiana State University Press, 2005.

Rifkin, Mark. *The Erotics of Sovereignty: Queer Native Writing in the Era of Self-Determination*. Minneapolis: University of Minnesota Press, 2012.

Rieger, Christopher. *Clear-Cutting Eden: Ecology and the Pastoral in Southern Literature*. Tuscaloosa: University of Alabama Press, 2009.

Rody, Caroline. *The Daughter's Return: African-American and Caribbean Women's Fictions of History*. Oxford: Oxford University Press, 2001.

Romine, Scott. "God and the Moon Pie: Consumption, Disenchantment, and the Reliably Lost Cause." In *Creating and Consuming the American South*, edited by Martyn Bone, Brian Ward, and William A. Link, 49–71. Gainesville: University of Florida Press, 2015.

———. *The Real South: Southern Narrative in the Age of Cultural Reproduction*. Baton Rouge: Louisiana State University Press, 2014.

Rosenthal, Gregory Samantha. *Living Queer History: Remembrance and Belonging in a Southern City*. Chapel Hill: University of North Carolina Press, 2021.

Ruti, Mari. *The Ethics of Opting Out: Queer Theory's Defiant Subjects*. New York City: Columbia University Press, 2017.

"S. A. Cosby on *Razorblade Tears*." *New York Times Book Review*. Podcast audio, 16 July 2021, https://www.nytimes.com/2021/07/16/books/review/podcast-razorblade-tears-s-a-cosby-murderous-dr-cream-dean-jobb.html.

Saturday Night Live. "Colonel Angus Comes Home." YouTube, 25 September 2013, https://www.youtube.com/watch?v=3l2oi-X8P38.

Saunders, George. *CivilWarLand in Bad Decline*. New York City: Random House, 1996.

———. *Lincoln in the Bardo*. New York City: Random House, 2017.

Sayers, Daniel. *A Desolate Place for a Defiant People: The Archaeology of Maroons, Indigenous Americans, and Enslaved Laborers in the Great Dismal Swamp*. Gainesville: University of Florida Press, 2014.

Schwartz, Josh and Stephanie Savage, developers. *Gossip Girl*. 2007–2012; Burbank, CA: Warner Brothers Television.

Scott, Darieck. *Extravagant Abjection: Blackness, Power, and Sexuality in the African American Literary Imagination*. New York City: New York University Press, 2010.

Sedgwick, Eve. *Between Men: English Literature and Male Homosocial Desire*. New York City: Columbia University Press, 1985.

Shenk, Joshua Wolf. *Lincoln's Melancholy: How Depression Challenged a President and Fueled His Greatness*. New York: Houghton Mifflin Harcourt, 2005.

Simal-Gonzalez, Begoña. "Judging the Book by Its Cover: Phantom Asian America in Monique Truong's *Bitter in the Mouth*." *Concentric* 39, no. 2 (2013): 7–32.

Simpson, Lewis. "The Closure of History in a Postsouthern America." In *The Brazen Face of History: Studies in the Literary Consciousness of America*. Baton Rouge: Louisiana State University Press, 1980.

Siodmak, Robert, director. *Son of Dracula*. Universal Pictures, 1943. 1 hr., 20 min.

Smith, Dina. "Cultural Studies' Misfit: White Trash Studies." *Mississippi Quarterly* 57, no. 3 (2004): 369–87.

Smith, Donna Jo. "Queering the South: Constructions of Southern/Queer Identity." In *Carryin' on in the Lesbian and Gay South*, edited by John Howard, 370–87. New York City: New York University Press, 1997.

Smith, Jon. *Finding Purple America*. Athens: University of Georgia Press, 2013.

———. "For They Know Not What They Do: Southern Studies Centers, Normativity, and Fantasies of White Redemption." In *Navigating Souths: Transcdisciplinary Explorations of a US Region*, edited by Michele Grigsby Coffey and Jodi Skipper, 249–64. Athens: University of Georgia Press, 2017.

———. "Hot Bodies and 'Barbaric Tropics': The US South and New World Natures." *Southern Literary Journal* 36, no. 1 (Fall 2003): 104–20.

———. "Toward a Post-Postpolitical Southern Studies: On the Limits of the 'Creating and Consuming' Paradigm." In *Creating and Consuming the American South*, edited by Martyn Bone, Brian Ward, and William A. Link, 72–94. Gainesville: University of Florida Press, 2015.

Snorton, C. Riley. *Black On Both Sides: A Racial History of Trans Identity*. Minneapolis: University of Minnesota Press, 2017.

soft era Cris (@realdealcwill). "Y'all Tiger King on Netflix is some crazy white people shit." Twitter, 21 March 2020, 1:25 am, https://twitter.com/realdealcwill/status/1241249600310304768.

Somerville, Siobhan. *Queering the Color Line: Race and the Invention of Homosexuality in American Culture*. Durham: Duke University Press, 2000.

Sontag, Susan. "Notes on Camp." *The Partisan Review* 31, no. 4 (1964).

Sorenson, Lief. "Modernity on a Global Stage: Hurston's Alternative Modernism." *MELUS* 30, no. 4 (2005): 3–24.

Spillers, Hortense. "Mama's Baby, Papa's Maybe: An American Grammar Book." *Diacritics* 17, no. 2 (1987): 64–81.

Stanonis, Anthony. "Introduction: Thoughtful Souvenirs." In *Dixie Emporium: Tourism, Foodways, and Consumer Culture in the American South*, edited by Anthony Stanonis, 1–19. Athens: University of Georgia Press, 2008.

———. "Just Like Mammy Used to Make: Foodways in the Jim Crow South." In *Dixie Emporium: Tourism, Foodways, and Consumer Culture in the American South*, edited by Anthony Stanonis, 208–34. Athens: University of Georgia Press, 2008.

Stockton, Kathryn Bond. *The Queer Child, or Growing Sideways in the Twentieth Century*. Durham: Duke University Press, 2009.

Stokes, Ashli Quesinberry and Wendy Atkins-Sayre. *Consuming Identity: The Role of Food in Redefining the South*. Oxford: University Press of Mississippi, 2016.

Sublette, Cammie and Jennifer Martin. "Let Them Eat Cake, Caviar, Organic, and Whole Foods: American Elitism, White Trash Dinner Parties, and Diet." *Studies in Popular Culture* 36, no. 1 (2013): 21–44.

Tate, Allen. "The New Provincialism: With an Epilogue on the Southern Novel." *Virginia Quarterly Review* 21, no. 2 (1945): 262–72.

Taylor, Melanie. *Reconstructing the Native South*. Athens: University of Georgia Press, 2011.

Taylor, Kristine. "Untimely Subjects: White Trash and the Making of Racial Innocence in the Postwar South." *American Quarterly* 67, no. 1 (2015): 55–79.

"Team Avatar vs. The Swampbenders," YouTube, 25 August 2021, https://www.youtube.com/watch?v=ae5JaLzOvUE.

Thananopavarn, Susan. "Digging Up the Past: Randall Kenan's *Let the Dead Bury Their Dead* and the Suppressed Histories of the US South." In *Swamp Souths*, edited by Kirstin Squint, Eric Gary Anderson, Taylor Hagood, and Anthony Wilson, 203–14. Baton Rouge: Louisiana State University Press, 2020.

"The ACLU Is Tracking Anti-LGBTQ Bills in the US" ACLU, accessed 12 December 2023, https://www.aclu.org/legislation-affecting-lgbtq-rights-across-country.

"The Vocabularist: Have We Gotten the Meaning of 'Whistle-Stop' Right?," BBC, 2 June 2015, https://www.bbc.com/news/blogs-magazine-monitor-32941311.

Thomas, Sara Gabler. "Queer Formalism: Synesthetic Storytelling in Monique Truong and William Faulkner." *The Faulkner Journal* 30, no. 1 (2016): 39–61.

Thompson, Graham. *American Culture in the 1980s*. Edinburgh: Edinburgh University Press, 2007.

Tompkins, Kyla Wazana. *Racial Indigestion: Eating Bodies in the 19th Century*. New York City: New York University Press, 2012.

Tripp, C.A. *The Intimate World of Abraham Lincoln*. New York City: Basic Books, 2006.

Truong, Monique. *Bitter in the Mouth*. New York City: Random House, 2010.

Tucker, Lauryl. *Unexpected Pleasures: Parody, Queerness & Genre in 20th Century British Fiction*. Clemson: Clemson University Press, 2022.

Tucker, Lindsey. "Gay Identity, Conjure, and the Uses of Postmodern Ethnography in the Fictions of Randall Kenan." *Modern Fiction Studies* 49, no. 2 (2003): 306–31.

Twitty, Michael. *The Cooking Gene: A Journey Through African American Culinary History in the Old South*. New York City: Amistad, 2017.

Vickers, Lu. "*Fried Green Tomatoes*: Excuse Me, Did We See the Same Movie?" *Jump Cut* 39 (1994): 25–30.

Wald, Patricia. *Contagious: Cultures, Carriers, and the Outbreak Narrative*. Durham: Duke University Press, 2008.

Walker, Antiwan. "Queering Black Nationalism: History, Geopolitics, and Sexual Identity in Randall Kenan's *A Visitation of Spirits*." *CLA Journal* 56, no. 1 (2012): 54–81.

Wallace, Maurice. *Constructing the Black Masculine: Identity and Ideality in African American Men's Literature and Culture, 1775–1995*. Durham: Duke University Press, 2002.

Wallace-Sanders, Kimberly. *Mammy: A Century of Race, Gender, and Southern Memory*. Ann Arbor: University of Michigan Press, 2009.

Watson, Jay. "So Easy Even a Child Can Do It: William Faulkner's Southern Gothicizers." *Mississippi Quarterly* 72, no. 1 (2019): 1–23.

Waugh, Patricia. *Metafiction: The Theory and Practice of Self-Conscious Fiction*. Milton Park: Routledge, 1984.

Weston, Kath. "Get Thee to a Big City: Sexual Imaginary and the Great Gay Migration." *GLQ* 2, no. 3 (1995): 253–77.

Wiegman, Robyn. "Eve's Triangles, or Queer Studies Beside Itself." *differences* 26, no. 1 (2015): 48–73.

Williams, Roger Ross, director. *High on the Hog: How African American Cuisine Transformed America*. 2021; Netflix.

Williams-Forson, Psyche. *Building Houses Out of Chicken Legs: Black Women, Food & Power*. Chapel Hill: University of North Carolina Press, 2006.

Wilson, Anthony. *Shadow and Shelter: The Swamp in Southern Culture*. Oxford: University Press of Mississippi, 2005.

Winter, Joseph. *Hope Draped in Black: Race, Melancholy, and the Agony of Progress*. Durham: Duke University Press, 2016.

Woodward, C. Vann. *The Burden of Southern History*. 1960. Baton Rouge: Louisiana State University Press, 2008.

Wray, Matt. *Not Quite White: White Trash and the Boundaries of Whiteness*. Durham: Duke University Press, 2006.

Wynter, Sylvia. "Unsettling the Coloniality of Being/Power/Truth/Freedom: Towards the Human, After Man, Its Overrepresentation—An Argument." *CR: The New Centennial Review* 3, no. 3 (2003): 257–337.

Yaeger, Patricia. *Dirt and Desire: Reconstructing Southern Women's Writing, 1930–1990*. Chicago: University of Chicago Press, 2000.

———. "Ghosts and Shattered Bodies, or What Does It Mean to Still Be Haunted by Southern Literature?" *South Central Review* 22, no. 1 (2005): 87–108.

Yurcaba, Jo. "DeSantis Signs 'Don't Say Gay' Expansion and Gender-Affirming Care Ban." *NBC News*, 17 May 2023, https://www.nbcnews.com/nbc-out/out-politics-and-policy/desantis-signs-dont-say-gay-expansion-gender-affirming-care-ban-rcna84698.

Žižek, Slavoj. "Melancholy and the Act," *Critical Inquiry* 26, no. 4 (2000): 657–81.

Index

Absalom, Absalom! (Faulkner), 161
African American folk tradition, 86, 87, 148–53, 179n95
Afrofuturism, 148, 151, 194n126
Agamben, Giorgio, 92
Agee, James, 44, 178–79n81
Agrarianism, 93, 106, 183n27
Ahmed, Sara, 6, 55, 93
AIDS epidemic, 22–23, 92
alienation, 6, 61, 93, 109, 183n19
Allewaert, Monique, 55, 56
Allison, Dorothy, 16, 19–20, 46–53
Anatol, Giselle Liza, 128, 148, 194–95n127
Anderson, Benedict, 4
anti-capitalism, 17, 69, 77, 93, 148, 157
antinormativity, 2, 7, 8–9, 15, 75, 164, 192n53
anti-relational queer theory, 6–7, 168n26
Anzaldúa, Gloria, 149, 152
Appalachia, rural, 6
appetite, food vs. sexuality, 15–16, 23–24, 49–50. *See also* foodways
"Appropriation of Cultures" (Everett), 121
archive: archival narrative technique, 113–17; "archive fever," 114; historical, 101; historical (fictional) archive, 26, 29, 38; story as, 66, 67
Asian identities in the South, 104–7, 109, 185n81
Auerbach, Nina, 132, 157
author's methodology, 14–18
Avatar: The Last Airbender (animated series), 55

Bakhtin, Mikhail, 88, 178n62
barbecue, 21, 24–25, 35, 37, 48, 172n66. *See also* cannibalism, trope of

Baudrillard, Jean, 122
Benjamin, Walter, 94, 95
Berglund, Jeff, 43
Berlant, Lauren, 22, 75
Bersani, Leo, 13
Betts, Doris, 66
Bibler, Michael, 5, 9, 58
Bitter in the Mouth (Truong), 17; archival narrative technique, 113–17; Asian identities in South, 104–7, 109, 185n81; and historical imagination, 122; historical narrative as structure, 101–3, 108; melancholy as theme, 117–21; synesthesia and melancholy, 107–12
Black community: Black resistance, 56–57, 80–86; "homeplace" as concept, 75–80; and queerness in *Fried Green Tomatoes at the Whistle Stop Cafe* (Flagg), 36–39; and resistance to surveillance, 80–86. *See also* race
Bone, Martyn, 93
Booth, Wayne, 13
Bradway, Tyler, 7
Brasell, R. Bruce, 4, 10, 129, 130
Brite, Poppy Z., 18, 128, 133, 141–47
Browne, Simone, 80
Butler, Judith, 90, 92, 126, 162

Caldwell, Erskine, 5, 129, 143
Calhoun, John C., 89
Camp, Stephanie, 56
Cane (Toomer), 178n60
cannibalism, trope of, 35, 37, 42, 146. *See also* barbecue
Cannon, Uzzie, 67

Cantrell, Jaime, 52
capitalism: anti-capitalism, 17, 69, 77, 93, 148, 157; late-stage, 11, 22, 27, 92–93, 122–24, 152, 168n38, 171n29; as normative paradigm, 7, 73; and slavery, 131, 183n27, 191n33; and white supremacy, 56–57
Capitol riots (2021), 89
Capote, Truman, 136, 162–63
The Carolina Table (Kenan, ed.), 63
Carpenter, Karen, 23
Carter, Jimmy, 11
Cash, W. J., 45
Chadd, Claire, 12
Cheng, Anne Anlin, 107, 108
Civil War, legacy of, 27, 81, 89–90, 96, 99, 106, 108–9, 122. See also slavery
CivilWarLand in Bad Decline (Saunders), 95, 121–25
Cohen, Cathy, 7–8
Cohen, Jeffrey Jerome, 126
"Colonel Angus" *Saturday Night Live* skit, 5
colonialism, 118, 131, 191n29
"colorblindness," 104
Confederate flag, symbolism of, 89, 121, 122
Confederate monuments/statues, 90, 116, 117, 189n190
The Cooking Gene (Twitty), 53
Cosby, S. A., 130
Cotton's Queer Relations (Bibler), 9
Cracker Barrel restaurants, 21
Crawley, Ashon, 73
Cruising Utopia (Muñoz), 157
Cruz, Denise, 104, 111–12

Dahl, Ulrika, 127
Dare, Virginia, 114–15
"dark sousveillance," 80, 82
Davis, Jefferson, 122
de Laurentis, Teresa, 13
Derrida, Jacques, 114
Desai, Jigna, 109

deviance: and appetites, 19–20, 26, 33; southern and queer intersection, 15–18, 43, 46, 52–53, 56; and southern culture, 2–3, 5, 8–10, 12–13, 127, 169n46; swamp as symbol of, 55, 59, 69, 86
A Dirty South Manifesto (Horton-Stallings), 12–13
disidentification, 152, 162
Douglass, Frederick, 130
Dracula (Stoker), 128, 131, 191n43
drag artists, 159–60, 162, 171n46; bans concerning, 164
Driving Miss Daisy (film), 10
Duck, Leigh Anne, 3–4
Dukes of Hazzard (television show), 10
Dunne, Michael, 34

eating disorders, 23
Ebert, Roger, 24, 42
Edelman, Lee, 14, 99, 156
Edge, John T., 44
Egerton, John, 43
Eng, David, 91, 104
eugenics, 45
Eurydice, 92, 188n173
Evans, Walker, 44
Everett, Percival, 121
"Everybody's Gay" (Lizzo), 164–65
exceptionalism, southern, 6, 167n9

"The Fall of the House of Usher" (Poe), 130
Faulkner, William, 5, 54, 90, 129, 130, 161
Fawaz, Ramzi, 14
femininity, Southern/traditional, 41, 161–62
feminism, 156–57; feminist activism (1980s), 10; "Sex Wars," 46–47; southern community of, 50–52
Ferguson, Roderick, 8
Ferris, Marcie Cohen, 21–22
Fevre Dream (Martin), 18, 127–28, 133, 137–41

218 Index

Flagg, Fannie, 15–16, 19–20. *See also Fried Green Tomatoes at the Whistle Stop Cafe* (Flagg)
foodways: barbecue, 21, 24–25, 35, 37, 48, 172n66; "Black" food, 173n79; chocolate rabbits, 31, 33; indulgent food, 19–20, 22; and intimacy, 31; queerness and Southern Foodways, 22–24; soul food, 45, 174n112; Southern comfort food, 62–63; Southern Foodways, 19, 20–22, 53, 63–64; taste-word synesthesia, 103, 108–12; Thanksgiving traditions, 117–18
Ford, Sarah Gilbreath, 27
"forms," 86–88, 182n194
Foucault, Michel, 182n184, 196n170
"Foundations of the Earth" (Kenan), 62–63
The Foxes of Harrow (Yerby), 152
Freeman, Elizabeth, 7, 147, 157
Freud, Sigmund, 22, 91–92
Fried Green Tomatoes at the Whistle Stop Cafe (Flagg), 15–16, 19–20, 24–43; conclusion of, 40–43; film adaptation, 24, 42–43; and queerness, 30–36; queerness and blackness, 36–39; reviews and popularity of, 24–26; structure and plot, 26–30, 40

Game of Thrones (television show), 137
Gates, Henry Louis, Jr., 59
gaze, transformative, 81, 82–83
ghosts, symbolism and significance, 95–96; in *Lincoln in the Bardo* (Saunders), 97–100
The Gilda Stories (Gomez), 18, 128, 133, 141–42, 148–53
Glasgow, Ellen, 129–30
Goddu, Teresa, 130
Gomez, Jewelle, 18, 128, 133, 141–42, 148–53
Gothic literature. See Southern Gothic genre
Great Dismal Swamp, 56–57
Greeson, Jennifer Rae, 4

Griffin, Farah Jasmine, 58
guilt vs. nostalgia, 23
Gwin, Minrose, 90

Hagood, Taylor, 132
Halberstam, Jack, 6, 93, 128, 130, 131, 156, 162
Hale, Grace Elizabeth, 8
Harker, Jaime, 5, 10
Harris, Trudier, 59
Hart, William David, 45
health-consciousness, 23, 44, 46, 49, 51–52
Hendrix, Grady, 18, 126, 127, 134–37
heteronormativity, 71, 73, 75, 94–95; white southern nostalgia, 38, 43, 53. *See also* normative ideologies
High on the Hog (Netflix series), 53
Hinrichsen, Lisa, 103
historical archive, 101; in *Fried Green Tomatoes at the Whistle Stop Cafe* (Flagg), 26, 29, 38
history: and capitalism, 122–23; "pornography of history," 116–17
HIV/AIDS. *See* AIDS epidemic
Hobbes, Thomas, 88
Holland, Sharon, 8, 74, 85, 156–57
Holmlund, Chris, 43
"homeplace" as concept, 72–73, 75–80
homophobia, 5–6, 75–76, 79. *See also* queerness
hooks, bell, 75
hope: and kitchen table, 120; opposite of melancholy, 93, 96, 122, 123; and transformation, 155
Horowitz, Andy, 155
Horton, George Moses, 114–15
Horton-Stallings, LaMonda, 12, 58, 151
Huckleberry Finn (Twain), 25
Hughes, William, 129, 142, 146–47
humanism, 18, 128, 149–50, 156
Hurston, Zora Neale, 59, 88, 179n95
Hutcheon, Linda, 11, 12

Index 219

identity-based analysis, 9
identity formation: Asian identities in the South, 104–7, 109; based on sensation, 146; and foodways, 20–24, 51–52; queerness, 7–9, 14, 51–52, 58, 70; racial, 8, 70; southern, 111, 122–23, 160; "white trash," 44, 51
If I Had Two Wings (Kenan), 16, 54, 59, 62, 63
I'll Take My Stand (Kline), 70
In Cold Blood (Capote), 136
intersectionality, 9, 12–13, 15, 87, 91, 130, 148
intertextuality, 11, 17, 54
Interview with the Vampire (Rice), 126, 137, 158
Isenberg, Nancy, 44
"I Thought I Heard the Shuffle of Angels' Feet" (Kenan), 70–72, 78–80

Jameson, Fredric, 11
Janette, Michele, 102, 114–15
Jarvis, Christina, 51
Jenkins, Jerry Rafiki, 152
Jerng, Mark, 104
Johnson, Colin, 58
Johnson, E. Patrick, 7, 9, 75, 87–88
Johnson, Rashauna, 154, 155
Jones, Suzanne, 72
Joshi, Khyati, 109

Kant, Immanuel, 92
Kazanjian, David, 91
Keeling, Kara, 55, 56
Kenan, Randall, 16–17, 54–59; approaches to nature, 70, 75; culinary pursuits, 63–64; "homeplace" as escape from surveillance, 80–86; *Let the Dead Bury Their Dead*, 64–70; queerness and "homeplace," 75–80; "Requiem for Tobacco," 86; "Run, Mourner, Run," 86–87; *A Visitation of Spirits*, 59–62
Kent, Sarah, 130

kinship, 186n105; family structures and vampirism, 146–47, 148; kincoherence, 7; and melancholy, 92–93; queer family structures in *Lincoln in the Bardo* (Saunders), 99
Kreyling, Michael, 12
Ku Klux Klan, 24, 34, 43, 173n99

Lacan, Jacques, 92, 94
Lee, Bill, 159–60, 163
Lee, Harper, 25, 44, 108
"A Lesbian Appetite" (Allison), 50–52
The Lesbian South (Harker), 10
"Let the Dead Bury Their Dead" (story by Kenan), 65–70, 88
Let the Dead Bury Their Dead (story collection by Kenan), 16, 54, 59, 62, 64–70
Let Us Now Praise Famous Men (Agee & Evans), 44, 178–79n81
Lewis, Christopher, 149
LGBTQ rights, erosion of, 1–2, 18, 164
Lincoln, Abraham, 184–85n61
Lincoln in the Bardo (Saunders), 17, 94–95, 96–101; and historical imagination, 122
Lindenmeyer, Antje, 50, 52
Littler, Lucy, 74
Lizzo, 18, 164–65
Lorde, Audre, 157
Loss (Kazanjian & Eng, eds.), 90–91
Lost Cause mythology, 4, 17, 89–90, 91, 93–94, 108–9, 116, 130; *CivilWarLand in Bad Decline* (Saunders), 121–25
Lost Objects, 90, 92, 107–8, 111. *See also* melancholy; nostalgia
Lost Souls (Brite), 18, 128, 133, 141–47
Love, Heather, 6, 92–93
Lovers and Beloveds (Richards), 9
Lowe, Lisa, 105
Lugosi, Bela, 128
lynching trees, 58, 70, 72, 75

Malatino, Hil, 154
Malinowski, Bronislaw, 49, 175n135

"Mamiwata" (Kenan), 76–77, 78, 82–83
Manalansan, Martin, 7, 114
Mandingo (film), 5
March on Washington (1979), 10
maroon communities, 54, 56–57, 65
Martin, George R. R., 18, 127–28, 137–41
Martin, Jennifer, 45–46
masquerade, as play, 162, 163
McBride, Dwight, 75–76
McCullers, Carson, 9–10, 110
McKittrick, Kat, 56
McPherson, Tara, 4, 10–11, 23, 161
melancholy, 90–95, 117–21; in *Bitter in the Mouth* (Truong), 107–12; melancholy vs. melancholia, 183n1; in racialized South, 107; of South, 100–101. *See also* hope
The Member of the Wedding (McCullers), 110
menopause, 31–32
metafiction, 11–13
metronormativity, 6
Mickler, Ernest Matthew, 16, 20, 43–46
The Mind of the South (Cash), 45
monstrosity: intersection of southernness and queerness, 154–55; monsters, 126–27; "monstrous" communities, 141; queer monstrosity, 157
Morris, Susana, 151
Morrison, Toni, 112
Mortimer-Sandilands, Catriona, 70
"Mourning and Melancholia" (Freud), 91–92
Muñoz, José Esteban, 92–93, 115, 124, 152, 156, 157, 162
Munro, Niall, 93
Murfreesboro, Tennessee, 159
"Muscles of the Mind" (Allison), 49–50

narrative forms: narrative theory, 169n64; "pornographies of history," 102–3; and queerness, 12–15
narrator, omniscient: in *Fried Green Tomatoes at the Whistle Stop Cafe* (Flagg), 26, 30, 31, 34–35, 38, 39

nationalism, 90, 94
natural foods movement, 22, 170n10
nature: concept of, 54; Kenan's approaches to, 70–75. *See also* swamp, symbolism of; wilderness
New Orleans, 145, 192n63; Bourbon Street, 147, 154; history and symbolism, 154–55
New South, 58, 70, 174n115
New Southern Studies (NSS), 3, 6, 168n38
Nguyen, Marguerite, 105
normative ideologies, 6–7, 52, 55–56, 80; normativity/deviance binary, 9–10; and public space, 114, 116. *See also* heteronormativity
North Carolina Parade, 114–15
nostalgia: in *Fried Green Tomatoes at the Whistle Stop Cafe* (Flagg), 29–30; nostalgia vs. guilt, 23; for Old South, 42, 70
"Now Why Come Is That" (Kenan), 80–82
Nunes, Zita, 35–36
Nurka, Camille, 154, 157–58
Nyong'o, Tavia, 6–7

Obama, Barack, 189n188
obesity epidemic, 23
O'Connor, Flannery, 48–49, 130, 143
"Ode to the Confederate Dead" (Tate), 106
Old South, 10–11, 15; cooking traditions, 53; gender roles, 160–61; mythology, 69; nostalgia for, 42, 70
oral history, 66
otherness: appetites for, 16; and perceived sexual deviance, 7–8; South as "internal other," 4; and southern deviance, 2; swamp symbolism, 57
Other Voices, Other Rooms (Capote), 162–63
Our Vampires, Ourselves (Auerbach), 132
Owen, Gilman, 105–6

Index 221

panopticism, 182n184
Parrish, Timothy, 101
Parton, Dolly, 161–62
patriarchal frameworks, 131, 160
plantation system, 54, 58; surveillance, 58, 66, 80–86; and swamp ecology, 55, 56. *See also* slavery
Poe, Edgar Allan, 130
politics: conservatism, 4, 5–6, 10–11, 23, 75; contemporary, 18; of food, 20; of melancholy, 91–93, 95; of narrative, 12–15; political aspects of publishing, 20; progressive, 52, 165; of South, 3, 58, 125; South and "identity politics," 159
postregionality, 12
postsouthernism, 11–12, 132; and sense of place, 183n27
poverty, 47, 49, 127, 129, 173n99. *See also* "white trash"

queerness: anti-narrativity, 13; and blackness in *Fried Green Tomatoes at the Whistle Stop Cafe* (Flagg), 36–39; definitions, 2–3, 14; in *Fried Green Tomatoes at the Whistle Stop Cafe* (Flagg), 30–36; and "homeplace" as concept, 75–80; and "homeplace" as escape from surveillance, 80–86; identity formation, 58; masquerade, 163; Pride events, 159; queer alimentarity, 22–24; queer sexuality and swamp symbolism, 55–56, 68; "queer time," 173n88; racial aspects, 172n61; and southernness, 163–64; and vampire themes, 138–39, 148–53, 155–56. *See also* homophobia
queer theory, 6, 14; and melancholy, 92–93; and swamp symbolism, 55–56

race: Black queerness and swamp symbolism, 55–56; paternalistic, in *Fried Green Tomatoes at the Whistle Stop Cafe* (Flagg), 28–29; racialized sexual violence, 115; racism and sexuality, 7–10; and slavery, 181n151. *See also* slavery
rape, 47, 115, 135
recombination and narrative technique, 113
recontextualization and narrative technique, 113
relational/anti-relational debate, 6–7, 168n26
"Requiem for Tobacco" (Kenan), 86
"Resurrection Hardware" (Kenan), 63, 77–78
rhyme, 33, 72, 86–87
Rice, Anne, 126, 137, 158
Richards, Gary, 9
Rieger, Christopher, 70
"River of Names" (Allison), 47–49
Rody, Caroline, 152, 153
Romine, Scott, 3, 20–21, 122
Rosenthal, Gregory Samantha, 6
"Run, Mourner, Run" (Kenan), 72–73, 78, 79, 86–87
Ruti, Mari, 7

Said, Edward, 4
Saturday Night Live skit, 5
Saunders, George, 17, 122; *Lincoln in the Bardo*, 94–95, 96–101
Sayers, Daniel, 56–57
Scott, Darieck, 22
Sedgwick, Eve, 55, 129, 130
sexual deviance, 5–7, 169n46; and race, 7–10
sexuality: and food/hunger, 15–16, 23–24, 49–50; and race, 7–10. *See also* queerness
The Sexual Life of Savages (Malinowski), 49, 175n134
sexual violence/assault, 47, 115, 135
Simal-González, Begoña, 120–21
Sinkin Spells, Hot Flashes, Fits and Cravins (Mickler), 46
"sinthomosexuality," 156
The Sixth Sense (film), 97

222 Index

slavery: legacy of, 8, 54, 154–55, 191n29; maroon communities, 54, 56–57, 65; neoslave narratives, 148–53, 194n126; slave trade, 139; and vampire symbolism, 130–31. *See also* plantation system
Smith, Andrew, 125, 129
Smith, Dina, 44, 45
Smith, Jon, 3, 90–91, 94
Snorton, C. Riley, 165
soil: native soil, 54, 59; and vampires, 150–52
Somerville, Siobhan, 8
A Song of Ice and Fire (Martin), 137
Son of Dracula (film), 131–32
Sontag, Susan, 174n109
soul food, 45, 174n112
South: migration from, 57–58; physical space vs. abstraction, 58–59; sense of place, 183n27; tradition and heritage, 4, 16. *See also* Tennessee
The Southern Book Club's Guide to Slaying Vampires (Hendrix), 18, 126, 127–28, 132–33, 134–37
Southern Gothic genre, 4, 18, 48, 128–34, 188n150, 194n109; and male homosexuality, 129; new southern gothic, 130; southern gothic conventions, 142–45
southern literature: individual geographies, 54; literary canon, 9–10; postmodernism, 11–12; "trashy" literature, 46–47
southernness: and antinormativity, 7, 8–9; definitions, 2–3; and food, 64; hyperfeminization, 161–62; masquerade, 163; as myth, 3; in popular culture, 3–5, 10–11; and queerness, 163–64; and sexual perversion, 5–7; southern belle stereotype, 29, 40, 160; southern exceptionalism, 6, 167n9; Southern Foodways, 19, 20–22; stereotypes, 3, 20, 23, 44
Southern Renaissance, 12
Southern studies, 6–7, 90, 94
Steel Magnolias (film), 10

Stockton, Kathryn Bond, 96
Stoker, Bram, 128
storytellers, 16, 17, 26–29, 40, 48
Sublette, Cami, 45–46
Suddenly Southern: A Yankee's Guide to Living in Dixie, 22
Sumner, Charles, 89
surveillance, 58, 66, 80–86
swamp symbolism, 16–17, 54–59, 86, 176n9; in *Let the Dead Bury Their Dead* (Kenan), 64–70; and queer sexuality, 68
Sweet Tea (Johnson), 87
synesthesia, 95–96, 103, 106, 108–12, 113

Tate, Allen, 90, 106
Taylor, Melanie, 94, 95
temporality: modern temporality, 30; queer, 79; rejection of, 93
Tennessee: contemporary situation, 14, 18; during COVID, 1; drag bans, 2, 164; Lizzo in Knoxville, 164; Pride in Murfreesboro, 159
Thananopavarn, Susan, 57, 67, 68
Thomas, Sara Gabler, 104
Tiger King (television show), 1–2
To Kill a Mockingbird (Lee), 25, 108–9
Tompkins, Kyla Wazana, 22–23
transformation, 74–76, 83, 114–16, 147, 153, 154–55; and New Orleans, 155; transformative gaze, 81–82; and written word, 152
trans identities, 154, 164, 165
trans studies, 154
Trash (Allison), 16, 19–20, 46–53
"trashy" literature, 20, 46–47
Traynor, Elise, 98
True Blood (television show), 5, 132, 155, 157
Trump, Donald, 189n188
Truong, Monique, 17. *See also Bitter in the Mouth* (Truong)
Tucker, Lauryl, 162
Tucker, Lindsey, 67
Twitty, Michael, 53

Undead Souths (Anderson et al.), 127
utopian ideals, 92–93

vampires, 18, 126–27; and gay identity, 142, 145–46, 192n71, 193n78; symbolism, 128–34, 144–45, 195n142, 195n145
Vietnam War, 105–6, 186n94. *See also* Asian identities in the South
violence: and plantation system, 58; sexual violence/assault, 47, 115, 135; and "white trash," 45
A Visitation of Spirits (Kenan), 16, 54, 59–62, 73–74, 83–86

Wald, Patricia, 133
Watson, Jay, 129
Waugh, Patricia, 11
Welty, Eudora, 130
white supremacy, 56–57, 149. *See also* race

"white trash," 20, 174n115, 174n117, 174n122; depictions of, 23; food, 174n112; stereotypes and clichés, 44–45, 51
White Trash (Isenberg), 44
White Trash Cooking (Mickler), 16, 20, 43–46
Whitman, Walt, 185n64
Wiegman, Robyn, 14–15
wilderness, 54, 55, 71, 73–74, 175n2. *See also* swamp symbolism
Willis, Bruce, 96–97
Wilson, Anthony, 55
Women in Print movement, 10
writing, transformative possibilities, 152

Yaeger, Patricia, 95
Yerby, Frank, 152
You Have Seen Their Faces (Caldwell), 143

Žižek, Slavoj, 4, 92, 125l